This book is simple, but not simplistic, and it is accessible to those who are reading the Bible for the first time and helpful for those who have read the Bible their entire lives.

—THOMAS R. SCHREINER, James Buchanan Harrison
Professor of New Testament Interpretation, The
Southern Baptist Theological Seminary

It's hard to imagine a more reliable guide to understanding the Bible for new believers, church members, and small group leaders.

—CHRISTOPHER W. MORGAN, dean and professor
of theology, California Baptist University, Riverside

A pastor and a scholar team up to explain the Bible's storyline accessibly and skillfully. This book is a gift to the church.

—ANDY NASELLI, associate professor of New Testament
and theology, Bethlehem College and Seminary

What if you could take the lifelong learning of a seminary professor and have it translated by the preaching ministry of a former student turned pastor so that everyone in the church can apply it? That's what you hold in your hands. Think of it as the best class you never got to take.

—JUSTIN TAYLOR, managing editor, *ESV Study Bible*;
blogger, The Gospel Coalition

This book is a gem for its treatment of the way the Old Testament contributes to our grasp of what it means for Jesus to be the Christ. It will repay careful reading from cover to cover.

—GRAEME GOLDSWORTHY, former lecturer in
biblical theology, Moore College, Sydney

Wellum and Hunter have craft-roasted the fine beans of sound doctrine and biblical theology, put them through the burr grinder, measured them into the French press, and poured the filtered water just off the boil. Four minutes have passed, which means the time has come for you to relish the rich, thick, and frothy cup they've prepared for your edification and delight. Drink deeply, which is to say, read and relish.

—JIM HAMILTON, professor of biblical theology,
The Southern Baptist Theological Seminary

Readers of all levels will find this accessible book a fascinating guide to God's unfolding story. It's sheer pleasure to commend this book.

—FRED G. ZASPEL, pastor, Reformed Baptist Church

Wellum and Hunter have produced the best, and most accessible, "along the Bible" tool I've found for helping people understand the unfolding drama of redemption. Read it for yourself, and then again with your leaders, your kids, and your study group.

—DAVID W. HEGG, senior pastor, Grace Baptist Church, Santa Clarita

This book is a rich, instructive, faithful, and clear unfolding of our promise-keeping God's gracious purposes in Christ. Highly recommended!

—ALAN J. THOMPSON, Sydney Missionary and Bible College, Croydon

This is the kind of resource to put in the hands of small group leaders, Sunday school teachers, youth group leaders, and staff. But it's also for parents who want to know how to read the Bible to their children, and anyone who would like to better understand the storyline of Scripture. Highly recommended!

—MICHAEL LAWRENCE, pastor, Hinson Baptist Church, Portland

If you want to revel in seeing the beauty and glory of God in the face of Jesus Christ from all of Scripture, then pick up copies of this book for yourself and other Christians you want to encourage. I know I will.

—JUAN R. SANCHEZ, senior pastor,
High Pointe Baptist Church, Austin

A few years ago, Steve Wellum shared with our church "a bird's-eye view of the Bible." Our church turned out eagerly to hear these presentations and loved every minute. We are so thankful that this simple tool for orienting believers to the storyline of Scripture is available to all. You will be too.

—JIM ELLIFF, a pastor of Christ Fellowship of Kansas City

Hunter and Wellum cause their readers to love Christ more deeply in response to the full picture of redemption seen through all of Scripture. I'm excited about and grateful for this beautifully written resource. It couldn't be more timely.

—RUTH CHOU SIMONS, artist and bestselling author, *GraceLaced*

This book will help you know Jesus Christ better and enable you to understand how all of Scripture points to the surpassing glory of his perfect life, substitutionary death, and victorious resurrection. I only wish it had been around forty-five years ago when I became a Christian!

—BOB KAUFLIN, director, Sovereign Grace Music

This excellent book deserves wide reading. For an overview of the Bible with a focus on Christ, this will be the text I recommend!

—GREG STRAND, executive director of theology and credentialing, Evangelical Free Church of America

Reading the Bible with Jesus as the unifying center is as revolutionary today as it was in the early days of the Christian church. Hunter and Wellum are both committed to the value of this approach, and their work winsomely makes the case.

—DAVE HELM, lead pastor, Hyde Park Congregation, Holy Trinity Church

CHRIST

from BEGINNING

to END

CHRIST

from BEGINNING *to* END

*How the
Full Story of Scripture
Reveals the
Full Glory of Christ*

TRENT HUNTER AND
STEPHEN WELLUM

ZONDERVAN

Christ from Beginning to End
Copyright © 2018 by Trent W. Hunter and Stephen J. Wellum

This title is also available as a Zondervan ebook.

Requests for information should be addressed to:
Zondervan, *3900 Sparks Dr. SE, Grand Rapids, Michigan 49546*

Library of Congress Cataloging-in-Publication Data

Names: Hunter, Trent, 1981– author. | Wellum, Stephen J., 1964- author.
Title: Christ from beginning to end : how the full story of scripture reveals the full glory of
    Christ / Trent Hunter and Stephen Wellum.
Description: Grand Rapids, MI : Zondervan, [2018] | Includes bibliographical references and
    index.
Identifiers: LCCN 2017049119 | ISBN 9780310536543 (hardcover)
Subjects: LCSH: Jesus Christ—Person and offices. | Jesus Christ—Biblical teaching.
Classification: LCC BT203 .H86 2018 | DDC 232—dc23 LC record available at https://lccn
    .loc.gov/2017049119

Cover design: Darren Welch Design
Cover photo: Shutterstock.com
Interior design: Kait Lamphere

Printed in the United States of America

18 19 20 21 22 23 24 25 26 27 28 /DCI/ 15 14 13 12 11 10 9 8 7 6 5 4 3

CONTENTS

FOREWORD

The Bible is God's Word, and this book helps us to read it better. That alone is sufficient to gain it readers. At least it has brought you and me to its pages! So what is this book that you hold?

This book is a kind of gospel-recovery project. Trent Hunter and Stephen Wellum understand that we are in a day that is marked by both interest in the Bible and profound ignorance of it. People today don't know its basic storyline. But our authors are convinced that without the Bible, we can't understand Jesus. So they've written this short book as a way of helping us understand Jesus by understanding the Bible's full story. They do this by orienting us to the major landmarks. They make sure that we notice that God is our creator, who is independent and self-sufficient and who has revealed himself to us. And what we find that he has revealed about us is that we've rebelled against God and that he will, therefore, judge us. It's only when we've grasped this that the news about who Jesus is and what he's come to do makes sense. Only then does it appear to us as good news!

"The Bible's nature is tied to God's nature." So Hunter and Wellum teach us that as big as the Bible is, as many human authors as it has, it also has one author behind it all: God. And it is his intention that we need to follow in order to read the whole Bible, to learn its full story. This book helps us to do just that. We are helped to read the Bible in the individual contexts of each book and also together as one connected story with God as its author.

Wellum and Hunter uncover the basic structure of the Bible's message as creation, fall, restoration, and new creation. And they also

11

walk us through the promises (covenants) that God made to his people. Those promises become the scenes of the story, progressing from Adam to Christ. In part 1, they give us the tools to use, such as covenants and types. In part 2—most of the book—they walk us through the story of the Bible in eleven episodes.

Geerhardus Vos wrote that "the truth is inherently rich and complex, because God is so Himself." It is this richness and complexity that the authors convey to us in these short, clearly outlined chapters. If God's nature really is reflected in God's book, the Bible, it is no wonder that we should find it so endlessly fascinating. And it is no surprise that studying it repays any amount of effort. What this book does is to help us make sure that that effort is properly directed and spent.

In these pages, familiar characters take on new significance. Stories which we've known are important (like the first sin in the garden of Eden) are placed in their full context where we can understand that they are even more important than we had realized. We find that God is the creator and humanity his greatest creation. But God and sin do not mix, and so we have the riddle of the Old Testament: How can God be both merciful and yet not clear the guilty, as he claims in Exodus 34:6–7? This, our authors say, "is the central question of the Bible." But the greatness of our problem simply magnifies the greatness of God's answer.

Here we come to understand the story of Noah as not only the story of a man in a boat but also an extension of God's covenant with Adam. To Abraham, God symbolizes with a smoking firepot and a blazing torch that he himself will fulfill his own covenant with Abraham. What can this mean? These authors carefully trace the storyline of God's grace, always pausing to look back and then turning to point ahead in the biblical narrative, showing us how one person relates to the next, how this event foreshadows that. We relish the irony of God's providence as Pharaoh adopts as a grandson one of the very boys he ordered to be killed. We are heartened by previews of heaven like the one we get in Joshua 21.

I could go on, but I'd rather you enjoy learning more about David and the prophets and Jesus and the church and the book of Revelation from the pages ahead of you. I already know of one way I hope to use this book: helping me to think about how to lead the congregation that I serve in prayers of praise as we focus on this theme or that in the character of God. Page after page of this book presents beautiful tapestries of God's similar faithfulnesses from different pages of our Bible. And they all make sense together.

And that makes sense because the Bible really is all about Christ, from beginning to end.

—MARK DEVER, *Capitol Hill*
Baptist Church, Washington, DC

ACKNOWLEDGMENTS

This book arose out of a twofold conviction. First, it is of vital importance for the church that we know and proclaim "the whole counsel of God" (Acts 20:27 ESV), which is all about our glorious triune God's redemptive plan centered in our Lord Jesus Christ (Eph. 1:9–10). Second, books that discuss how the Bible is about Christ from beginning to end are not merely for academic interest but for the entire church. The planning of this book arose out of our partnership for five years in leading a ministry to young couples at Ninth and O Baptist Church in Louisville, Kentucky. Stephen had been teaching these truths in the seminary classroom, and Trent, then a student and now a pastor, began to strategize how to make more accessible for a wider audience the amazing story of God's sovereign grace centered in our Lord Jesus Christ. This book is the result of that planning and strategizing which began many years ago and which has been tested on numerous occasions in the context of local church ministry. For any book to see the light of day, there are many people to thank. Our first word of thanks goes to the couples with whom we shared those great years.

From Trent:

Several people deserve special thanks.

Kristi, you're my faithful wife and partner in life. You're never going to give me up, never going to let me down, never going to run around and desert me. You're a beautiful picture of covenant faithfulness, and you cheered this project on from the start. I dedicate this book to you.

Carson, Madalyn, and Shae, you didn't know it, but you added energy to my work with playful interruptions. We played Connect Four, passed notes under the door, and I sat in the garage while you rode bikes. There I prayed for you to believe in Christ.

Brett Isselhardt had something to do with this book. He invited me to church repeatedly in the eighth grade, told me about Christ, and prayed for my salvation. I am ever thankful.

Dad raised us boys to do things that matter and wouldn't let me quit, and I can still hear Mom singing me to sleep with the heartbeat of this book: "Holy, Holy, Holy! God in three persons, blessed Trinity."

Drew, my brother and friend, has been my conversation partner in Christ for twenty years and made this book better with many suggestions.

To the saints at Desert Springs Church and Heritage Bible Church who receive the Word with joy, here's to our partnership and your prayers.

Finally, to the preachers: Leron Heath, Scott Berglin, Larry Dyer, Keith Spaugh, Erwin Lutzer, Steve Mason, Bill Cook, and Ryan Kelly. May this book stir and strengthen more preachers like you for the glory of Christ, from beginning to end.

From Stephen:

There are so many people to thank from my immediate and extended family who have encouraged me to know Christ and to glory in him alone. I especially want to thank our triune God for the remembrance of and gracious gift of my father, Dr. Colin L. Wellum Sr., who went home to be with the Lord on October 11, 2017. My father, along with my mother, faithfully taught me about the glories of Christ and made sure that I and my brothers heard the faithful exposition of God's Word at Trinity Baptist Church, Burlington, Ontario, Canada, under the ministry of William E. Payne. As he awaits the glorious resurrection in the presence of Christ, I thank the Lord for such a wonderful father who dearly loved his family. He served his family by being an example of a godly husband and father who sought to know, love, and serve Christ Jesus as Lord.

I also want to thank the administration and trustees of The Southern Baptist Theological Seminary for allowing me the opportunity to teach Christ from beginning to end. What a joy and privilege to train another generation for gospel ministry and proclamation.

However, I dedicate this book to two foundational pastors in my life, the late William E. Payne and John G. Reisinger. These two faithful servants of Christ repeatedly preached the glory of our Lord Jesus and demonstrated in their lives their faithful commitment to all that Scripture teaches. In the most formative years of my life, I learned firsthand that the full story of Scripture reveals the full glory of Christ.

Finally, both of us would like to thank Ryan Pazdur, our editor at Zondervan, for getting behind this project and making it much better due to his careful editorial eye. We are also indebted to our marvelous illustrator, Caleb Greene, for capturing the heart of each chapter simply and with intrigue. Our prayer is that this book, in some small way, will help the truth of Scripture to come alive and the glory of our triune God to be seen in greater ways in the face of our wondrous Lord and Savior, Jesus Christ.

INTRODUCTION

Getting the Story Straight

Both of us were typical boys growing up. We liked to take things apart and discover how they worked. In grade school, we took apart our calculators, fascinated to discover what made them tick. But when we broke open the cover, we discovered nothing but a confusing mess. The casing and the soft sheet of buttons made sense to us, but everything else looked like the pieces of a jigsaw puzzle. And there was no apparent connection between microchips and the math on our screens. Eventually we gave up opening calculators and trying to decipher their inner workings. Figuring them out was for the smarter people.

Maybe you feel the same way about the Bible. You know that the Bible is a book about Jesus, but when you crack it open and poke around inside, you're not quite sure how it all fits together. Maybe at some point you found yourself interested in knowing more about Jesus and how the entire Bible speaks about him and his work, and you started reading it with curiosity. But then a few chapters into the book of Leviticus, perhaps, you lost heart. The Bible's many seemingly disconnected characters, events, and places—not to mention its many pages!—wore down your interest. You expected to comprehend what you read, but it just didn't happen. You closed the book, opening it only occasionally to read a verse or to follow along with the pastor on Sunday morning. *Pastors and theologians can understand the Bible*, you reasoned, *but not me*.

Many years ago we gave up trying to figure out how calculators work. We left the mysteries of LCD displays and microcircuitry to the engineers and lost nothing in that decision. But when it comes to the study of the Word of God, none of us should quit so easily. After all, the Bible is *God's* Word! When we give up on the Bible, we miss what is most important in life, the words that our Creator and Lord wants to say to each one of us.

Yes, the Bible is complex. And some sections can be quite complicated. But what if the Bible's complexity isn't a hurdle to jump but a scenic trail to run? What if the Bible's many characters, events, and places are not in the way of getting to know Jesus but *are* the way to know him? What if the Bible's numerous pages aren't a reason for intimidation but a call to exploration?

We wrote this book with several guiding convictions, which are summed up nicely in the title *Christ from Beginning to End: How the Full Story of Scripture Reveals the Full Glory of Christ.*

- Conviction 1: The Bible is a book about Jesus Christ.
- Conviction 2: The Bible is a unified story.
- Conviction 3: Through the Bible's story, we come to know Jesus in all his glory.

What do these convictions mean for you? They mean that the better you read the story of the Bible, the better you can fathom Christ's glory. But if you read the story inaccurately, you risk misunderstanding who Jesus is and why his work is necessary, incomparable, and unique. Getting the Bible's story right is foundational for knowing Christ.

For some people, even a suggestion that it's possible to interpret the Bible's story incorrectly can be distressing. Does the Bible teach that? Does it support the idea that there is a correct or right way to read the Bible? Let's start our journey together by exploring this question.

WHY GETTING THE STORY
STRAIGHT MATTERS

In many places, Scripture stresses the importance of getting the story right as necessary for knowing Christ. Here are four examples that show us four different ways this is true.

A Story for Seeing

In Luke 24, we witness two of Jesus' disciples as they grasp better Jesus' identity and why he has come. Although these men had lived with Jesus for several years and heard him speak about his future death and resurrection, they didn't fully understand who Jesus was or why he came. They rightly believed that Jesus arrived as the promised Christ (Messiah) and thus ruling King, but they couldn't comprehend a crucified Messiah. Jesus' death devastated them; they didn't expect it. After three days, even after reports of Jesus' empty tomb, they still hung their heads in confusion. Together, the men walked for miles, pondering Jesus' apparent failure: "The chief priests and our rulers handed him over to be sentenced to death, and they crucified him; but we had hoped that he was the one who was going to redeem Israel" (Luke 24:20–21). Clearly, they did not think of Jesus' cross as good news yet!

Then Jesus joined them on the road. At first, the men didn't discern that Jesus walked with them as they reeled in sorrow. What did he say to them? As Jesus always did in his teaching, he took them to the Scriptures. He gave them a whirlwind tour of the Scriptures' story, and he helped them see it correctly as a story about him. Jesus even rebuked them for not reading the Scriptures correctly. If they had, they would have discerned that his death and resurrection weren't discouraging news but good news! "'How foolish you are, and how slow to believe all that the prophets have spoken! Did not the Messiah have to suffer these things and then enter his glory?' And beginning with Moses and all the Prophets, he explained to them what was said in all the Scriptures concerning himself" (Luke 24:25–27).

That must have been an extraordinary Bible study! The response of the two disciples is telling: "Were not our hearts burning within us while he talked with us on the road and opened the Scriptures to us?" (24:32).

What explains their joyful response? It was more than Jesus' presence. At that moment, they didn't realize it was Jesus speaking to them. Instead their hearts burned because the light of Scripture had been turned on. As they looked at the Old Testament writings, they correctly saw—for the first time—how the Scriptures fit together and how all Scripture is fulfilled in Christ. To use another puzzle analogy, the disciples had all the pieces of the Old Testament in front of them, but until Jesus put the pieces together properly, they failed to grasp that the Scriptures' message centered in him. They had lived with Jesus for several years, yet it was there, on the pages of Scripture, that they truly saw Christ for the first time.

What is true about the Old Testament is also true about the New. Unless we grasp the Bible's story correctly, we'll miss the true significance of the New Testament message. Think of John 3:16: "God so loved the world that he gave his one and only Son, that whoever believes in him shall not perish but have eternal life." We hear this verse all the time, but what does it mean that God so loved the *world*, or that the Father gave his *Son?* These truths make sense only when we read them in light of the Bible's entire story. Or as Peter, one of the first followers of Jesus, writes, "Christ also suffered once for sins, the righteous for the unrighteous, to bring you to God" (1 Peter 3:18). Or when Paul, one of the leaders in the early church, proclaims that "in [Christ] we have redemption through his blood, the forgiveness of sins, in accordance with the riches of God's grace" (Eph. 1:7).

To grasp these truths accurately—why Christ had to suffer for our sins, why his blood was necessary to reconcile us to God, and what redemption is—we need to see how they fit into the rest of the Bible. The entire story of the Bible—not just verses pulled out here and there—helps us to know Christ and to know him for all that he is.

A Story for Growing

A second reason we need the whole Bible's story relates to our growth in the Christian life. The same thing that makes us Christians also grows us as Christians: the grace of God revealed in the gospel. The more faithfully we understand the whole Bible, the better equipped we are to faithfully follow him.

For example, the author of Hebrews instructs us this way in 12:1–2: "Let us throw off everything that hinders and the sin that so easily entangles. And let us run with perseverance the race marked out for us, fixing our eyes on Jesus, the pioneer and perfecter of faith. For the joy set before him he endured the cross, scorning its shame, and sat down at the right hand of the throne of God."

On its own, this verse is encouraging, but the context of the whole letter multiplies that effect. When the author urges us to "fix our eyes on Jesus," he sets our gaze on the glorious Savior he has written about for many chapters. Through a series of contrasts with Old Testament characters, events, and institutions, the author puts a spotlight on Jesus. To understand this exhortation, we must understand it in light of the entire Bible.

The letter to the Hebrews strengthened its Jewish audience, which knew the Old Testament well. Yet the letter to the Ephesians, written primarily for a gentile audience, also drew from the Old Testament. Paul reminds the gentile believers that they were once "separate from Christ, excluded from citizenship in Israel and foreigners to the covenants of the promise, without hope and without God in the world. But now in Christ Jesus you who once were far away have been brought near by the blood of Christ" (Eph. 2:12–13). Through Christ, Paul writes, God has now made Jew and gentile into "one new humanity" (2:15), and in Christ, Jew and gentile are "joined together and [rise] to become a holy temple in the Lord . . . a dwelling in which God lives by his Spirit" (2:21–22). The Bible's whole story helps us fully appreciate all that this means for us: how far we were from God, how near he has brought us to himself, and what it means to live a life worthy of our calling (3:18; 4:1).

The New Testament repeatedly encourages and warns us in our Christian lives by appealing to the Bible's story and drawing examples from it. Addressing Christians tempted to sexual sin, Paul asks, "Do you not know that your bodies are temples of the Holy Spirit, who is in you . . .?" (1 Cor. 6:19). Warning Christians under the threat of persecution, the author of Hebrews says, "We have come to share in Christ, if indeed we hold our original conviction firmly to the very end. As has just been said: 'Today, if you hear his voice, do not harden your hearts as you did in the rebellion'" (Heb. 3:14–15). Both examples draw directly from the Bible's story, referring to the temple and to the rebellion of the nation of Israel as they wandered in the desert. If you don't know the story, you'll miss these allusions.

Here's why this matters: The Bible's story propels our Christian growth. Until we grasp the Bible's content in the context of its unified story, the New Testament's instruction will lack compelling force. In many cases, our Christian lives will not be fully shaped by the truth of the entirety of Scripture.

A Story for Guarding

By reading Scripture correctly, we guard and defend the truth of the gospel. This is tragically illustrated in Paul's letter to the church in Galatia. The Galatians have subtly misread the Old Testament story. Yet this misreading has put them in danger of denying the gospel! With sharp words to the church, Paul writes, "If anybody is preaching to you a gospel other than what you accepted, let them be under God's curse!" (Gal. 1:9). What has happened that leads Paul to speak so strongly? Some in the church were forgetting the very heart of the Christian gospel: "[We] know that a person is not justified by the works of the law, but by faith in Jesus Christ" (2:16).

They got the story wrong and were in danger of missing salvation. So how does Paul counter their mistake? He retells the story properly to demonstrate the centrality of salvation by grace through faith. "So also Abraham 'believed God, and it was credited to him as righteousness.' Understand, then, that those who have faith are children of Abraham. Scripture foresaw that God would justify the Gentiles by faith, and announced the gospel in advance to Abraham: 'All nations will be blessed through you.' So those who rely on faith are blessed along with Abraham, the man of faith" (3:6–9).

The Galatian church needed to get Scripture's story straight. Properly read, the story of the Bible makes plain the way of salvation: in Christ alone, by grace alone, and through faith alone.

Sadly, we can misread the Bible in many other ways. The Corinthian church, for example, was vulnerable to teaching that the resurrection did not happen. To correct misunderstandings among these believers, Paul refers them back to the story. He argues that Christ died, was buried, and was raised, all "according to the Scriptures"—that is, the Old Testament (1 Cor. 15:3–4).

Do not miss this: the Bible itself teaches that we must know the Bible's story if we want to know Christ and defend this gospel.

A Story for Spreading

Here's one last example of the importance of knowing the Bible's story. We find it in Paul's proclamation of the gospel in Athens, Greece. When he preached Christ at the Areopagus, he faced a challenge similar to what we sometimes face today. His audience was diverse people with little or no knowledge of the Scriptures. Sound familiar? The Athenians were pluralistic. They embraced many religious perspectives. As Luke reminds us, they "spent their time doing nothing but talking about and listening to the latest ideas" (Acts 17:21). This intellectual center of the ancient world prided itself in diversity and openness to new ideas. To cover their bases, the Athenians even erected an altar among the many shrines in the city to an "unknown god" (17:23).

Distressed by their worship of false gods, Paul preaches the gospel of Jesus Christ, but he begins this sermon differently. Normally when Paul preached Christ to a Jewish audience, he began his message by emphasizing God's promises to Israel and reminding them of their hope of a future Messiah (Acts 13:13–52). But that's not what he does in Athens. Paul knows that his audience is not scripturally literate. So how do you appeal to Scripture when your audience knows nothing about its teachings or basic truths?

Notice that Paul does not begin his message with Jesus, since they don't know enough about Scripture to make sense of that. Instead he begins by establishing a larger framework from Scripture to help his listeners grasp who Jesus is, giving them a larger context by summarizing the Scriptures' storyline. Paul outlines the big picture of the scriptural worldview so that his proclamation of who Jesus is will make sense on Scripture's own terms and within its own understanding. Paul sets the Christian view up as true against the diverse, false worldviews of

Athens. Then he proclaims Jesus as the only Lord and Savior by placing his identity and role within Scripture's worldview and story. He does this in six steps.

First, Paul establishes the identity of God as Creator. He explains that this world is not the result of blind chance (contrary to the Epicureans) or the evolution of a world spirit (contrary to Stoicism). Instead he asserts that the world is the creation of one sovereign, personal God, who alone reigns as the Lord of heaven and earth: "The God who made the world and everything in it is the Lord of heaven and earth and does not live in temples built by human hands" (17:24).

Second, Paul establishes that God is independent and self-sufficient. Everything we receive comes from him, and he does not receive anything from us. God rules as the Lord of history all by himself: "And [the Lord of heaven and earth] is not served by human hands, as if he needed anything. Rather, he himself gives everyone life and breath and everything else" (17:25).

Third, Paul explains that God reveals himself. He created us in his image and locates us in our exact places. Why? So that we might know him. God isn't playing hard to get. The evidence for him is everywhere if you are willing to open your eyes to the truth. "From one man he made all the nations, that they should inhabit the whole earth; and he marked out their appointed times in history and the boundaries of their lands. God did this so that they would seek him and perhaps reach out to him and find him, though he is not far from any one of us. 'For in him we live and move and have our being.' As some of your own poets have said, 'We are his offspring'" (17:26–28).

Fourth, Paul declares that humans have rebelled against God as their Lord. We stand justly condemned before him. "Therefore since we are God's offspring, we should not think that the divine being is like gold or silver or stone—an image made by human design and skill. In the past God overlooked such ignorance, but now he commands all people everywhere to repent" (17:29–30).

Fifth, Paul then instructs the Athenians that all humans are to turn from their idolatry to the living God because a day of future judgment is coming: "For [God] has set a day when he will judge the world with justice" (17:31).

Finally, only after constructing the Scriptures' big picture does Paul proclaim Jesus as the man whom God raised from the dead to judge the world. He states, "For [God] has set a day when he will judge the world with justice by the man he has appointed. He has given proof of this to everyone by raising him from the dead" (17:31). The big picture reveals a big Christ. Jesus is not one religious leader among many. Set within Scripture's own framework and teaching, Jesus is presented as the exclusive Lord, Savior, and Judge of the world.

Here is what Paul's example teaches us: to preach Jesus rightly, we must do so from within Scripture's own story and worldview.

As you and I seek faithfully to communicate the gospel today, especially in places where the Bible is unknown or misunderstood, Paul is a helpful example. He teaches us that Scripture's storyline gives us the metanarrative in which the gospel is truly seen as good news. Only the true and whole story of Scripture can counter the false worship of our day. Growing in our knowledge of the Bible's full story will help us as we take the gospel to our neighbors and to the nations.

These four examples encourage us to get the story straight. As we learn to think God's thoughts after him and grasp the full story of Scripture, we will be better equipped to know, obey, and adore our triune, covenant God. He alone is worthy of our worship and our lives. Getting the story straight matters greatly.

PUTTING THE PUZZLE TOGETHER

Just as we shared a love for taking things apart (like calculators), we share a dislike for doing puzzles. Addressing two thousand problems in a pile on a kitchen table does not sound like a good way to relax. Yet despite our distaste for doing them, the puzzle analogy helps us think about how to understand the Bible.

If you've been puzzling over the Bible for a few years, you might be in a place where you're familiar with its many parts but are unsure of how they fit together. If you're new to the Bible, it's as if you've just poured the pieces out on the table. You're excited. But you may also feel overwhelmed. Sometimes, when we lack understanding and grow impatient, we try to jam the Bible's pieces together. Have you ever tried doing that with a puzzle? You aren't sure how they're supposed to fit, but if a piece *almost* fits, you think it's good enough. Yet as we know with puzzles, jamming pieces together won't give us the right picture in the end.

Like a puzzle, the pieces of the Bible—the various books, letters, characters, and stories—do fit together. The Bible contains mysteries, but its meaning is not intended to be mysterious or hidden from us, especially in its central teaching. God does not try to hide truth from us; he reveals it. The Bible reveals more than a picture for us to enjoy. It reveals a person for us to know.

Jesus is that person. On the last page of the Bible, Jesus makes an astounding claim: "I am the Alpha and the Omega, the First and the Last, the Beginning and the End" (Rev. 22:13). What does Jesus mean? Jesus says that the purpose and meaning of the universe, history, and every human life is tied to him (Col. 1:17). It should not surprise us to find that he is also the beginning and end of the Bible—and everything in between. We have written this book to help you see that. We want you to see Christ in all his glory in all of Scripture—in the cracks, corners, and turns of the Bible's complex and scenic story. We write "that you may believe that Jesus is the Christ, the Son of God, and that by believing you may have life in his name" (John 20:31).

To that end, this book has two parts. In part 1, we will look closely at what the Bible is and how to interpret it correctly. We will start by answering the question, What *is* the Bible? Moving from our answer to that question, we will turn to the subject of how rightly to interpret the Bible, the focus of chapters 2–4. In those chapters, we will discuss how to read the Bible in light of three crucial contexts. In the close context, we interpret the passage in front of us. In the continuing context, we read any biblical passage in light of what preceded it. Then in the complete or canonical context, we interpret the passage in light of the Bible's entire storyline.

In part 2, we will walk through the storyline of Scripture to discover how the Bible's full story reveals Christ's full glory. Three features of this section are worth noting. First, these chapters are organized to reinforce how the Bible is put together. Second, we will put into practice our reading of Scripture by using the three contexts we learned in part 1. Third, we will ask over and again a question that reveals a tension in the Bible's storyline: How will God keep his promise?

We hope that you will get a clear understanding of the Bible's unity and central message. And we pray that you will become more competent in reading the Bible for yourself. As Paul prays, so we pray that you may comprehend "how wide and long and high and deep is the love of Christ, and to know this love that surpasses knowledge—that you may be filled to the measure of all the fullness of God" (Eph. 3:18–19).

If you belong to Christ already, we pray you'll know him all the better, love his church more, and spread his gospel farther. If Christ is not your only hope in life and in death, we pray that he will become all of that for you by faith. That's a lot to ask, but it's not too much for our gracious Lord to grant.

"Now to him who is able to do immeasurably more than all we ask or imagine, according to his power that is at work within us, to him be glory in the church and in Christ Jesus throughout all generations, for ever and ever! Amen" (3:20–21).

PART 1

OPENING

the Book

Chapter 1

WHAT IS THE BIBLE?

"This is a football." These were the memorable words of NFL coach Vince Lombardi as he addressed his team at the start of training camp in the summer of 1961. Pretty obvious, right? But Lombardi chose to take nothing for granted, and starting with the basics, he built a great team that went on to win the national championship.

When we approach the Bible, our first question is usually, What does it say? Now that's a good question. But we need to ask another question first: What *is* the Bible? We ask this question because before we can understand what the Bible says, we need to understand what it is. We don't read a nutrition label like we would read a treasure map, nor do we read a novel like we would read a presidential biography. These are different kinds of writing, and we usually understand the difference. While the Bible is written with words like any other book, the Bible is not like any other book. After all, it's God's Word. As we get started, we need to know what kind of book it is so we can read it correctly and practice all that it teaches.

In the introduction, we introduced the illustration of a puzzle as a way of thinking about the Bible. Now consider the contrast between a puzzle and a mosaic. A mosaic consists of many pieces taken from different things, usually bits of pottery or panes of glass. Its pieces can be arranged in a variety of ways to make just about anything. A puzzle, on the other hand, is designed for a single purpose. It is intended to fit together, and if put together correctly, it results in the same picture every time.

We share this because we want you to see that the Bible is best viewed as a puzzle, not a mosaic. If the Bible were like a mosaic, it wouldn't matter how the pieces fit together. But because the Bible is like a puzzle, composed of many parts that God intends to fit together, then it greatly matters how all of its pieces fit in relation to the whole. If the Bible were a mosaic, its meaning would be ours to create. But because the Bible is a puzzle, we must discern how the pieces are intended to fit together.

This is what we mean when we talk about reading the Bible on its own terms. It requires that we read it according to what it is. So what is the Bible? This is a big question, so we'll break it into three separate questions:

- Who wrote the Bible?
- How does the Bible come to us?
- What is the Bible centrally about?

In this first chapter, we will focus on answering these three questions. Then in chapters 2–4, we will explore how to read the Bible in light of the answers to these questions.

WHO WROTE THE BIBLE?

When you pick up a book for the first time, you typically take note of the author. You might look into the author's experience, education, or credentials. It would be hard to take seriously a book on being a good mom written by a fourteen-year-old boy. The authorship of a book determines how seriously you'll take it and how carefully you'll read it. So it matters who wrote the Bible.

We will summarize the Bible's authorship this way: the Bible is the triune God's speech written through the agency of human authors. Let's unpack both parts of this statement.

From beginning to end, the Bible claims to be God's own speech or word in written format, and it makes this claim in a variety of ways. From the Bible's opening chapter, we meet God as a speaking God. One thing is definitely true about him: he speaks truth and he is faithful to his word. Reflecting on this, the psalmist writes, "By the word of the LORD the heavens were made" (Ps. 33:6). God speaks in such a way that, when he says it, it happens. Things come into existence!

But God also speaks words for us to read. Notice the repetition of words used in Psalm 19 to describe God's words to us:

> The law of the LORD is perfect,
> > refreshing the soul.
> The statutes of the LORD are trustworthy,
> > making wise the simple.
> The precepts of the LORD are right,
> > giving joy to the heart.
> The commands of the LORD are radiant,
> > giving light to the eyes.
> The fear of the LORD is pure,
> > enduring forever.
> The decrees of the LORD are firm,
> > and all of them are righteous.
> They are more precious than gold,
> > than much pure gold;
> they are sweeter than honey,
> > than honey from the honeycomb.
> By them your servant is warned;
> > in keeping them there is great reward.
>
> —PSALM 19:7–11

Though he doesn't say it directly here, the writer of Psalm 19 wants us to see that the Bible's nature is tied to God's nature. The Bible is the law, testimony, and precepts of the Lord. His perfection, his purity, his truthfulness, and his inestimable worth are reflected in what he says.

We rightly say that the Bible is inspired. But what does that mean, exactly? The use of this word is often unclear because of the varied meanings of it in English. Biblically, the word *inspiration* in reference to the Bible is best understood to mean "breathed out" (from the Greek word *theopneustos*). This is evident because the word for inspiration is used in 2 Timothy 3:16, where it emphasizes God's unique initiative and action in communicating to us in Scripture. Second Timothy 3:16 says this: "All Scripture is God-breathed." To say that God breathed out Scripture means that all of it comes from him: the Bible is God's own speech. This means that if we are to read Scripture on its own terms, we must read it as a divine book, a book authored by the triune Lord. We see this in the way Jesus, the divine Son, used the Scriptures in his own ministry. Jesus quoted from the Old Testament with authority (Matt. 4:4) because what it said, God said (Matt. 19:3–6). In this way, the Bible attests to its own divine authorship.

But while it is true to say that the Bible is God's speech, it's also God's Word, written through the agency of human authors. The Bible's human authorship is plain as well. Its authors name themselves and write about themselves. Their unique personalities and personal histories are evident throughout. For example, Luke writes as an educated doctor, Paul writes as a lifelong student of theology, and Peter writes as a fisherman. When they write, they do so from their unique and diverse human circumstances. Paul writes to Timothy about Demas, who "deserted me," and of Alexander the coppersmith, who "did me a great deal of harm" (2 Tim. 4:10, 14). He asks Timothy to "bring the cloak that I left with Carpus at Troas" (4:13). These are human circumstances, disappointments, and desires.

God did not dictate Scripture to these men. He sovereignly and supernaturally "breathed out" his words by acting through the human authors over time (Heb. 1:1–2). Theologians call this phenomenon dual authorship. It simply means that the Bible is simultaneously God's speech through the writings of human authors.

How do we summarize the relationship between the divine and human authors? Two biblical texts are crucial in answering this question.

- "For no prophecy was ever produced by the will of man, but men spoke from God as they were carried along by the Holy Spirit" (2 Peter 1:21 ESV).

- "All Scripture is God-breathed and is useful for teaching, rebuking, correcting and training in righteousness, so that the servant of God may be thoroughly equipped for every good work" (2 Tim. 3:16–17).

In the first text, Peter reminds us that the Bible's authors did not speak on their own. As they spoke, the Spirit supernaturally "carried" them along. As they freely wrote, God sovereignly worked so that what they wrote was what he wanted written. In the second text, Paul emphasizes that the text they wrote—Scripture—was God-breathed. Taking these passages together we can say that whatever the human authors of Scripture wrote is what God wanted written. "What the Bible says, God says," is a helpful way of summarizing what Scripture is. Scripture speaks with full authority and without error.

Not everyone accepts this view of Scripture. Some suggest that the human character of the Bible entails human error. They appeal to our human finitude and time-bound condition to establish this point, while also trying to say that Scripture is from God when it speaks on issues of faith and practice. Others suggest that the Bible is merely a record of God's revelation, so that Scripture is inspired in the sense that the men who wrote it had inspirational experiences with God that they put into writing. The experiences, not the writings, are from God. Still others suggest that the Bible gives us no doctrine of inspiration that demands that we identify its human writings with God's own word. They say that such a view of Scripture's full authority is only "a modern invention."

These alternative views are out of step with what the church has always believed about Scripture. More important, they deny the Bible's view of itself. If we read the Bible on its own terms, its self-testimony is clear: Scripture is God's authoritative speech through the writings of human authors. Jesus himself quoted Scripture as God's authoritative Word, saying things like, "It is written: 'Man shall not live on bread alone, but on every word that comes from the mouth of God'" (Matt. 4:4), or in reference to the Old Testament, "Scripture cannot be broken"

(John 10:35 ESV). For Jesus and the Bible's authors, the formula "it is written" introduced an appeal to Scripture as the highest authority. Even more explicit, when the author of Hebrews quotes from the Old Testament, he views it as God's own speech by the Spirit (Heb. 3:7).

These texts, plus many more, are reasons why we receive Scripture as God's word written. Let's conclude our discussion by considering how the book of Revelation teaches this truth. In Revelation, Jesus is called the "faithful and true witness" (3:14). Jesus affirms the truthfulness and the faithfulness of his own words when he says to John, "Write this down, for these words are trustworthy and true" (21:5). But how do we know what John wrote is trustworthy? Well, because Jesus said so. Speaking of John's writing, Jesus said, "These words are trustworthy and true" (22:6). Here Jesus' faithfulness extends from his character to his oral word, and from his oral word to its inscripturation by John. What John wrote is what God wanted written. And what is true here is true throughout the Scriptures. What Scripture says, God says, from beginning to end.

HOW DOES THE BIBLE COME TO US?

The Bible is a divine and human book, but there is more to the nature of Scripture than its origin. The Bible is also a progressively revealed book: it comes to us over time. God didn't drop Scripture down from heaven in a moment through the vision of a single person. He gave us the Bible over time, book by book. It comes to us as a compilation of sixty-six books written during a nearly two-thousand-year period. As later authors built on the work of previous authors, the Bible, as God's written revelation, reached its closure in the coming of Christ (Heb. 1:1–2).

God has given us his Word over time and in coordination with his redeeming activity in history. As God has acted throughout history, he has also breathed out his Word to provide us with his interpretation of his mighty acts. Scripture is best viewed as a "word-act revelation." God's Word is his interpretation of his acts in history to redeem.

Muslims believe that the Qur'an was transmitted from an eternal tablet in heaven. Mormons believe that the Book of Mormon was transmitted letter by letter to Joseph Smith. But Christians believe that our triune God acted personally in history and revealed himself across time. This truth is vital for a variety of reasons, but over the next few chapters, we'll see its importance specifically in how we correctly interpret and apply Scripture.

WHAT IS THE BIBLE CENTRALLY ABOUT?

Do the Bible's many words have a central subject and message? If you walk through a mall, you'll hear many words about many different things, but you'll ignore most of what you hear. You won't try to connect them together. You'll hear many words in a movie too, but you'll listen differently. You'll assume that these words are connected. Diverse characters and scenes come together to form a unified whole. So it is with the Bible.

Ultimately, the Bible has a single message uniting its diverse parts. As we assume unity when we enter the theater, so we assume unity when we open the Bible, given its divine authorship. The author of Hebrews makes this exact point. He reminds us that all of God's diverse revelation over time has reached its culmination in Christ: "In the past God spoke to our ancestors through the prophets at many times and in various ways, but in these last days he has spoken to us by his Son" (1:1–2). As God speaks through the prophets and inscripturates his spoken word, a canon is formed that reaches its closure in the New Testament books written about Christ.

Back to our question: What is the Bible about? Without trying to minimize the diversity of Scripture, we can say that the Bible is centrally about what our triune Creator-covenant God has done to redeem us and to make everything new in Jesus Christ our Lord. Ultimately, we cannot understand what God intends for us in any part of Scripture until we have understood that text in light of the fullness of revelation in Christ. Jesus, then, is the goal of all of God's previous revelation. Prior to Christ's coming, God's Word was authoritative but incomplete. Now, through Jesus, God's previous revelation has reached its fulfillment. Now all Scripture must be understood in light of him (Matt. 5:17–20). He is its subject and goal. You will recall from Luke 24 that Jesus' disciples were disillusioned about his death. How did Jesus enlighten his disciples? We are told, "Beginning with Moses and all the Prophets, he explained to them what was said in all the Scriptures concerning himself" (24:27). This is what Scripture is all about. Or, better, this is *who* Scripture is all about.

This doesn't mean that every Old Testament author understood how his writings and work would fit into the full plan of God. Peter reflects on this very point in one of his letters:

> Concerning this salvation, the prophets, who spoke of the grace that was to come to you, searched intently and with the greatest care, trying to find out the time and circumstances to which the Spirit of Christ in them was pointing when he predicted the sufferings of the Messiah and the glories that would follow. It was revealed to them that they were not serving themselves but you, when they spoke of the things that have now been told you by those who have preached the gospel to you by the Holy Spirit sent from heaven. Even angels long to look into these things.
>
> —1 PETER 1:10–12

According to Peter, the prophets operated in the "dark." They knew that what they did served a greater purpose, but they didn't know all the details. Given the Bible's view of inspiration, this isn't a problem for us. It just means that every text means something specific because of the author's intent, but the full significance of what was written and the text's ultimate referent becomes clearer only as the Bible's story unfolds. While the human author had a clear intent, as God's plan unfolded, God's ultimate intention became clearer, reaching its fullness in Christ.

It's important to note that the fullness of God's revelation is not at odds with the original writers' understanding. The author of any movie script knows things that the characters in the story he creates don't know. Every line in a movie has a specific meaning in that moment, and yet the end of the film brings a fuller, more complete meaning. That's why we can watch a movie a second time with new insight. Each biblical author may not have understood the Bible's whole story to which his life and writing is a contribution, but in its own context, what he did and wrote communicated something important to the overall plan. Yet because of the promises of God, the biblical authors knew that what they were writing was also leading somewhere, farther ahead in the story. As Peter reminds us, they didn't know the full storyline, but they longed to see where the story would lead. So, apparently, do the angels (1 Peter 1:12).

HOW THEN SHOULD WE READ THE BIBLE?

We've considered the question, What *is* the Bible? This is the first question we need to answer if we're going to read the Bible faithfully, but we cannot stop here. We also need to ask, How should we read the Bible? As with any book, there is a proper and an improper way to interpret the Bible. And given what Scripture is, a wrong reading is particularly serious. This is why Paul exhorts Timothy to be one who "correctly handles the word of truth" (2 Tim. 2:15), for Timothy's own life and the lives of his hearers are at stake (1 Tim. 4:16).

As we mentioned earlier, the idea that a person can read the Bible incorrectly surprises some people. Isn't God speaking to each of us through the Bible? Isn't what we read from God clear? Yes, but this is not always true in the way we sometimes think. Over the next three chapters, we will address this crucial question with the goal of making us all more faithful readers and doers of God's Word.

Before we get started, we offer a word of warning. Chapters 2–4 may stretch you at times. You might have to read some sections twice or put the book down and think about them for a bit. Think of them as you might the task of reading the directions before playing a board game or attending a briefing on the rules of football before watching or playing it. If you know the rules, the game will make sense and you might even enjoy it. But learning those rules can be a bit tedious and frustrating until you start to see how they fit into the larger game. Be encouraged. If you invest the time it takes to wrestle with the crucial matters in the next few chapters, you'll have much more enjoyment exploring the Bible's story in part 2 of this book.

Chapter 2

LOOKING DOWN

The Close Context

Most children experience that moment of amazement when they realize their parents always know how to find their way. When it comes to navigation, adults know something kids don't.

Whether you're driving across town or across the country, if you want to get to your destination, you need to pay attention to your context. Or more accurately, to several contexts. First, you need to consider what immediately surrounds you. Second, you must take into account where you've been. Third, you must remember where you're going. Children are confused because they don't track these contexts. They don't know where they are, they don't know how they got there, and they don't always know where they're going.

Wherever you're going, these three contexts are present. If you don't know them, you're probably lost. Understanding this helps explain why many of us feel lost when we open our Bibles. In the last chapter, we looked at three features of Scripture: its divine-human authorship, its progressive nature, and its central message that God has redeemed us and made everything new in Christ. In light of these three features, it's best to think of three interlocking contexts when we interpret and apply the Bible:[1]

- The *close context*. We saw that the Bible is a divine-human revelation. So when we *look down* at the page, we seek to understand the words in their immediate context. The close context takes into account the divine inspiration and human character of the words written.

- The *continuing context*. We also noted that the Bible is a progressive revelation. Thus we *look back* in the story to read a given passage according to the Bible's unfolding drama. The continuing context takes into account where the words are in relation to what has come before them in the unfolding story.
- The *complete or canonical context*. Because the Bible is a book centered on Jesus, we *look ahead* in the story, even when we read the earlier parts before the coming of Jesus, so that we read them in light of the whole of Scripture. The complete context takes into account the whole Bible's message centered in Christ and brought to bear on our lives.

To help you grasp these three contexts, let's return to the puzzle illustration. If we want to fit a given puzzle piece into the puzzle, we must do three things: study the individual piece with its colors and shape (close context), examine what has been done so far and what remains undone (continuing context), and look at the box for the big picture (complete context). All three steps are necessary to understand and appreciate the significance of any one piece of the puzzle.

The same is true when we're reading the Bible.

Let's start by looking at this first context in the puzzle, the work of looking at individual pieces with all their colors and varying shapes. As we interpret Scripture, we'll call this the close context—the context of the words, ideas, and book we're reading as it's understood within its historical setting. This is what we see when we look down at the page in front of us.

When putting together a puzzle, we can't ignore the specific features of the pieces. And when we're reading Scripture, we can't ignore the specific features of each text. When we look at the words in any given book of the Bible, we must read them in a way that fits both their divine and human character. Let's think about what this entails.

READ THE BIBLE AS A DIVINE BOOK

Most of us reflexively throw away junk mail. We assume that the mail we receive from people we don't know is meaningless. Even our email inboxes are programmed to trash spam. Yet when we receive a letter from a family member, friend, or romantic interest, we read with interest. Some of this mail we may choose to keep for a lifetime. The message contained in this correspondence directly affects our lives.

Consider what it means to read Scripture as a divine book—a book from God to us! If God wrote every word, sentence, paragraph, chapter, and book, then the Bible is unified. The Bible's sixty-six books really do form one book from one Author. It's also coherent. If we're confused about the meaning of a certain text, we may assume that we're the ones confused, not God. The Bible coheres with itself and with the world in which its readers live. It's complete—the Bible is what God wanted us to have. If it raises questions that it doesn't completely answer, then that must be on purpose. And not only is it complete, but it's also sufficient for what we need. The Bible is perfect. There's nothing wrong with it. Every word is good and true. The Bible is also urgent. If God has spoken to us, then nothing is more important than for us to listen to its message.

All of these truths about Scripture have major implications for how we interpret the Bible. We should read it with creaturely humility because these words are from our Creator and Lord. We are to read with expectation. If we look forward to the release of a new novel by a favorite author, how much more should we look forward to reading God's Word!

We should also read with caution, recognizing that we are inclined to misunderstand what God has written, given our finitude and sinfulness. That means we should read the Bible patiently to accurately discern what God has said. We cannot assume that what first comes into our minds matches what's in God's mind. We read and we reflect, and once we settle on an interpretation that is faithful to the text and aligned with previous interpretations, we submit to God's Word.

If we disagree with something the Bible teaches, we assume that our thinking must change, not God's. We don't stand over Scripture; we stand under it in submission to God (Isa. 66:1–2). We are aware of the Bible's divine authorship, and we are aware of our creaturely position as readers.

READ THE BIBLE AS A HUMAN BOOK

Since the Bible is also a human book, we must not neglect its human character. There is a danger in focusing on the Bible's divine character to the extent that we forget to read its poetry as poetry and its stories as stories. Again, we cannot assume that the thoughts that pop first into our heads as we read are always God's thoughts. God speaks to us through what the authors wrote, which demands hard work from us to discern what the authors intended to say. Reading a given text in its close context means reading it in its literary and historical context.

Consider the Literary Context

Two words are helpful in thinking about the literary context: flow and form. Reading a text in its literary context involves interpreting it in light of its flow of words and the form the words take. Let's explore both of these aspects of literary context.

First, consider reading a text in terms of the flow of words around it. Words mean something in the sentences, paragraphs, chapters, and books in which they are used. We don't begin reading a novel in the middle of the book. If we try, we'll miss the details that give shape to the characters and the plot, and we'll spend most of the book trying to figure out what is happening and why. Yet that's how many people approach the Bible. Since it's a long book and pastors preach out of different sections each week, we get used to entering and exiting portions of Scripture without considering the context of the books in which they are found, let alone their location in the rest of the Bible's storyline.

There are, of course, good reasons why preaching begins and ends with a text in the middle of a book of the Bible. Sometimes the preacher is picking up where a previous sermon left off. But this practice can also reinforce our tendency to read passages in isolation. There's an easy way to fix this, thankfully! Be encouraged: if you take the time to read and reflect on a book as a whole, then every part of that book will start to make more sense.

Second, we must learn to read texts by considering the form the author chooses to employ in writing. The Bible's words are written in the form of minimally three different kinds of texts: discourse, narrative, and poetry. Learning to spot the form or the kind of text the author writes will greatly help you in your personal Bible reading.

Discourse texts are simply words spoken or written from one person to another. They are structured in several common ways. They rely on logic, moving from one idea to the next and connecting those ideas with words like *therefore* and *but*.

Narrative texts are words that tell a story. From English Lit class, you may recall that narrative texts have an unfolding plot, a narrative arc. Narratives have settings, which include details about the characters and the place. Typically, a conflict rises to a point of climax, after which the action reaches a point of resolution. This resolution leads to a new setting, which further unfolds the plot.

Poetic texts are yet another form. Poetry conveys its meaning through images, and it is structured, at least in English poetry, by rhyming lines. Instead of rhyming lines, most biblical poetry is structured by parallel lines. Knowing the structure of Hebrew poetry can be crucial to interpreting poetic texts correctly.

Often different kinds of texts are combined in a book of the Bible to create an entire genre or literary form. For example, the genre of New Testament epistles is similar to written letters. An epistle contains discourse, but it may also include poetry. Old Testament narrative is a genre that includes a great deal of narrative, but it may also include poetry and some discourse. Old Testament Wisdom and Prophetic Literature, two separate genres, include mostly poetry, but other text-types are present at times as well. Here are the common genres found in Scripture: Old Testament Narrative, Wisdom, Prophetic, Gospels and Acts, Epistolary, Apocalyptic.

We must interpret each passage of Scripture in its literary context. This means understanding it in light of the *flow* of words around it and the *form* the author employs.

Consider the Historical Context

Every passage of Scripture emerges in the course of history. To understand the historical context of a passage, we begin with the *author* and the *original audience*. When thinking about the original audience, we should distinguish the original characters in the story from the original readers, those who were reading Scripture about those characters. For example, when we read the story of Abraham, we do so from the standpoint of Moses, who wrote the story of Abraham while he led the nation of Israel in the wilderness as they prepared to enter the promised land. In considering the historical context, we ask, What is Moses teaching the Israelites about Abraham and the Patriarchs?

Or consider the historical context for reading the Gospels. The Gospels were written after Christ's resurrection to explain to people who Jesus is, but the authors included details about events *prior to* Jesus' death and resurrection. For example, in his Gospel account, John tells his post-resurrection readers about events that weren't fully understood until *after* the resurrection, not only preserving historical accuracy but also reminding us that the original audience was reading the Gospel *after* Christ's resurrection (John 2:12–22).

The historical context also includes *circumstances* that gave rise to the book and *cultural features* of life at that time. For example, in Revelation 3:14–22 we are told that John writes to seven churches. We should not forget that these were real churches with real locations in the first century, and the details in chapters 2 and 3 reflect this fact. Jesus tells the church at Laodicea that they are neither "hot" nor "cold" (3:15–16). How would they have heard this? As it turns out, Laodicea neighbored two cities, Hierapolis and Colossae. The hot springs of Hierapolis were of great medicinal value, while the cold springs of Colossae brought nourishment and refreshment. Laodicea, on the other hand, had a water supply that was lukewarm, tasteless, and useless. Unfortunately, the spiritual life of the church had become like her city's water supply—lukewarm and useless.

This is what it means to read the Bible *according to its close context*. We take seriously every word and read them in keeping with their divine *and* human intent.

Chapter 3

LOOKING BACK

The Continuing Context

The Bible was written over time, spanning several centuries from beginning to end before it was compiled into the single book we have today. This may seem like an obvious point, but it's a reality we easily neglect. To fully appreciate this truth, we need to read the Bible in light of its continuing context: we must *look back* in the story to discover how a given passage relates to what *preceded* it.

When you're putting together a puzzle, you need to periodically stop, look at what you've already completed, and then look at the box top to see what is yet undone. In a similar way we need to interpret a biblical passage by thinking through what comes before it and then thinking about what comes after it. We often do this when we watch a play with several acts. We know that one act leads to another, and the successive acts make sense only in the context of what happens before and after that act.

How do we discern the sequence of the Bible's unfolding story? One simple way to start is by considering the Bible's chronology—when the various parts were written. For example, Moses wrote the first five books of the Bible, commonly known as the Pentateuch, in a specific order for a purpose. He wanted us to read the story of the exodus in light of what happened in Genesis. The exodus and Israel's role as a nation should be understood in light of the stories of creation, Adam, the fall, and the Patriarchs. Or consider when we read the Prophets as another example. When we read these books, we must understand them in light of everything that preceded them. The Prophetic Books build on the books that came before them, often picking up on key themes from those writings.

But we need to clarify that the Bible's chronology is not always determinative. If we push the chronology too far, confusion results. Consider the placement of the Wisdom Literature, the books of Job, Psalms, Proverbs, and several others. These books are not ordered by chronology but are arranged together for a different reason. Job was likely written very early, but it is placed in a collection that appears much later. And think of the arrangement of the Psalter. It contains psalms from diverse time periods, but they are all arranged in a common book. Psalm 90 is written by Moses, and Psalm 137 is written during the Babylonian exile—a span of many centuries between the two. This means that the Psalter, as a unified collection, is post-exilic—it was arranged in its current form *after* the Babylonian exile and placed along with the other Wisdom Literature. We need to consider this final arrangement and the context for that arrangement when reading the Psalter.

We should also know that while the Prophets come later in the arrangement of the Bible, they are not placed in order of chronology but according to length. The New Testament letters, similarly, are ordered according to length or kind, and not according to when they were written. The chronology of the Bible's books is important, but we need something more to discern the true shape of the story they tell.

In discerning the *continuing context*, then, we are attempting to discern the deeper shape and flow of the story. A helpful example of how this works comes from the world of geology. Geologists tell us that the earth's land masses are composed of large plates that shift from time to time. Scientists call this plate tectonics. The movement of these unseen plates brings volcanic eruptions, earthquakes, tsunamis, and the slow movement of continents. The shifting of these plates explains the action on the surface.

The Bible is much like that. The movements of characters and events are related by an underlying structure. What is that structure? The most significant chronological marker is Christ's coming—the division between the Old and New Testaments. The Old Testament contains books written *before* the incarnation, while the New Testament is written *after* the coming of Christ. Galatians 4:4 gives a clue to why this is so significant, speaking of Christ's coming as the culmination of history: "When the set time had fully come, God sent his Son." Everything *before* Christ anticipates him, and everything *after* Christ expounds him. Paul sees all of history as subsumed under two heads, Adam and Christ (Rom. 5:12–21). The coming of Christ divides history into two parts.

While the coming of Christ divides the story in two, the Bible also highlights several other important turns in the story, resulting in momentous change. Here are a few to note:

- Before the fall of Adam, and after the fall (Gen. 1–2 versus Gen. 3; see Rom. 8:20)
- The Patriarchs, the Old Covenant, the exile, and the Coming of Christ (Acts 7:1–53)
- Abraham to David, David to the exile, the exile to Christ (Matt. 1:1–17)
- Before the cross, after the resurrection (John 2:20–22)

To honor the most significant divisions of the Bible's story, we will focus on two sets of divisions. The first will be akin to a wide-angle photographic lens, helping us to gain the "big picture." The second will be more like a narrow lens, giving us an up-close perspective. The wide-angle view will trace the Bible's broad plot movements, while the close-up view shows us the Bible's unfolding story *through* the biblical covenants. Seeing how these views work together gives us a flyover of the Bible's basic shape and helps us understand how the Bible is put together *on its own terms*.

TRACE THE BIBLE'S PLOT MOVEMENTS

The Bible's long and layered story can be outlined in four major plot movements: *creation*, *fall*, *redemption*, and *new creation*. These four plot movements are helpful because they follow the Bible's own plot and help us think about the Bible's unique worldview against other worldviews. Thinking through the Bible's plot movements helps us answer the questions that every person asks and must ultimately answer:

- Where did we come from?
- What went wrong?
- What is the solution to our problem?
- Where is history ultimately going?

These are questions the world perennially asks, and the Bible's answers are clear, satisfying, and true.

Creation

Where did everything come from? Genesis 1–2 gives the account of God's creation of all things, including human beings like you and me, his creatures and image-bearers. This initial section of the Bible is short, but it is theologically significant, packed with meaning. Why? Because it's foundational to everything that Scripture teaches, setting the stage for the rest of the Bible's unfolding drama. Here we meet several key characters and first grasp the setting for Scripture's story. We also learn several of the major themes and patterns that will be progressively unpacked through the later covenants, all working toward an ultimate end.

Fall

What went wrong? In Genesis 3, everything changed in the world God made, including his relationship with his created people. Adam, the first man, forever changed the direction of space-time history with his choice to rebel against God. When tempted by Satan, Adam disobeyed God and plunged his descendants, the entire human race, into sin, death, and condemnation. The fall establishes the terrible problem that the rest of Scripture is written to address. Apart from Genesis 3, we cannot make sense of God's glorious plan of redemption. The question that creates tension in the story is, How can sinful and rebellious human beings ever be acceptable before the triune, holy God, given sin's impurity and pollution? How can you and I stand before God without being condemned? Because of Adam's choice to rebel and our banishment from God's presence, our only hope is found in God's gracious initiative to redeem and to reverse the effects of sin and death caused by Adam.

Redemption

The world is broken and condemned. Where do we find hope? In Genesis 3:15 God promises that a son—the "seed" of the woman, a human offspring—will one day come to crush the enemy who tempted our first father and mother. This enemy is the serpent, or Satan, and the promised son will crush his head. Although human beings merit nothing but death for their sin—the wages of sin is death (Rom. 6:23)—death will not get the last word. God says that death itself will be put to death! The rest of the Bible, with all the stories and details in that storyline— the people, the sacrificial system, its saving events—slowly unfolds this initial "good news" promise, which is fulfilled in the person and work of Jesus Christ.

What is that work? The life and death of Christ and his resurrection from the dead. Through Messiah Jesus—God's own Son—the Father creates a new humanity, the church, that can enjoy the full forgiveness of sins, new hearts, and uninhibited access to the Father through the Spirit. The fall crippled God's original intention for his image-bearers, yet Christ redeems it through his work on the cross. We receive the benefits of the work Christ has done by grace alone through faith alone, trusting in the promise he makes to us.

New Creation

In light of all this, where is history now going? The direction of history is toward a new creation, the goal and end of God's redeeming promise. The present order is the old creation in Adam, but Christ will bring a new creation. The Old Testament prophets describe this new creation as arriving in the coming of God's King and Messiah. Through his life, death, and resurrection, Jesus brings the new creation. In his return, he will bring the new creation in its fullness. In Revelation 21–22, the exalted Jesus gives John, his apostle, a symbolic vision of this future age, and it is beautiful to behold. Even now some of what John envisioned is present in Christ's people, who are a new creation, a colony of the future age, although we still await the fullness of that new creation when Christ returns.

These four plot movements serve as the wide-angle lens of Scripture. They help us grasp the broad contours of the Bible's story. But as helpful as they are, more must be said to make sense of the diversity of material between these broad divisions. Thankfully, in addition to the four primary plot movements, Scripture gives us some clues about its own internal structure, clues that help us navigate the Bible's storyline with confidence.

TRACE THE BIBLE'S COVENANTS

In 1930, the University of Chicago's law school hired Mortimer Adler to teach "the philosophy of law," and to help in teaching the class he wrote a helpful little book titled *How to Read a Book*. Here's how Adler begins a chapter titled "X-Raying a Book": "Every book has a skeleton hidden between its covers. Your job as an analytical reader is to find it. A book comes to you with flesh on its bare bones and clothes over its flesh. It is all dressed up. You do not have to undress it or tear the flesh off its limbs to get at the firm structure that underlies the soft surface. But you must read the book with X-ray eyes, for it is an essential part of your apprehension of any book to grasp its structure."[2]

The Bible's four plot movements give us the rough outlines of the skeleton that underlies the Bible's structure. This helps us, but if we want to see with finer details and understand what shapes the Bible's deeper structure, we need to grasp something called a *covenant*. The word *covenant* tells us something about who God is and how he acts. It tells us that God enters into relationships. And he chooses to enter into relationships with us, human beings he has created. "I will take you as my own people, and I will be your God" (Ex. 6:7). As God's plan progressively unfolds, he makes a series of covenants with different people.

These biblical covenants bring order, direction, and focus to the story of God's redemption of the fallen human race.

Covenants are simply God's way of relating with his people. You can think of covenants like you think of the interstate highway system in the United States. Among the thousands and thousands of roads in the country, a few facilitate movement at a high speed from one side of the country to the other. Covenants are how the Bible's story moves along from beginning to end. And to pick up on the metaphor Mortimer Adler used, covenants are the backbone of Scripture's grand story, holding its four-part skeleton together.

What exactly is a covenant? *Covenant* is an older word that has fallen largely out of use today. It refers to a means by which we structure a relationship. Our contemporary word *contract* is the most familiar way we structure relationships today, and a covenant and a modern contract have some similarities. For example, both types of agreements involve parties and require obligations. If you buy a car, hire an employee, or rent a home, you need to enter into a contractual relationship with another person or party. But a contract and a covenant also have important differences. While a contract involves a relationship for the sake of obligations, a covenant involves obligations for the sake of a relationship. A covenant is *a chosen relationship between two parties ordered according to specific promises.*

In a contract, if one party fails to fulfill his or her obligations, certain consequences follow. The emphasis falls on the performance of obligations and completing that transaction. The relationship is somewhat secondary. But in a covenant, the relationship is primary, and the promises made to each other serve the higher purpose of the relationship. Though many people today think of marriage as a contract, in the biblical understanding it is not. In marriage, a husband and a wife make a covenant. Even if a person today doesn't have a precise sense of what makes a covenant, he or she understands that marriage is different from a typical business deal. Whatever else may be involved in a marriage, it's about the relationship between a husband and a wife, as well as their relationship with the children who result from that union.

Covenants were quite common in the Ancient Near East, the time and place where most of the Bible occurs, and the biblical covenants reflect this. They have many similarities to other covenants at the time, similar structures and procedures, yet the biblical covenants exhibit important differences. Those differences reveal the uniqueness of what God is doing to redeem us and usher in his new creation in Christ. Let's take a close look at how God unfolds his one plan through these biblical covenants.

God's Covenant with Creation through Adam and Noah

The Bible begins with the creation of the world and the special creation of human beings, who were created in God's image. Adam, the first man, is not merely the first biological man; he is also the representative head of humanity and of creation itself. For this reason, when Adam disobeys God's command, his sinful choice affects *all* people and the entire creation. Yet according to God's gracious promise (Gen. 3:15), a son/seed of Eve will undo the curse of sin on the world and restore humanity to God. God has not given up on his plans for his creation, nor has he abandoned his image-bearers.

When God later judged the world with a flood, he saved Noah, his family, and two of every creature. The story of Noah and his family bears some similarities to the original story of creation, giving us hints that this is a "restart" on creation. As God commanded Adam before him, Noah was to fill the earth and rule over it. When God made a covenant with Noah, he placed his rainbow in the sky as "the sign of the covenant between me and the earth" (Gen. 9:13). God's covenant with Noah is a *reaffirmation* of the foundational covenant with Adam and creation. Yet unlike the original covenant with Adam and creation, the Noahic covenant is established in the context of a fallen world subject to God's judgment. Because of God's promise to Noah, we know that God will graciously preserve creation and the created order of things until a day of judgment and the coming of a new creation, despite ongoing human sin and depravity. God's covenant with Noah is an extension of his relationship with Adam, but it also gives us hints of how salvation will come to this world—God will work through creation by providing a seed of the woman, who will reverse all the effects of Adam's sin.

God's Covenant with Abraham and His Children

As Noah's children multiplied, they lived just like their ancestors had, carrying on humanity's sinful rebellion and the curse of Adam. The Tower of Babel is evidence that humanity's Adam-like, God-defying ambition continues. We see evidence that sin is passed on from generation to generation, and we wonder how God will reverse the effects of sin and death and restore us to our image-bearing role.

The answer to that question is the Abrahamic covenant. Set in the context of Genesis 1–11, the Abrahamic covenant is how God will fulfill his promise to redeem and restore the world. Through *one family*, Abraham and his seed, God will make good on his promise to reverse the effects of sin and death. By sovereign grace—not according to anything Abraham had done or any special quality he possessed—God chose Abraham, an idol worshiper, and promised to bless him with a great name, land, and offspring to bring salvation to all nations (Gen. 12:1–3; cf. Josh. 24:2–4). Through the Abrahamic covenant, God clarifies further how his saving promise will take place. In its inauguration in Genesis 15:9–19, he demonstrates how *he* alone will keep his promise to save, underscoring the truth that salvation is of the Lord (Jonah 2:9). God's promises rely on his commitment to his word alone, and so we receive its blessings through faith alone (Gen. 15:6).

In the garden, God banished Adam and the human race from God's presence. Now Abraham's children, identified as those who trust and obey God, will be God's people, restored to his presence and remade to fulfill God's intent for human beings—to be his image-bearers and servant kings.

God's Covenant with Israel through Moses

Abraham's descendants multiply into a nation—the people of Israel. And as the story continues, God makes an additional agreement with them. In God's covenant with Israel, mediated through a man named

Moses, God's promise is now focused on an entire *nation*—a holy nation and a kingdom of priests who are to act as God's son (Ex. 4:22; 19:6). When the promise God made to Abraham began looking dim, God delivered his people from Egyptian slavery through Moses in an event known as the exodus. The exodus gave birth to Israel as God's covenant people and served as a paradigm for all of God's saving acts to follow.

In this part of the biblical storyline, God delivers his people from Egypt to a mountain, where he gives the Law to them (Ex. 19–20). Moses serves as the mediator of this covenant, and God outlines his plans for the nation. These plans include the key roles of prophets, priests, and kings, each role touching on an aspect of Adam's original role in Eden. Again, we see that God's covenant with Israel builds upon the previous covenants, continuing to unfold God's one plan of redemption and his original purposes for us. The structure of God's covenant with Moses included blessings for obedience and curses for disobedience, and through her obedience Israel would experience the blessings of God's covenant.

As the story unfolds further, it becomes clear that while Israel sometimes obeys, the pattern of her life as a nation is largely one of disobedience to God's Word. Despite her special calling and God's promises and blessings, Israel acts just like Adam in her rebellion and rejection of God. This covenant, often called "the old covenant," although given by God, also points beyond itself to something greater. In itself it was insufficient because it foreshadowed what was necessary to save us, but it did not provide that salvation in full.

In God's plan, we discover that God, in a whole host of ways, intended for this covenant to point beyond itself to the coming of Christ and the new covenant (Jer. 31:31–34). In God's plan, the covenant with Israel through Moses—the old covenant—was intended to be temporary as part of God's unfolding plan through the covenants. It graciously allowed God to dwell in Israel's midst as their Covenant Lord, but it also revealed the need for a greater covenant tied to a greater mediator and sacrifice. As part of God's plan, the old covenant served several purposes: it revealed the hideous nature of human sin (Rom. 7:13), it unveiled the greatness of God's grace, and it prophetically anticipated the righteousness of God in the gospel (Rom. 3:21) by serving as a guardian to lead us to the promised seed of Adam and the true son of Abraham, Jesus Christ (Gal. 3:19–4:7).

God's Covenant with David and His Sons

As the nation of Israel is established in the land God had promised to his people, they call for a king to rule over them. Through the Davidic covenant, God's promise is now focused on an *individual:* the king. Each of God's previous covenants are now brought to a head in this covenant with the king of the nation. From Adam as a kind of "kingly" ruler, to the promise that kings would come from Abraham (Gen. 17:6), to the anticipation of the king in the establishment of the old covenant (Deut. 17:14–20; Num. 24:7; Judg. 21:25), we finally have the arrival of the king. Before David is inaugurated as king, Israel sinfully trusts man instead of God's Word and demands a king to rule them like the kings of the nations. In a king named Saul, the people got what they demanded, along with the tragic consequences of such a ruler. In contrast, David, Saul's successor, would be *God's* king, his choice as a ruler for his people, the promised one from Judah's line (Gen. 49:8–12). In his covenant with David, God promises a "son/king," a throne, and a kingdom that will never end (2 Sam. 7:14).

In the promise God makes to David of a "son," we hear echoes of Israel as God's son (Ex. 4:22). And we hear echoes of God's promise to provide a man who will undo Adam's work (Gen. 3:15). This seed/ son will be descended from David's line, and he will fulfill all of God's promises. The storyline of the Bible now centers on David's dynasty. Yet as we soon witness, David and his sons disobey as well and fail, leaving God's salvation promises in question, at least from a human perspective.

God's New Covenant in Christ

The question of the entire first half of the Bible—what we commonly call the Old Testament—is when and how God will honor his promises, his covenants with Adam, Noah, Abraham, Moses, and David. With the arrival of Jesus of Nazareth—who is revealed to be God's eternal Son, born into history as a descendant of Adam, Abraham, and David—all of

God's promises are now a yes and the covenants reach their fulfillment (2 Cor. 1:20). As God planned from eternity, through the new covenant established by our Lord Jesus Christ, our triune God inaugurates his kingdom and saving reign in the world. In his incarnation, the divine Son becomes the promised son of Eve, Abraham's seed, the true Israel, and David's greater Son, and he achieves our redemption from the effects of sin and the curse by his work. By Jesus' life, death, resurrection, ascension, and the pouring out of the Spirit at Pentecost, *he* pays for our sin, remakes us as his new creation, and removes the curse of sin upon creation. In Christ alone, all of God's promises are fulfilled, and the original purpose of our creation as God's covenant people living in relationship with him is now accomplished forever.

CHARACTERISTICS OF BIBLICAL COVENANTS

It may be helpful to clarify several characteristics of biblical covenants that are important to grasp as we look closely at the Bible's unfolding story.

God's covenants are part of God's one plan of salvation. Multiple covenants do *not* entail multiple ways of salvation. There is *one* plan of God for redemption, and the covenants unfold that *one* plan. Sometimes theologians and biblical scholars will speak of a covenant of works and a covenant of grace, but it's better to think in terms of *one* plan that each of the *covenants* unveil as they progressively unfold God's plan, which culminates in our Lord Jesus Christ. The covenants are interrelated, beginning in creation and finding their fulfillment in Christ. Yet it's equally important to think through how each covenant uniquely contributes to God's overall plan as it is fulfilled in Christ. Each covenant has its own part to play in preparing us for the coming of Christ and the culmination of God's glorious and unified plan of salvation.

God's covenants progress from one to another. Across Scripture, we see many different covenants, but as we just noted, they aren't separate or isolated from one another in God's plan and purposes. How do these covenants relate to one another and unfold God's plan? We'll cover that in detail in part 2 of this book. For now, it's enough to note that God's various covenants *progress* from one to another, revealing his one salvation plan as it leads us to Christ. We'll also see that grasping *how* the covenants relate to one another makes a difference for how we understand any given passage in the Bible and apply it to our lives today.

God's covenants are unconditional and conditional. Some people divide the biblical covenants into either unconditional or conditional covenants, based on differences that were common in the Ancient Near East. But it's not as simple as dividing or categorizing the biblical covenants in this way. It's best to think of the biblical covenants as consisting of both unconditional and conditional elements. On the one hand, each covenant is unconditional and unilateral because of God's gracious initiative to redeem and to keep his own promises. On the other hand, each covenant is conditional because it involves a human partner who is called to obey God. God, as our Creator and Lord, demands perfect love, loyalty, and obedience, which highlights the conditional aspect of each covenant.

Why is this important? Because as the Bible's storyline unfolds, it becomes clear that God always keeps his promises, but human beings do not. In each covenant that God makes, we eventually find that *no human partner loves and obeys God perfectly.* What hope can there be for us? The only hope is that God keeps his own promise to redeem us through the provision of his Son, who does perfectly keep his promises. Jesus Christ simultaneously meets God's own righteous demand *and* acts as our obedient covenant representative and substitute. Through his obedience, sinners can be saved.

God's covenants are revelatory; they reveal who God is and his plan. The covenants include many different elements, including laws and commands, but they are far more than a collection of rules. In all of their elements, the covenants reveal the nature of God and his plan to save. In studying each covenant, we learn more about the God who makes these promises, who he is and why he does what he does. We learn that our God is a gracious God, faithful to his Word, and he saves through his Promised One. In numerous ways, the covenants reveal who this Promised One is, the need he comes to address, and what he does to save. As we read the Bible's story, we are always asking ourselves, How does *this* covenant reveal the God who saves and the Savior he sends?

Chapter 4

LOOKING AHEAD

The Complete Context

The Bible is a unified book centered in Jesus Christ. The complete context—what we can also call the *canonical* context—is where we *look ahead* to discover the fullness of God's intent in light of the fullness of Scripture's message.

Let's return to our puzzle illustration. If you recall, to put together a puzzle, we must locate the place for each piece in light of the "big picture" we see on the box. Individual pieces in isolation from that big picture can be confusing. Even with the big picture in view, it takes time to discern how exactly a given piece relates to the whole. It's much that way with Scripture. We know the Bible is about Christ, but how can we relate its various parts to that big picture truth?

There are at least two ways Scripture puts together the diverse details of God's plan into an overall unity in Christ—the big picture that helps us unlock the puzzle of the Bible. The two ways are the *promise-fulfillment* theme and the unfolding of *typology* through the biblical covenants. As we explore the ways God has stitched his story together, we will grow in our ability to see the glory of Jesus Christ.

FOLLOW PROMISE TO FULFILLMENT IN CHRIST

There was a time when my [Trent's] son would make a connection between almost any topic and monster trucks. He would find connections where they did not exist because monster trucks were always on his mind. The hidden meaning of *Moby Dick*—monster trucks. The latest movie playing—monster trucks. Obviously, he was guilty of reading his obsession into everything he saw and experienced.

In fairness to my son, we should admit that we are all vulnerable to making superficial connections. And we often do this when we read the Bible, especially when we're looking for connections to Christ. On the one hand, this makes sense. We should look for Christ in our reading of Scripture because he is on our minds and we know that he is central to the storyline of the Bible. That said, we also need to remember that the Bible moves *from promise to fulfillment* in Christ *through the biblical covenants*. There is continuity between the promises God makes and the fulfillment he brings. Promise and fulfillment glue the Bible's diverse phases together. Knowing this helps us discern how a given part of Scripture relates to the Christ of Scripture.

The distinction between the Old and New Testaments best shows us the promise-fulfillment structure of Scripture. This significant division reminds us how God's promises are now fulfilled in Christ. As the covenants unfold from Adam to Christ, we discover how God's initial promise in Genesis 3:15 is accomplished with greater clarity and detail. The simple way to grasp this is to say that *the Old Testament is the story of God's promise and the New Testament is God's fulfillment of all he has promised.*

FOLLOW THE TYPOLOGICAL PATTERNS FULFILLED IN CHRIST

One of the crucial ways the Bible moves from promise to fulfillment is by using *typology*. This is an unusual word, and it's a word we don't use in everyday conversation. But it's a biblical word, and its meaning isn't difficult to grasp.

We find it helpful to start with the English word *typical*. When we say that something is typical, we mean it follows a certain pattern. Earlier, when we examined the *continuing context*, we considered the central significance of "covenant" as the way the Bible's story unfolds.

Here we want to explore how the Bible's thematic patterns—or *types*—are traced through the covenants.

The concept of typology, the study of these types, comes from the New Testament authors' use of the Greek term *typos*. Most of the primary types that we study are given to us in the apostolic writings. They help us see how the revelatory features of God's unfolding plan in the past relate to his new revelation in Christ. For example, Paul refers to Adam as "a type of the one who was to come" (Rom. 5:14 ESV), and Peter refers to baptism as an "antitype" of Noah's flood (1 Peter 3:18–22).

We should note that when the writers of Scripture use *typos*, they are not using it as a technical term. It's used in a variety of ways, most frequently with reference to an "example" or "pattern" of living worthy of imitation. The concept of typology takes its cue from this word group, but it's also derived from the wider context of Scripture. Biblical authors note that in God's plan, he has established the story and unveiled its significance through various patterns. These patterns are *not* accidental but are intended to point forward and reveal his glorious plan of redemption. Since our triune God is the Lord of history and the single author of Scripture, through various types he prepares us for the fulfillment of his plan centered in the coming of our Lord Jesus Christ.

Types are categorized in several ways. One popular and useful way to think of types is in terms of *people*, *events*, and *institutions*. The types are real, present on the grand stage of human history, but they have a significance beyond themselves. As later biblical authors interpret salvation history through these patterns, we gain insight into how God's plan anticipates and predicts the coming of Jesus. Jesus, as the center of God's plan, is the ultimate fulfillment of every biblical type.

People

Scripture lists countless names, many of them obscure and ancient. Nonetheless, because God plans all things, including the people mentioned in the Bible, every person we read about is important in some way. Every name in every genealogy moves the story along. In thinking about people, we should note that some are especially significant because God intends them to function as types that point to Christ. When these people first appear in the story, we see something of their importance, but we especially discover God's intent as *later* biblical authors refer back to them.

For example, the Bible tells us that Adam is intended to point us to Christ. When Adam is first introduced, we know he is important because he represents the entire human race. This truth is reinforced as "Adam-like" people continue to carry on Adam's role through the covenants (e.g., Noah, Abraham, Israel, David), which ultimately reaches fulfillment in Jesus, who is called the last Adam (Rom. 5:12–21; 1 Cor. 15:21–28; Heb. 2:5–18). In a similar way, Moses points to Christ, speaking of a prophet greater than himself (Deut. 18:15–18; Acts 3:17–26). David, likewise, died expecting a son/king to sit forever on his throne (2 Sam. 7:14; Matt. 1:1–18). Each of these people served as a type for the greater one to come, Jesus Christ.

Events

In addition to specific people, many of the events in the Bible are significant in God's plan. They not only had meaning for the people of the day in which they occurred, but they also point forward and anticipate Christ's coming and work. The exodus is the best example of this. In the exodus, God redeems Israel from Egypt, an event tied to his covenant promises. He does this through a sacrifice whereby they escape God's judgment and experience deliverance. As later biblical authors anticipate what God will do in the future, the exodus serves as a type/pattern of what is to come. Ultimately God will redeem us from our sin and not merely from political oppression (Isa. 11:10–16; 53:1–12; Hos. 11:1).

In the New Testament, Jesus' cross is understood as an act of redemption or exodus (Luke 9:31; Eph. 1:7), fulfilling what God had previously done for his people but now revealing something even greater. By his atoning sacrifice, Christ redeems us from slavery to sin, death, and Satan. The prophets predicted that the coming Messiah would bring a new and greater exodus (e.g., Isa. 11:1–16), while the New Testament announces that this is precisely what Jesus has done.

Institutions

Specific institutions by their very nature, structure, and purpose also anticipate the Redeemer to come. For example, the prophets speak God's Word to the people, but the entire prophetic institution anticipates a Prophet-to-come who will speak God's Word perfectly. Jesus comes as *the* Word made flesh, Truth incarnate (John 1:1, 14; Heb. 1:1–2). The same is true of the priests—especially the high priest, who acts as a mediator between God and the people (Heb. 5:1–2). The entire priestly role anticipates a greater priest, Jesus (Heb. 5:1–10; 7:1–8:13).

The priestly work transpires in the context of the tabernacle and temple and by means of the sacrificial system that functions to forgive sin. This entire system—with its priesthood, its sacrifices, and its temple—anticipates a redeemer who will fully deal with sin and bring full access to God (Heb. 9:1–10:18).

The institution of the kings also functions in this way. By the Davidic promise, the kings anticipate a true and greater king who will rule in righteousness and rescue his people from their sins (2 Sam. 7:14; Isa. 9:6–7; 11:1–16; 53:1–12; Ezek. 34).

CHARACTERISTICS OF BIBLICAL TYPES

Typology exists because God is not random in what he says and does. He makes plans. He has chosen to reveal *who* and *how* he will save by various people, events, and institutions—all of which point us to Christ. Types have several characteristics:

- *Types are patterns rooted in history*. Each pattern is real history. Types are not merely imaginative ideas; they are real people, events, and institutions that signify something greater to come. Types also involve repetition. They reveal the way God works, giving us clues regarding his future work and how he will keep his future promises.

- *Types are designed by God.* Types are not random; they are purposeful in God's plan. Scripture alone warrants determining what is a type; we cannot decide what a type is apart from biblical warrant. Through the covenants, the biblical authors interpret specific persons, events, and institutions as purposely reaching their fulfillment in Christ. A pattern is first given, then repeated and picked up by later authors in the Bible, and we discover that the pattern and its significance were intended by God.

- *Types involve progression toward fulfillment in Christ.* As types are unpacked through the covenants, they move from lesser *to* greater in scope and significance for God's purposes, especially as they come to final fulfillment in Christ. When the last Adam finally arrives, or we meet the prophet Moses predicted or David's son, we see that he is *greater* than those who preceded him. In Christ all the previous patterns are fulfilled, and we as his people become the beneficiaries. Without Christ, the Bible's story makes no sense and God's salvation promises are left unfulfilled. Yet in Christ all of God's promises are yes (2 Cor. 1:20) because he alone is God the Son incarnate who can save us completely. This is one of the key ways the New Testament explains the glory, superiority, and uniqueness of our Lord Jesus Christ.

IT'S TIME FOR A STORY

A faithful reading of Scripture requires that we read it according to what it is. To this point, we have asked and answered two crucial questions: *What is the Bible?* and *How do we read the Bible?* We won't know how to read the Bible until we know what it *is*. And we won't read the Bible well unless we think carefully about how the Bible's nature affects how it should be read.

That's why in part 2 of this book we lay out the Bible's storyline according to the Bible's structure. In this first part we have examined the story in brief, giving you the big picture and the outline of the broad storyline. Now in part 2 we will work our way from one side of the Bible to the other, from creation to new creation, from the garden to the New Jerusalem. As we do so, we'll tell the story in a way that rightly reflects the shape and emphasis of the Bible's own telling. We'll employ all three of our contexts as our primary tool for interpretation.

Are you ready? Let's get started!

PART 2

READING

the Story

Chapter 5

CREATION

A Garden Full of God's Glory

GENESIS 1–2

Every culture has a creation story because the question of our origins is foundational to almost every other question of life. Children who ask their parents, "Where did everything come from?" are asking a profound question, one that adults should not brush off or ignore. Many argue that the most basic question of philosophy, the question that underlies all other questions, is, Why is there something rather than nothing? The origins question speaks to our most basic beliefs about God, the world, and how we understand who we are. Creation stories are vitally important.

They are also connected and bound up with various worldviews. The naturalist believes that the world is solely material, the result of an impersonal beginning. Matter, then, isn't created or directed by a personal God. The worldviews of ancient Greeks, Hindus, and Buddhists are also shaped by their respective creation stories. Our understanding of origins is integral to the way we think and live, to how we see the world.

Thankfully, God hasn't left us in the dark regarding our ultimate origins. He has revealed the true account of origins in the story of the world's creation. It's the first story in the Bible's first book, and it's foundational to Scripture and the Christian worldview. In this story, we meet the Bible's main characters, we are acquainted with its original setting, and we discover crucial trajectories for the Bible's unfolding storyline.

THE MAIN CHARACTERS

My [Trent's] daughter recently wrote a story. It went like this: *The fairies were with their mommy in their princess house.* I was not all that impressed, but her teacher commended her for including characters and a setting. Fair enough. At the very least, any story should have characters and a setting, so as we enter into the Bible's story our first order of business is to look for the main characters in this drama. Who are they and what can we learn about them from the story of creation?

Creation Introduces the God of the Bible

God is the first character we meet in Scripture. This should give us a clue that he is the most important person in the story. The entire Bible has much to say about God, and the Bible's opening lines give us much to ponder. From creation, we learn that God is *not* an impersonal force but a personal being of majestic power who simply speaks and the universe comes to exist. "In the beginning, God created the heavens and the earth" (Gen. 1:1).

That God is the Creator of all things means he is the *source of everything*, having created everything by means of his word. We hear the refrain "And God said" seven times in Genesis 1. Psalm 33:6 reflects on this: "By the word of the LORD the heavens were made, their starry host by the breath of his mouth." As Creator, God is the source of all existence. He isn't created by anyone or anything, nor is he dependent on anything else for his life. He has life in himself, and he is self-sufficient. He has no needs (Ps. 50:12–14; Acts 17:24–25).

God is also the source of all authority. He is the standard of knowledge and truth. His knowledge is complete and perfect, and his word accomplishes his will (Ps. 139:1–4; Isa. 46:9–11). God is also the source of all morality. His will and character are the standard of goodness, justice, and righteousness (Ex. 20:1–17). He created his world good, and he executes his perfect justice against all injustice against him (Gen. 18:25; Rom. 1:18–32).

As the Creator, God is *separate from his creation*, distinct; he is transcendent. The Creator is *not* the creation. This point distinguishes the biblical view of reality from most other worldviews. Eastern religions are monistic, which means that they think of the world and "god" as one and the same. Yet while the Bible teaches us that God is distinct from his creation, this doesn't mean that he is spatially distant. He is present everywhere with his creation, what is commonly referred to as being immanent. God is Lord over creation, and he is actively involved in it. He is everywhere present, yet present in a special way with his people, as demonstrated by his unique covenantal presence in Eden.

As the Creator, God is also *sovereign over what he has made*. This means that nothing is outside of his control or rule. He is the King over all his creation. Psalm 115:3 states, "Our God is in heaven; he does whatever pleases him." Psalm 95:3–5 says, "The LORD is the great God, the great King above all gods. In his hand are the depths of the earth, and the mountain peaks belong to him. The sea is his, for he made it, and his hands formed the dry land." In the Ancient Near East, people assigned separate "gods" to the sea, to the mountains, and to other features of the world. But according to the Bible, these "gods" were not gods. There is only one true God, the Creator of all things (Jer. 10:10–12; Rev. 4:11).

As the Creator, God is perfectly *satisfied in his creation*. We know this because after he creates, he rests. Genesis 2:1–3 tells us of the culmination of God's work of creation: "Thus the heavens and the earth were completed in all their vast array. By the seventh day God had finished the work he had been doing; so on the seventh day he rested from all his work. Then God blessed the seventh day and made it holy, because on it he rested from all the work of creating that he had done."

God does not rest because he runs out of energy. His rest indicates that he enters into the enjoyment of his handiwork and into covenant relationship with his creation. As Scripture later teaches, in God's rest we fully experience him as our God and know what it means to be his people (Heb. 3:7–4:11).

Creation Introduces Human Beings

The second main character introduced into the creation story is humanity. The creation narrative reaches its high point in the crown of God's creation—us! In Genesis 2, God creates humanity as his final work of creation. When the story reaches this point, the pace slows down and the camera zooms in to give us a careful account of God's thoughts, purposes, and designs for human beings.

This is clearly a special moment: a creation and coronation.

> Then God said, "Let us make mankind in our image, in our likeness, so that they may rule over the fish in the sea and the birds in the sky, over the livestock and all the wild animals, and over all the creatures that move along the ground."
>
> > So God created mankind in his own image,
> >   in the image of God he created them;
> >   male and female he created them.
>
> > God blessed them and said to them, "Be fruitful and increase in number; fill the earth and subdue it. Rule over the fish in the sea and the birds in the sky and over every living creature that moves on the ground." . . .
> > God saw all that he had made, and it was very good.
>
> —GENESIS 1:26–31

Important people get proper introductions. For human beings, the crucial truth about us is that we are created in the image of God.

But what exactly does this mean? Many have written on this subject, but its central meaning is that we were created to be like God and to represent him in the world. In the ancient world, kings represented the gods. They were the "image" of the gods. In the story of the Bible, however, it's not merely the king who represents God but all of humanity. Every human being—male and female—was created to represent God by ruling over creation. We are "little" kings and queens, made to rule God's grand creation. We are God's image-bearers. That makes us royalty!

Humans are also created for one another. Genesis 2 details our creation as male and female. Genesis 1 describes the seven days of creation, and Genesis 2 focuses on the single day of *our* creation. While God has repeatedly declared creation good (Gen. 1:31), one striking feature of the story is that something God does is *not* good. He makes it clear what he means: "It is not good for the man to be alone. I will make a helper suitable for him" (Gen. 2:18).

A perfect Adam, in a perfect place, and in relationship with a perfect God, yet he still needs someone to complement him. He even needs help to recognize this need. The Lord parades the animals before Adam "to see what he would name them" (2:19). Adam named them all, yet for him "no suitable helper was found" (2:20). For this reason, God custom-builds a wife for Adam. He causes Adam to sleep, "and while he was sleeping, he took one of the man's ribs and then closed up the place with flesh. Then the LORD God made a woman from the rib he had taken out of the man, and he brought her to the man" (2:21–22). Mere words are not enough to express Adam's awe at meeting his wife for the first time. Only a poem will do, and the Bible gives us the first love song:

> This is now bone of my bones
> and flesh of my flesh;
> she shall be called "woman,"
> for she was taken out of man.
>
> —GENESIS 2:23

The woman complemented Adam in every way. Even young children see the physical differences although they don't know all the details of how male and female bodies work. God's design, of course, runs deeper than the physical body. At her core, the woman is different from Adam, yet she equally bears the divine image.

The man and the woman fit together in a way that bonds them at the deepest levels of their experience. In God's plan, the design of male and female not only binds them together but in the establishment of marriage serves as the building block to the family and by extension to human society. The foundation of marriage is stated this way: "That is why a man leaves his father and mother and is united to his wife, and they become one flesh. Adam and his wife were both naked, and they felt no shame" (Gen. 2:24–25).

As we will see, this God-ordained institution of marriage will figure prominently in the Bible's story.

We haven't yet mentioned one final but enormously significant truth about humans: we were created, as the Bible says, *in Adam*. Adam isn't merely the first human being God made. He also serves as humanity's covenant head and representative. The magnitude and significance of this role will become apparent as history and the Bible's story unfolds. As the representative of all his later descendants, Adam was the one to whom God first spoke and gave the command to obey. This speaks of his unique, singular role in creation, and of God's continued expectation of obedience from us, Adam's descendants. "The LORD God commanded the man, 'You are free to eat from any tree in the garden; but you must not eat from the tree of the knowledge of good and evil, for when you eat from it you will certainly die'" (Gen. 2:16–17).

As the Bible's story continues, Adam's role and headship will be contrasted with that of the last Adam, our Lord Jesus Christ, who comes as the head of the new creation. Many prominent people are in Scripture, but Adam and Christ are the most significant. The entire Bible is structured in terms of these two men. We are either "in Adam" by our natural birth, or we are "in Christ" by a new, spiritual birth (Rom. 5:12–21). No other options are available to us.

Later in the Old Testament, 1 Chronicles confirms the importance of Adam by tracing our lineage back to him (1 Chron. 1:1), and in the New Testament Luke traces Jesus' genealogy back to Adam, whom he refers to as the son of God (3:38). Jesus and Paul viewed Adam not only as an historical figure (Matt. 19:4–6; 1 Tim. 2:13–14; Rom. 5:12–21; 1 Cor. 15:22–23, 45–47) but as the one whose role and actions define all of humanity.

Without a grasp of Adam and his representative role—for good and, sadly, for ill—the Bible's story makes little sense.

SETTING THE STAGE

Just as every story has characters, every story has a setting. The setting of the Bible's story establishes the *where* and *when* of the story at its beginning.

Creation Establishes the Reality and Goodness of Creation

The creation story teaches that God created the entire universe—its galaxies, planets, stars, land, water, animals, and of course, us! The Bible also teaches that God created everything *good*. This truth is repeatedly stressed by the refrain "and God saw that it was good" (Gen. 1:9, 12, 18, 21, 25), along with the final summary statement, "God saw all that he had made, and it was very good" (1:31).

Unlike the pagan myths that viewed material reality as bad or unclean, Scripture teaches that God delighted in his creation and that it was good. Every aspect of God's creative work was consistent with his intention, and God delighted in his handiwork, including his creation of humans. In light of the Bible's whole story, we know that Adam was not created in a glorified state, as we will be in the future because we are in Christ. Yet this does not mean that there was something wrong with Adam. Adam was created in a good state, and God delighted in the man he made.

Creation Establishes the Beginning of History

Creation begins the story, but what was there *before* the beginning? Only God—the triune God who existed in perfect love, communion, and fellowship with himself. Jesus, the eternal and divine Son, hints at this in John 17:5, where he speaks of the glory he shared with the Father "before the world began."

By the act of creation, the eternal God brought into existence a universe that had not existed before. Unlike pagan worldviews that view history as cyclical, the Bible views history as linear. History has a definite starting point with creation, and it moves forward to God's appointed end. Creation can be seen as God creating a stage by which "his-story" begins to unfold. It unfolds step-by-step as humans are created, have children, build societies, and interact with God and one another. God enacts his eternal plan on the stage of human history, and he will do so until Christ returns and he unveils his new creation. Genesis 2:4 captures this point with a phrase repeated throughout Genesis, moving the story forward: "These are the generations" (2:4; 6:9; 10:1; 11:10; 11:27, etc. ESV).

TRAJECTORIES FOR THE STORYLINE AHEAD

In creation, several features take on greater significance as we move ahead into the storyline of Scripture. Here are three of the most significant trajectories for the story yet to come.

1. Creation Defines God's Relationship with His People as Covenantal

Adam is not just the first man in God's story. He is the representative of humanity and the head of creation itself. He is God's image-bearer and king, and his role defines this role for all his descendants—the entire human race. In creation, we meet the triune God, see his purpose for creation, and learn that human beings, as defined by Adam and his role, stand in special relationship to God.

Later in the Old Testament, the responsibilities that God gave to Adam are uniquely expressed in various other people—specifically, those who function as prophets, priests, and kings. Prophets mediate God's Word. Priests mediate God's presence as worshipers. Kings mediate God's rule.

In embryonic form, each of these functions first belonged to Adam and then by extension to the entire human race. We see this in several ways. Consider that God spoke directly to Adam, and Adam (in a prophetic role) was responsible to mediate God's word by trusting, keeping, and preaching it to his wife and children. And while God is distinct from creation, we learn that he is uniquely present through covenant relationship. Adam (in a priestly role) was responsible to mediate God's presence to the world by universally expanding Eden's borders, filling it with image-bearers, and ruling over creation. And while God is King of the universe, he has chosen to exercise his rule through humans, as his royal kings and queens. Adam (in a kingly role) was given dominion over the world as a servant king, who was to act as God's image, his representative and son. As Psalm 115:16 says, "The highest heavens belong to the LORD, but the earth he has given to mankind."

In function, though not in any explicit title or office, Adam was a prophet, priest, and king. Later in the Bible's story, these titles are revealed to identify people who carry on the tasks that originated with Adam.

To put it another way, these roles express the deeper role God originally intended for humans. That role was first established in Adam, but then only Jesus as the last Adam and God the Son perfectly fulfills it. Then he restores it in us (Heb. 2:5–18).

2. Creation Defines Marriage as Foundational for the Story Ahead

God created two kinds of image-bearers: male and female. Why? Together they can procreate. That's an obvious and important reason, but it's not the only reason. The Bible tells us that God created Adam *alone* for a reason, and ultimately Scripture teaches us that this order— creating Adam first, and then Eve—serves as instruction for us.

By parading the animals before Adam, God helped him recognize his need for a companion. When God made him a companion, he did not make another male to be his friend; he made a female to be his wife: one who was like him yet different to the core. In creating male and female, God not only established proper limits to the use of our sexuality but also established the foundational institution of marriage as the building block to human society, a gift for our flourishing and something we distort to our peril.

Even further, God created marriage as a type or pattern to point beyond itself to a greater relationship—God's covenant relationship with his people. Marriage is a crucial, created means to a larger end. This is why the Bible teaches that, as weighty and important as marriage is, it's *not* eternal, nor is it part of the new creation to come (Matt. 22:29–32). What is eternal is what marriage typifies—God's exclusive love for his people as shown in the new covenant relationship of Christ's love for his church (Eph. 5:32).

3. Creation Defines Rest as the Goal of Creation

Significantly, the creation story climaxes with God's rest on the seventh day (Gen. 2:1–3). This is one crucial way to communicate God's goal for creation. "Rest," which refers to God's full enjoyment of his handiwork, is an easy theme to miss, but it is not unimportant. As we'll see in later chapters, "rest" gives us unique insights into the Bible's larger storyline.

The seventh day of rest is an important type and pattern that begins in creation and is picked up in the Mosaic law in relation to the promised land and the Sabbath-day command (Josh. 21:43–45; Ex. 20:8–11; Ps. 95:11). More significant, God's creation rest ultimately points forward to Jesus, who by his work brings salvation rest and restores us to full relationship with our covenant God (Matt. 11:28–30; Heb. 3:7–4:11).

With creation, the setting of the Bible's story has been established. We have met several of the key characters, we have a setting, and we've been introduced to some key features that give direction to the story. Sadly, we will soon discover that God's good world and our role in it goes terribly wrong, all through a tragic and rebellious choice. We now turn to this next chapter in the story.

Chapter 6

FALL

A Day Full of Death

GENESIS 3

For several months, my [Trent's] daughter would regularly ask me to take her to the park down the street. There was just one problem: there was no park down our street. There was a cemetery. But to my daughter, the flowers and trees, the sprinklers and well-groomed grass, were all clear marks of paradise. Of course, I knew all of the visitors there were burying and visiting their dead. After several confusing conversations with her, I eventually made the connection and took her there to play. I shared with her that this wasn't a typical park. This park was filled with the bodies of the dead—brothers and sisters, mothers and fathers, grandmothers and grandfathers. Each of them lived. Then each of them died.

This was an important moment for my daughter, and each one of us experiences it at some point. We must all come to terms with the reality of death. What if I told you we can also know the *reason* for death? We can.

In the Bible's storyline, Genesis 3 is a text of extraordinary significance because it explains what went wrong with humanity and why God's good world is now so flawed. Death is part of that story, but there's more to the story than simply death. We also learn *why* there is death, that it is abnormal and not natural to our human condition, and about its awful consequences.

The fact that we die is directly related to the existence of sin and evil in this world. We can ask the question, What is wrong with us? Everyone must answer that question. We fight as kids, and we kill as adults. Not everyone commits every evil, but we, the human race, do so collectively. If put in the right circumstances, each one of us—without exception—is capable of atrocious acts.

Some worldviews blame the problem of evil in this world on spiritual powers. Other worldviews claim that evil is simply an illusion. Other views accept the fact of evil but then claim that morality is merely relative to each culture's perspective. Christianity, based on the teaching of the Bible, tells us that as diverse as these answers are, they *all* have something in common: they explain our problem in terms of our creatureliness. They accept the idea that we have *always* been this way. The human problem, then, is *normal* to us. It is part of our humanity—our nature. We came off the assembly line, as it were, structurally flawed and engineered for failure.

The Bible rejects all of these views. Our problem is not our creatureliness. The Bible says that we were created good. The human problem is rooted, instead, in history and is directly related to the moral choice of the first man, Adam. Genesis 3 tells this story—a story necessary to make sense of the Bible's later salvation story and of our lives today. Death is a problem for us. As it turns out, death is also *our* problem. It started with human sin.

In the previous chapter, we looked at the characters, the setting, and the trajectories of the Bible's storyline. Any good story has conflict, and the Bible's story is no exception. By unpacking Genesis 3, we discover how sin brings an awful deformity in the relationship of the *characters* to one another, in the *setting*, and in the *trajectories* of the Bible's story. The story will end well, but things will get worse before they get better.

THINGS TURN UGLY

Where we left off with the story, the main *characters* were on wonderful terms. As Genesis 1–2 ends, everything is good. It's paradise. God said it was very good (Gen. 1:31), and at the heart of this goodness was the moral uprightness of Adam and Eve and how they related to God and to each other: "Adam and his wife were both naked, and they felt no shame" (2:25).

Then something goes desperately wrong. Genesis 3 gives us the how and why. It starts in the garden of Eden, where human needs are fully satisfied. Adam, created as God's representative and servant king, is called to trust, love, and obey God fully and completely. He is to demonstrate his devotion with loving obedience to God's command. "The LORD God commanded the man, 'You are free to eat from any tree in the garden; but you must not eat from the tree of the knowledge of good and evil, for when you eat from it you will certainly die'" (Gen. 2:16–17).

God didn't make a bad tree with defective or poisonous fruit. He placed the tree in the garden to test Adam. Consider who Adam is. He is an image-bearer of God. He is a prophet, priest, and king. Adam is made to rest in God's covenantal presence. As its head, he represents the human race. He is the greatest creation of a great Creator. He was made to know, to treasure, and to obey his Maker. Given *who* God is, what should God expect other than perfect obedience from Adam? Given *who* Adam is, what higher vocation is there than to know, love, and obey God? Will Adam trust God or trust himself? Will Adam treasure his Creator, or will he seek the creation instead? These are the questions the narrative sets up.

Tragically, Adam's awful and disastrous choice is recounted in Genesis 3. The serpent is introduced and conflict begins. The serpent is a troublemaker "more crafty than any of the wild animals the LORD God had made" (3:1). For now, we know this, and that's all. Later Scripture identifies him with the name Satan, which means "the accuser." Revelation 12:9 speaks of "that ancient serpent, who is called the devil and Satan, the deceiver of the whole world" (ESV). We are not told how the serpent got into the garden, nor is that the burden of this story. But he is there, and the encounter he has with Adam and his wife, Eve, and the conflict that follows have effects that reach into every corner of God's creation and down through eternity. From this point forward, the relationship between God and humanity is broken and takes an ugly turn for the worse.

A Deadly Choice: Humanity Turns Against God

How did the world go wrong? The Bible says that it all started when something went wrong with us. As the narrative unfolds, we see the serpent interacting with the first couple. A question is asked, an exchange of ideas takes place, and a process of desire climaxes in a deadly choice. At the core of this interaction is the questioning of God's goodness, integrity, and character. It all begins with a provocative question from the serpent to Eve: "Did God really say, 'You must not eat from any tree in the garden?'" (Gen. 3:1).

In asking this question, the serpent isn't being curious! Like many questions we ask, it was calculated to throw the woman off-balance, to cause her to mistrust God. The woman's reply? Initially, it sounds fine. "We may eat fruit from the trees in the garden, but God did say, 'You must not eat fruit from the tree that is in the middle of the garden, and you must not touch it, or you will die'" (3:2–3).

Yet there is a subtle and possibly dangerous direction in her answer. Notice how she has added to God's command. God didn't say *not* to touch the fruit of this one tree, but only *not to eat it*. She made a slight addition, and she has downplayed God's kindness and generosity. *All* trees were at the couple's disposal, except one. Downplaying God's sheer generosity, the woman is now vulnerable to the serpent's direct attack on God's trustworthiness and moral character. "'You will not certainly die,' the serpent said to the woman. 'For God knows that when you eat from it your eyes will be opened, and you will be like God, knowing good and evil'" (3:4–5).

The serpent directly questions God's character, his intentions, and his word. Who will she believe? Whose word will she trust? And where is Adam while this is happening? He was the one who directly received the command, the one blessed by God with a wife. Surely he would speak up and protect his wife from these lies, wouldn't he?

"When the woman saw that the fruit of the tree was good for food and pleasing to the eye, and also desirable for gaining wisdom, she took some and ate it. She also gave some to her husband, *who was with her*, and he ate it" (3:6, emphasis added).

We learn, after the act of disobedience, that he was "*with* her, and *he ate it*"—some of the most consequential words in the Bible. Trusting the serpent instead of ruling over him, Adam presumed to be like God. The world would never be the same as we see in verse 7: "Then the eyes of both of them were opened, and they realized they were naked; so they sewed fig leaves together and made coverings for themselves."

At the end of Genesis 2, the couple is naked and they have no shame, but now because of their disobedience, they are ashamed of their nakedness and they hide from their Creator-covenant Lord. The world has been turned upside down.

Adam and Eve experienced firsthand the fourfold effects of sin. Vertically, they experienced alienation and condemnation from God. Horizontally, they experienced alienation from each other. Internally (and schizophrenically), they experienced alienation within themselves. Cosmically, they experienced alienation in the world they were created to rule. These four effects of sin play out across the Bible's story, but they are immediately apparent from the very moment sin enters the world.

A New Normal: God Now Stands Against Humanity

Verses 8–9 of Genesis 3 are haunting: "Then the man and his wife heard the sound of the LORD God as he was walking in the garden in the cool of the day, and they hid from the LORD God among the trees of the garden. But the LORD God called to the man, 'Where are you?'"

God does not ask, "Where are you?" out of ignorance. He is the omnipresent and omniscient Lord. No, this question is God calling Adam and Eve to account for their actions. Will Adam speak the truth? No. He deflects his responsibility and blames his wife. He also hints that God himself is somehow to blame. "He answered, 'I heard you in the garden, and I was afraid because I was naked; so I hid.' And [God] said, 'Who told you that you were naked? Have you eaten from the tree that I commanded you not to eat from?' The man said, 'The woman you put here with me—she gave me some fruit from the tree, and I ate it.' Then the LORD God said to the woman, 'What is this you have done?' The woman said, 'The serpent deceived me, and I ate'" (3:10–13).

The right answer would have been, "I have sinned. According to your word and because I rebelled against *you*, I deserve to die. Please forgive me." Instead Adam pins his sin on God. Our pervasive internal corruption and perversity are clear. So is our propensity to blame others for our sin.

True to his word and his righteous character, God responds to this treason with judgment on everyone involved. He punishes each party according to their creation domain. The serpent will crawl on his belly. The woman will experience pain in childbearing and discord with her husband. Adam will be in conflict with Eve, and the earth under his rule is now cursed. While the ground belongs under Adam's feet, Adam will eventually find himself six feet under, as will every human who comes from him. For this reason, Scripture roots the human problem of sin and death back to Adam, and then to each one of us: "Sin entered the world through one man, and death through sin, and in this way death came to all people, because all sinned" (Rom. 5:12). Yes, tragically, "in Adam all die" (1 Cor. 15:22). We are all born condemned and corrupt because of our association with him.

A CORRUPT AND CONDEMNED PLACE

When the relationship between God and humans breaks down, everything else falls apart too. The world after the fall is not the same. The *setting* of the Bible's story is no longer the good creation of Genesis 1–2. It is the fallen creation, marred and distorted by Adam's choice and our ongoing sin. The effects of the fall are immediate and long-lasting.

God's Good Creation Is Now Corrupt

All people since Adam now enter this world "in Adam," under the guilt and pollution of sin. Humans, created to rule over the earth, now experience the earth turned against them in the form of hurricanes, tornadoes, earthquakes, tsunamis, fires, volcanoes, and wild animals. In Adam, we do not rule or reign as intended.

But the effects of sin's curse run deeper than these deadly disasters;

sin also corrupts the very fabric of the material world. Children are now born with mental and physical disabilities, living under the curse of corruption. Human sin has mutilated the entire created order.

Some think of sickness and death as "natural." But biblically, sickness and death are *unnatural*. They are abnormalities, which are all departures from God's design for humanity. We resist death because we were created to live. Cemeteries remind us of Satan's lie and the truth of God's Word—"The wages of sin is death" (Rom. 6:23). When my [Stephen's] children were younger, to remind them of this truth as we drove by a cemetery, I would often say, "Remember, Satan is a liar!" Everything wrong with this world traces back to Adam's sin, God's curse, and the outworking of Adam's rebellion among his descendants. Paul explains this sad fact as he unpacks the connection between the fate of creation and the fate of humanity:

> The creation waits in eager expectation for the children of God to be revealed. For the creation was subjected to frustration, not by its own choice, but by the will of the one who subjected it, in hope that the creation itself will be liberated from its bondage to decay and brought into the freedom and glory of the children of God. We know that the whole creation has been groaning as in the pains of childbirth right up to the present time. Not only so, but we ourselves, who have the firstfruits of the Spirit, groan inwardly as we wait eagerly for our adoption to sonship, the redemption of our bodies.
>
> —ROMANS 8:19–23

Romans 8 is a profound commentary on the effects of sin on creation. Creation is screaming to anyone who will listen, "Sin is bad!" God has cursed this world in response to our sin so that every awful thing that happens in this world, from disabilities to hurricanes, serves as a reminder that *we* are in rebellion against our Creator, and that the condition of this world is no longer normal.

The universe was placed under a curse at humanity's fall; now the universe waits for humanity's fix.

Ominous Clouds on the Horizon

"In the beginning, God created" signals the beginning of time. Adam's tragic choice signals the movement of history from its glorious beginning to its end in judgment. In Adam, we're born guilty and under the sentence of death. Judgment awaits all of us unless God graciously chooses to redeem us. Thankfully, the story is not over! Exactly how God will reverse sin and death and reconcile us to himself will be seen only as God's plan unfolds further. But the fact that God chooses to redeem doesn't minimize the truth that there is still coming a final judgment for sin. The New Testament is clear about this: "People are destined to die once, and after that to face judgment" (Heb. 9:27). Peter writes of "the day of God [which will] . . . bring about the destruction of the heavens by fire, and the elements will melt in the heat" (2 Peter 3:12). The Bible ends with the tragic destruction of humanity in Adam, outside of Christ (Rev. 21:8).

Although many people deny the coming of final judgment, the reality of our death is a constant reminder from God. Scripture tells us that we are "held in slavery by [our] fear of death" (Heb. 2:15), and this fear explains the existence of the world's diverse religions. Human beings are frantic for a solution to death and judgment, but they cannot find one apart from God.

The fact of coming judgment presents us with a deeply theological and personal question: How can any of us escape the judgment of God given our sin? How can polluted sinners find acceptance with a God of perfect purity? How can the guilty escape condemnation before a God of perfect justice? These questions of Scripture are inescapable for us.

Thankfully, there's good news yet to come.

TRAJECTORIES FOR A STORYLINE EAST OF EDEN

Adam's fall changed everything. Working from the *three trajectories* identified in the story of creation, let us consider how they have now changed because of human sin and the curse.

1. Adam Is a Failed Prophet, Priest, and King

Adam traded the truth of the Creator's word for the creature's lie, so God's word changed from a promise of blessing to a word of judgment.

Adam was now a failed prophet, unable to speak truth or blessing. He was also a failed priest, unable to stand in God's presence. When Adam traded the glory of God's presence for the opportunity to become God, God's presence became a presence of holy wrath for him. He was also a failed king. When Adam traded the rule of God as Creator for the authority of a serpent, God's sovereign rule brought judgment. The earth created for Adam's rule now rules over him.

Adam wanted to be *like* God instead of *with* God, and he failed to keep his covenant responsibility.

2. The First Marriage Is on the Rocks

The Bible is ancient, but its description of our relationship problems feels timeless. Adam sins, hides from God, and then blames his wife. This pattern sums up so many of our relational problems.

In Adam, our human relationships have been warped and broken. From our broken relationship with God flows trouble with one another. Though we were created for communion—a life of oneness and unity with God and with other human beings—because of our sin we are isolated and we hide. We may not use leaves to cover our shame, but we hide behind the "leaves" of our jobs, our pedigrees, and our good works—our attempts to justify and prove ourselves as people of worth and value. Because we're self-absorbed, it's no wonder that our relationships with others are fractured.

Nowhere is this more evident than in the intimacy of marriage. Though marriage was created to illuminate the love and unity that God has for his people, the good news that marriage was intended to typify is now distorted. As the story continues to unfold, marriage will still function as a picture of our relationship to God, but our sins of infidelity and unfaithfulness now reflect our awful sin against the God who is worthy of all of our love, devotion, and trust.

Thankfully, this is not the end of the story.

3. Rest Is Lost

When God finished his work of creation, "he rested" (Gen. 2:2). That day, which had no morning or evening, was "blessed" and made "holy" (2:3). It was a glorious day that signified our triune Covenant God entering into the joy of his creation and into covenant relationship with his creatures. Yet because of Adam's sin, we no longer experience that rest. Covenant relationship with our glorious God is the goal of our creation, but now we are alienated from him, and the world we live in is a restless and unfulfilling place. We need God to act in grace to save us to recover the rest we have lost and to be restored to the purpose of our creation.

The first human couple walked out of the garden of God's presence under a cloud of shame. They were banished, and so are we. East of Eden stand cherubim and a "flaming sword flashing back and forth" (3:24) to block us from the garden and the tree of life.

How can we regain access to the garden? Will we taste again of the tree of life? Thankfully, the Bible's story does not end here. Our Creator-covenant God has not left us to ourselves. In the story that follows, God will make saving promises and repeatedly give his people a word of hope. In keeping his promises, access to his rest will come again. God will reestablish his covenantal presence with his people; he will remove our sin and reestablish his rule.

But how?

Chapter 7

REDEMPTION

A Story Full of Promise

GENESIS 3:15

As we saw in the previous chapter, the burning question of the Bible is this: Given God's holiness and human sin, how can God reconcile and justify sinners without compromising his own moral demand? By "reconcile" we mean make things right between us and God. By "justify" we mean clear our account of guilt. No righteous judge merely clears the guilty without justice being served. You see the problem. We are guilty of cosmic high treason. We will state this problem a few different ways before the chapter is out. Every command, story, and character in Scripture makes sense only when we grasp the fundamental tension between our sin and who God is in his holiness and justice. Like an explosive chemical reaction, God and sin do *not* mix, and God, in all of his glory and majesty, always triumphs over human sin.

Unfortunately, the Bible's central question is *not* the central question of our day. At a superficial level, we know we have a problem. We create religions to deal with our guilt and systems of morality to keep us in line. Still, we are blind to the real problem. And the fact that people don't take this problem seriously is itself symptomatic of our problem. In the blindness of our sin, we are ignorant of our true condition, and we distort who God is. This means that we grossly underestimate the depth of our sin *before* God. Like fools who think ourselves wise, we vainly try to remake God in our own image. In our morality making, we make ourselves into gods. Have you ever noticed that we are easier on ourselves than we are on other people? In all of this, we underestimate both God's holiness and human sin. We are farther from God than we think. For all our hard work, we are without hope. In our sin, we stand before him condemned, and nothing we do can change that reality.

Yet there is reason for hope. Because of God's grace alone, the Bible says, he has chosen to redeem us. How can a righteous, holy God who does not tolerate sin allow sinful people to stand in his presence? How can he love a people who have become stained by evil and corruption? *This* is the central question of the Bible. Reading Scripture correctly requires that we read it to discern the answer God has given us, the answer that fundamentally addresses our greatest need in life and death.

A PROMISE OF LIFE IN A PROMISE OF DEATH

After the passing of time, Adam died, just as God promised (Gen. 2:16–17; 5:5). Yet Adam did not die immediately, and before he died, God made *another* promise to him and his wife. Genesis 3 is a dark chapter of the Bible, but there is a crack of light. In a promise of death for the serpent is a promise of life for humanity. Listen for it in God's cryptic words to the snake:

> I will put enmity
> between you and the woman,
> and between your offspring and hers;
> he will crush your head,
> and you will strike his heel.
>
> —GENESIS 3:15

God's curse and judgment still rang in their ears. Life would never be the same, and they knew it. The ongoing pain of work, childbearing, and strained relationships would serve as a daily reminder of their sin.

Yet nestled among these declarations of God's judgment we find a precious word of comfort—a *promise*. This rang in their ears as well, and its sound would get sweeter in the course of time. This short verse is a seed—a small promise that will eventually grow into the full-blown tree of God's good news, the storyline of Scripture. Early biblical interpreters rightly called this text "the first gospel" (*protoevangelium*). Death and the curse would reign, but not entirely. Adam and Eve would have a child, and the human race would continue to grow and multiply. We learn that the battle with the serpent was not over, and discord would be constant between the serpent's offspring and that of the woman. We learn that the woman's seed would be like Adam—a man. But unlike Adam, he would obey God and defeat the serpent. The woman's seed would crush the serpent's head, destroying him, and, we can infer, reversing the disastrous effects of the fall. Although the woman's seed would suffer, he would live and triumph in victory.

How is any of this possible? Because the Creator-covenant God acts in sovereign grace.

Adam seems to have understood that God had been gracious to him. With the promise still ringing in his ears, we are told, "the man called his wife's name Eve, because she was the mother of all living" (Gen. 3:20 ESV). Though they were still under the curse of death, Adam named his wife Eve—mother of the living—in the hope of future life.

But how could a son of Eve possibly solve humanity's problem? To answer this question and grasp the *kind* of salvation he would bring, we must first learn more about the nature and extent of the problem of our sin.

WHAT'S THE REAL PROBLEM AND HOW BAD IS IT?

The serpent is a problem. But the serpent is *not* our primary problem, although he is an enemy of the human race. Our primary problem—what keeps you and me from personally knowing our Creator—is our sin *before* God. Given who God is and our sin, how can God reconcile and justify sinners without compromising his own moral demand? Yet to appreciate the Bible's *good news* in addressing our problem, we need to fully grasp how dire our standing before God is. To get this across, God has given us several rich metaphors to convey the sheer incompatibility of God's holiness with our sin.[3] Our situation is quite desperate, and these metaphors are given to reorient our moral sense so we can accurately feel remorse and grief over our sin.

The first metaphor God gives us relates to *height*. God is the God "Most High" (Ps. 7:17), a phrase that does not connote spatial height but refers to God's transcendent lordship. He is the "Most High over all the earth" and "exalted over all the nations" (97:9; 99:2). If God is Most High, then his position and authority exceed that of any other person. In one of the Bible's most vivid and memorable encounters between God and man, Isaiah says, "I saw the Lord, high and exalted" (6:1). In the book of Isaiah, this vision comes after five chapters in which Isaiah writes of the condition of Israel as a disobedient people and under the judgment of God for their sin. In this context, Isaiah knows of his own unworthiness before God, and in God's holy presence he confesses, "Woe to me! . . . I am ruined!" (6:5). God is high and lifted up, and Isaiah is brought low.

The second image that portrays God's utter inaccessibility to sinners is *distance*. Although God is omnipresent, in relation to sin, he is far from us. When God spoke through Moses to Israel, he did so through an unapproachable mountain (Ex. 19:12–25). In the tabernacle-temple, God designed a way he could be present with his people. Yet even in that system, he separated his holy presence from the sinful people with a thick curtain, allowing access to the place of intimacy, the holy of holies, only once a year through the high priest, and only by a blood sacrifice. We learn that approaching God wrongly results in death, graphically illustrated when Aaron's sons, Nadab and Abihu, mishandle the sacrifice (Lev. 10:1–2; cf. 2 Sam. 6:6–7).

While some of these images may feel obscure to modern readers, that's okay. As we read the story on its own terms, what follows makes sense of these ancient stories. The primary point being communicated to us is that God's covenantal presence is inaccessible to sinners—unless God does something to remedy the situation.

The third image is of *light and fire*. When God appeared to Moses, he appeared in a burning bush (Ex. 3:1–6). Don't picture the warm camp-fire you might find in a Bible-story book. It's likely a terrifying scene: a bush that burns yet is not consumed. Moses is commanded to remove his sandals because the ground is holy. He immediately understands that God is there.

The connection between light and holiness is developed later in the Bible as well. Paul reminds us that God "lives in unapproachable light" (1 Tim. 6:16), and concerning God's moral purity, John writes, "God is light; in him is no darkness at all" (1 John 1:5). Concerning his terrifying justice, we read, "God is a consuming fire" (Heb. 12:29). This imagery not only conveys God's response to our sin; it also strikes fear in the hearts of sinners (Heb. 10:27, 31).

Each of these metaphors teaches that God's holiness and human sin do not mix. At times the imagery is even more graphic and shocking. At one point, we read that sin causes the world God has made to *vomit*. When God brings Israel into the promised land, a symbolic return to Eden, the nation is reminded to obey God "so that the land . . . may not vomit you out" (Lev. 18:25–28; 20:22). It's a vivid reminder that sin is never welcome in God's presence. Later, John tells us that it's not only the world God has made that vomits out sin; God also metaphorically "spits" sin from his presence (Rev. 3:16). God's vitriol at sin does not contradict his inherent goodness but serves as proof that he *is* good. The Lord is so morally pure—he is high, distant from sin, a consuming fire whose purity cannot tolerate evil, and sin rightly disgusts him—that sinners cannot stand or defend themselves before God.

GOD HAS A PROBLEM TOO

After looking at the hellish truth about our sin, let's return with fresh eyes to our opening question: Given God's holiness and human sin, how can he reconcile and justify sinners without compromising his own moral demand? What's crucial to note is that sin is not only *our* problem; it's also a problem *for God*. Why? Because God has created us for a covenant relationship with him, and given the reality of our sin, that relationship is now impossible. God cannot overlook our sin without denying himself and his fundamental justice and goodness. Nor can he "grade on the curve." God is the moral standard of the universe, and every sin is personally against *him*—not simply the breaking of an abstract set of rules or laws. But how can we dwell in his presence without the just Judge we have personally rejected bringing his judgment against us?

To answer that question, we're going to jump ahead in the story to a paragraph in the New Testament that helps to explain God's solution. As we work through the Bible's story toward this New Testament solution to sin, let's focus on the Bible's answer to this central question.

Be forewarned! This is one of the most important paragraphs ever written. Speaking about God's solution to the problem of human sin, Paul, a leader in the early Christian church, writes,

> But now apart from the law the righteousness of God has been made known, to which the Law and the Prophets testify. This righteousness is given through faith in Jesus Christ to all who believe. There is no difference between Jew and Gentile, for all have sinned and fall short of the glory of God, and all are justified freely by his grace through the redemption that came by Christ Jesus. God presented Christ as a sacrifice of atonement, through the shedding of his blood—to be received by faith. He did this to demonstrate his righteousness, because in his forbearance he had left the sins committed beforehand unpunished—he did it to demonstrate his righteousness at the present time, so as to be just and the one who justifies those who have faith in Jesus.
>
> —ROMANS 3:21–26

A great deal of information is packed into this short paragraph. You may not recognize every word or fully understand what is being said, but here are some of the key truths taught in this text.

First, it teaches us that God is the standard of justice (another word for righteousness). God is making known his justice, revealing and demonstrating it because it's a reflection of who he is—a holy God. We also learn that sinners are unjust—we all fall short of God's glory and do not accurately reflect his image, his moral goodness, back to him, the creation, or to one another. We learn that this is a problem because God's justice—his moral goodness in rendering the right judgment according to who he is as the moral standard of the universe—is questioned if he allows sin to go unpunished. God cannot sweep moral offenses against him under the rug; it would be a denial of himself.

We also learn, however, that God has come up with a solution to this problem. He has satisfied his own justice by making a payment for our sin through the blood sacrifice of Christ, the righteous one. How can this solution become effective for you and me? By grace and through faith in Christ alone, God now declares sinners to be just because *he* has paid the debt of their sin and satisfied his own righteous demand in God the Son incarnate, our Lord Jesus Christ. God saves in such a way as to display the glory of his grace, which is why Scripture says elsewhere, "It is by grace you have been saved, through faith—and this is not from yourselves, it is the gift of God—not by works, so that no one can boast" (Eph. 2:8–9).

This is how the Bible's central problem of alienation between God and humans is solved! In Christ, we are redeemed from the penalty of our sin, God's justice is fully met, *and* the serpent is defeated. Hebrews 2 says it this way: "Since the children have flesh and blood, he too shared in their humanity so that by his death he might break the power of him who holds the power of death—that is, the devil—and free those who all their lives were held in slavery by their fear of death" (vv. 14–15).

Human beings are scared to die. We were created to live forever, and death interrupts God's original intention for us. We fear death, but God provides us with hope. Jesus, the divine Son, became a man to destroy sin and death, a clear echo of God's promise to Adam and Eve in Genesis 3:15. The author continues: "For this reason he had to be made like them, fully human in every way, in order that he might become a merciful and faithful high priest in service to God, and that he might make atonement for the sins of the people" (Heb. 2:17).

In paying for our sin, Jesus defeats Satan, who has power over us because of our sin. When sin is paid, Satan no longer has the power to accuse us before God. His primary weapon has been taken away, and he is defeated. This is the glorious solution first hinted at in Genesis 3:15.

We apologize for leaving out the spoiler warnings in this chapter. As you can tell, we have now given the story away. But we have done this because, as Christians, we read the Old Testament with an understanding of where the story has been and where it is going. Since Moses wrote the first five books of Genesis after the exodus from Egypt, even the first readers of Genesis 1–3 had something of a preliminary understanding of salvation, reading this *after* the events of the exodus story. Hopefully an understanding of the Bible's central problem will allow us to grasp better the story that unfolds.

WHY SO MANY PAGES?

We know the problem that emerges in Genesis 3, and Romans 3 tells us how God will solve it in Christ. But why so many pages between Genesis 3 and Romans 3? Romans 3:21 gives us one hint: "But now apart from the law the righteousness of God has been made known, to which the Law and the Prophets testify."

"The Law and the Prophets" is shorthand for the Old Testament, which Paul says prophesy or testify of the salvation that later comes in Christ. Later in his letter, Paul says it this way: "Everything that was written in the past was written to teach us, so that through the endurance taught in the Scriptures and the encouragement they provide we might have hope" (Rom. 15:4).

Here's the reason there are so many pages between the problem and the solution: God is providing for our instruction, endurance, encouragement, and, ultimately, our hope. As we see how God unfolds his glorious plan of redemption in Christ and how he keeps all of his promises, we learn to trust, love, and obey him. The Bible is long and layered for a reason. It prepares us to see and receive Jesus as the only solution to our problem and the only Savior from our sin.

The Bible is written in such a way as to perfectly portray the greatness of our problem *and* the greatness of God's grace in Christ.

HOW WILL GOD DO IT?

For the rest of this book, we will walk from God's promise in Genesis 3:15 to its fulfillment in Messiah Jesus, God's own dear Son. We may agree that the Bible's characters, events, and story all point to Christ, but that doesn't mean we know *how* they point to Christ. *How* is the concern of the rest of this book.

Chapter 8

NOAH

A Boat Full of Life

GENESIS 4–11

Noah is one of the best-known people in Scripture, mostly because of his association with animals. It's perfect for decorating the nursery and engaging two-year-olds. Kids love animals, right? But if we dig a little deeper into the story, we find that the ark, the flood, and the animals all leave a vivid impression on the mind. What's amazing about the story of Noah's ark is not that Noah built a giant ship or that he got two of every kind of animal on it. What's amazing about Noah's ark is that there was any life on it at all.

Adam named his wife Eve, which means "mother of the living," possibly related to God's promise. God promised to reverse sin and death through her offspring. Through a son, he would destroy the serpent. That was Genesis 3. Genesis 4 opens with the birth of a son, Cain, and then a second son, Abel. In a fit of jealous rage, Cain killed his brother Abel. He murdered him in a field, away from the view of his parents, but not from God's view. When the Lord asks about Abel's whereabouts, Cain replies with these infamous words: "I do not know; am I my brother's keeper?" (4:9 ESV). Similar to the actions of his father, Adam, Cain evades the question and avoids taking responsibility for his sin. Will either of these sons reverse the curse and restore rest for God's people? Clearly not.

After the birth of more of Adam and Eve's children, along with children from Cain and his wife, chapter 4 closes with a note of hope: "At that time people began to call on the name of the LORD" (4:26).

Yet the hope is short-lived, for the following list of genealogies in chapter 5 reminds us that life continues, but it is overshadowed by the reign of death. Repeatedly, each person's life, except for Enoch's, concludes with the haunting refrain "and then he died" (vv. 5, 8, 11, etc.). Life continues, but death reigns. This is the setup to Noah's story that begins in Genesis 6. Noah, as Lamech his father hopes, "will comfort us in the labor and painful toil of our hands caused by the ground the LORD has cursed" (Gen. 5:29).

LOOKING DOWN: A STORY FLOODED WITH JUDGMENT AND FAVOR

When Genesis 6 opens, we find a mixed bag. Humans continue to multiply as God had commanded (6:1), but the situation is not good. The story of God's covenant with Noah tells us the story of what happened when fallen humanity began to multiply and fill the earth.

Only Evil All the Time

As humans multiplied, so did human sin and evil: "The LORD saw how great the wickedness of the human race had become on the earth, and that every inclination of the thoughts of the human heart was only evil all the time" (6:5). This news is similar to learning that the entire human race has stage 4 cancer. We knew we had a problem, but now we know that it's deep within us and universal. Adam's first sin led to Abel's murder, and now that same evil is alive and well in all humanity. What Scripture later declares in the New Testament is borne out in human history: "All have sinned and fall short of the glory of God" (Rom. 3:23). The story of Noah's ark is not a comforting story of friendly animals to entertain children—it's a horror story.

Given God's justice and holiness, the real surprise in learning about God's response to our sin is that it took so long. God declares, "I will wipe from the face of the earth the human race I have created—and with them the animals, the birds and the creatures that move along the ground" (Gen. 6:7). God says he will do this through a flood, and only

Noah and his family will survive, for "Noah found favor in the eyes of the LORD" (6:8).

Hurricanes, tornados, earthquakes, and tsunamis claim entire civilizations. Yet even though *all* disasters have their origin in Adam's sin and the curse that followed, we must be careful not to assign specific disasters to specific sins. In the case of the Genesis flood, however, we know exactly why the rain came and why it stopped after life on the earth was destroyed. The flood was God's direct judgment on human sin.

The severity and extent of the flood corresponds to the severity and extent of human sin. Today, we cannot imagine the devastation described. Imagine rain. Now imagine a downpour that doesn't let up for over a month. Picture the waters rising, the ensuing panic, and witnessing the drowning multitudes of people helpless before the waters of destruction. Before we can appreciate the story of Noah's ark as something wonderful, we must first see it as the Bible does, as something tragic.

Enter the Ark

Repeatedly throughout the Bible, we will find God making and keeping promises to people. In this story, Noah is more than a master shipbuilder. We are told that he was a "righteous man," who "walked" with God and "found favor" in his sight (Gen. 6:8–9). Noah was unlike the others of his generation. The Lord announces a word of judgment to Noah and, by grace, a way of salvation for him—and in a manner that has ramifications for the entire world. "I am going to bring floodwaters on the earth to destroy all life under the heavens, every creature that has the breath of life in it. Everything on earth will perish. But I will establish my covenant with you, and you will enter the ark—you and your sons and your wife and your sons' wives with you" (6:17–18).

There in the middle of that paragraph is an important word. Did you catch it? It's the word *but*. Everything was slotted for death, *but* Noah would live. The world would be judged, but God would establish his covenant with Noah, which would mean life for the world. Noah's entire family was invited to join him, thus continuing the human race, along with the animals, and ensuring their survival.

Noah obeyed the Lord in everything (6:22). He loaded up the boat, the rain came, and "the LORD shut him in" (7:16). The water utterly covered the earth so that even its high mountains were submerged. Every living thing was killed, and "only Noah was left, and those with him in the ark" (7:23). After many months, and after the water subsided, at God's command Noah and his crew left the ark.

The carnage was indescribable. Human sin was crushed under the weight of an ocean as wide as the earth. Noah, a son of Eve, saved the world. It was a chance to start over and begin again. Never had things looked this good for humanity since Eden.

Drunk and Naked in a Tent

In Genesis 6, Noah is a shining figure against the backdrop of a tragic and wrecked humanity. After his obedience in building the ark, our expectations and hopes are high. When he steps off the ark, the first thing Noah does is build an altar to worship God. Then God makes this amazing promise to Noah: "'I establish my covenant with you: Never again will all life be destroyed by the waters of a flood; never again will there be a flood to destroy the earth.' And God said, 'This is the sign of the covenant I am making between me and you and every living creature with you, a covenant for all generations to come: I have set my rainbow in the clouds, and it will be the sign of the covenant between me and the earth'" (9:11–13).

With God's covenant promises comes a commitment of the earth to Noah and a restatement of the original "creation mandate" of Genesis 1—to be fruitful, to multiply, and to fill the earth (9:1–3).

If you knew Hebrew and heard Noah's name in that language, you would hear a sound much like the word for "rest." Noah's father had given him that name because "[Noah] will comfort us in the labor and painful toil of our hands caused by the ground the LORD has cursed" (5:29). Yet even with these promises and the hope of imminent rest, we soon learn that Noah, too, had Adam's problem. Noah built a boat and saved the world, yet a short time later we find him drunk and naked in his tent (9:20–27).

We don't know why he got drunk, and we don't know why he was naked. Still, the Bible indicates that this was a thing of shame for Noah, and it reminds us that as faithful as he was, Noah wasn't the son of Eve who would turn back sin and death. Noah himself needed a redeemer.

As we read on, we find that it's only a matter of time before Noah's descendants unite to defy God by building a tower to "make a name for [themselves]" (11:4). Adam's self-exalting ambition to usurp the place of God endures in the generations that follow Noah as well.

LOOKING BACK: GOD'S PROMISE REBOOTED

How does the story of Noah fit into the larger story we've been looking at so far? It's best to think of the flood as God's means to *restart* the world and his plans for humanity. Noah walked off the boat into a *new* creation as *a new Adam*.

A New Creational Breeze

God's creation purposes will not fail. That is what the Noahic covenant teaches us. The Noah story anticipates that the old creation will ultimately give way to a new creation. Noah's ark is a vessel for passage from the old world to the new one. Some interesting literary clues help us to see this parallel. In Genesis 1:2 the earth was described as "formless and empty," with "darkness . . . over the surface of the deep" and "the Spirit of God . . . hovering over the waters." After the flood, we read that "[God] sent a wind over the earth, and the waters receded" (8:1). The word used here for "wind" is the same word for "Spirit" in Genesis 1:2. This is a clue that when Noah steps off the boat we should see him stepping out into a new or renewed creation, a restart on the original.

Yet as the story unfolds, we see that this is not the ultimate new creation. It doesn't offer a final answer to the problem of sin.

Noah as Another Adam

Noah's world is a new creation, and Noah himself is a new Adam. We see this through a series of significant parallels that help us to consider how God's commission to Noah was a restatement of the charge he gave to Adam.

God blessed them and said to them, "Be fruitful and increase in number; fill the earth and subdue it" (Gen. 1:28).	Then God blessed Noah and his sons, saying to them, "Be fruitful and increase in number and fill the earth" (Gen. 9:1).
"Rule over the fish in the sea and the birds in the sky and over every living creature that moves on the ground . . . And to all the beasts of the earth and all the birds in the sky and all the creatures that move along the ground—everything that has the breath of life in it . . ." (Gen. 1:28, 30).	"The fear and dread of you will fall on all the beasts of the earth, and on all the birds in the sky, on every creature that moves along the ground, and on all the fish in the sea; they are given into your hands. Everything that lives and moves about will be food for you" (Gen. 9:2–3).
"I give you every seed-bearing plant on the face of whole earth and every tree that has fruit with seed in it. They will be yours for food . . . I give every green plant for food" (Gen. 1:29–30).	"Just as I gave you the green plants, I now give you everything" (Gen. 9:3).

Here's an important lesson we learn: God's covenant with Noah is not a covenant that begins with Noah but a covenant that is *extended* through Noah, one originally made with Adam. In Scripture, covenants are either started or extended. "To cut a covenant" refers to when the covenant begins, while the word that means "to establish a covenant" describes when it is extended. Although the word *covenant* first appears in God's dealings with Noah, this mention of the covenant hints at something earlier. When God says to Noah, "I will establish my covenant with you," he is not referring to the start of something new but indicating to Noah that what he began with Adam, he is continuing through Noah. The Noahic covenant is with Noah *and* creation: "and every living creature with you, a covenant for all generations to come" (9:12). It is a reaffirmation that God is still committed to his entire creation; he has not abandoned it, but he will continue to honor the plans he had, as we first saw in Genesis 1–2.

What God intended through Adam, he will fulfill through Adam's race. God promises *not* to wipe away the human race and constantly start over again (8:21–22). While the world remains in a fallen and cursed state, God tells Noah that he has hung his rainbow in the sky as a reminder of his promise (9:9–17). From Noah to the end of the age, God will allow for the simultaneous existence of two kingdoms. There will be the kingdom of man, but it will be set in opposition to the kingdom of God.

Salvation will come in due course, and it will come through God's provision of a godly seed. With Noah intoxicated and naked in his tent, we are left to wonder how the promise of Genesis 3:15 will come about now. Someone greater than Adam and Noah must still come.

LOOKING AHEAD: A FORETASTE OF WHAT'S TO COME

Noah was a new Adam in the story of salvation. He received Adam's charge and opportunity, but like Adam, he failed. Yet God's promise will never fail. Ultimately, God will provide a true Adam, the *last* Adam. He will be what Adam was supposed to be and will undo the consequences of Adam's sin by saving us from our sin. When we consider Noah's place in the Bible's storyline, two themes emerge—*judgment* and *salvation*.

A Foretaste of Coming Judgment

As we ponder Noah's flood, we are confronted with the harsh reality of what humanity deserves for its sin and rejection of God. More accurately, the flood is a *foretaste of coming judgment*, of what humanity will receive. Jesus, in describing his return and the future judgment, compares the judgment in Noah's day with the judgment that will come. Like Noah's judgment, it will take people by surprise: "As it was in the days of Noah, so it will be at the coming of the Son of Man. For in the days before the flood, people were eating and drinking, marrying and giving in marriage, up to the day Noah entered the ark; and they knew nothing about what would happen until the flood came and took them all away. That is how it will be at the coming of the Son of Man . . . Therefore keep watch, because you do not know on what day your Lord will come" (Matt. 24:37–39, 42).

No one saw the flood coming, and that was the problem. The only thing more tragic than the entire world wiped out by a flood is a world that defies God to invite such judgment. Yet that is what we find in Genesis 6. The flood comes by surprise to the people of that day, as will the final judgment Jesus describes.

But final judgment is far worse. The judgment by flood was only partial and temporary, yet the final judgment is eternal. In the final judgment there is no relief, and in this way Noah's flood becomes a reminder to us of a greater judgment to come, which we ought to take seriously.

A Foretaste of Coming Salvation

Positively, God's salvation of Noah is also a *foretaste of coming salvation*—a salvation that God will accomplish in the future. Isaiah 54:9–10 beautifully pictures this truth:

> "To me this is like the days of Noah,
>   when I swore that the waters of Noah
>   would never again cover the earth.
> So now I have sworn not to be angry with you,
>   never to rebuke you again.
> Though the mountains be shaken
>   and the hills be removed,

> yet my unfailing love for you will not be shaken,
>   nor my covenant of peace be removed,"
>   says the LORD, who has compassion on you.

Our God has unfailing love and compassion! God's promise to Noah is proof of this, and it is a warrant for trusting him about a far greater promise of a new covenant, sometimes called the "covenant of peace."

As water covered Noah's world, all appeared lost. Yet on the surface of the water floated a vessel containing the lives of eight people and many animals. By God's grace and provision, they "were saved through water" (1 Peter 3:20). In the New Testament, Peter, one of the followers of Jesus, tells us that our baptism "corresponds to this" (3:21). As Noah passed through the waters of God's judgment, now men and women will pass safely through the greater downpouring of God's wrath. How? Peter says, "Not [by] the removal of dirt from the body but [by] the pledge of a clear conscience toward God. It saves you by the resurrection of Jesus Christ, who has gone into heaven and is at God's right hand—with angels, authorities and powers in submission to him" (vv. 21–22). Jesus will save us from God's judgment by taking that judgment on himself.

Together, both the judgment and the salvation we see in the Noah story serve to strengthen New Testament Christians, who, like Noah, find themselves living amid a generation set against God. Peter appealed to the story of Noah in just this way: "If he did not spare the ancient world when he brought the flood on its ungodly people, but protected Noah, a preacher of righteousness, and seven others . . . then the Lord knows how to rescue the godly from trials and to hold the unrighteous for punishment on the day of judgment" (2 Peter 2:5, 9).

One day God will, in a final and definitive way, judge the unrighteous *and* save his people. As Noah reminds us, he will save in mercy and grace.

Noah also teaches us that God will need to do the saving completely. Righteous Noah walked with God, but he was still a sinner needing a savior. Even a total reset on creation and a fresh start could not cure humanity from the pollution of sin. Neither could it remove the problem of sin's guilt. While humans have turned on God, he is nonetheless committed to humanity and to creation. He will provide *a savior greater than Noah.*

At this point in the biblical storyline, we learn that God is not done with us, but the way forward is still unclear. Yet one thing is always certain: God will keep his promise to save us. He will undo all of the disastrous effects of sin and death on his creation.

Chapter 9

ABRAHAM

A Sky Full of Stars

GENESIS 12–50

S tars are not easy to count. If you are surrounded by city lights, they appear too faint to count. But if you travel far from any sign of civilization, the stars appear far too numerous to count. Even having a powerful telescope isn't much help. Stars may become clearer, but then you realize that some of the lights you thought were single stars are really galaxies full of even more stars.

Our sky is full of stars—and we cannot count them. God knew this when he came to Abram and said, "Look up at the sky and count the stars—if indeed you can count them" (Gen. 15:5). The night sky is filled with infinite lights—a massive quantity that speaks to the greatness of God's promise of salvation. Shortly after this point in the story, God gave Abram a new name, "Abraham," which means "father of many nations" (17:5). From this point forward, unless we're quoting Scripture directly, we'll refer to this man as Abraham, and to his wife, formerly called Sarai, as Sarah (17:15).

With the story of Noah, it seemed as if God's promises had taken two steps forward and one step back. By grace, God chose righteous Noah to restart creation, but to no avail. When later generations followed Noah and looked up to the stars, they weren't humbled before God but sought, apart from God, to "make a name" for themselves (11:4). The Tower of Babel gets its name from the judgment God leveled on humanity in that place. The descendants of Noah multiplied, but they did not fill the earth! So God confused their language and forced them to scatter abroad. This confusion of language was God's judgment, but it was also God's grace at work to restrain human sin.

Given the nature and extent of human sin, we might at this point wonder where this promised son/seed of Eve will come from? The story of Abraham brings clarity and focus to God's promise.

LOOKING DOWN: A STORY OF STARS, SLEEP, AND A SACRIFICE

Noah's family is *not* a successful restart for Adam's race, yet God is *not* thwarted. Out of fallen humanity, God calls one man to receive a big promise. This is the story of that promise in God's covenant with Abraham.

I Will, I Will, I Will

When God says, "I will," that can be a good thing or a bad thing. It was a good thing when God said to Adam, "I will make him a helper suitable for him" (2:18), and a bad thing when he said to the woman, "I will make your pains in childbearing very severe" (3:16). It was a good thing when God said to the serpent, "I will put enmity between you and the woman" (3:15), but a word of judgment when God said, "I am going to bring floodwaters on the earth" (6:17). Of course, whether God's promise is ultimately a good thing or a bad thing for us depends on its context, content, and the person God addresses.

Most definitely, God's promise to Abraham is good and gracious. Set in the context of the Noahic promise never again to judge the world with a flood, God now promises that through Abraham and his offspring, he will bring salvation to the world. Here is the promise in a series of "I will" statements: "The LORD had said to Abram, 'Go from your country, your people and your father's household to the land *I will* show you. *I will* make you into a great nation, and *I will* bless you; *I will* make your name great, and you will be a blessing. *I will* bless those who bless you, and whoever curses you *I will* curse; and all peoples on earth will be blessed through you'" (Gen. 12:1–3, emphases added).

Abraham did not deserve these promises. They were not based on anything special he had done. Joshua later reminds us that Abraham's family worshiped other gods before God chose him for this special task (Josh. 24:2–4). God chose Abraham by his grace, and now we learn that the world's fate is tied to this man!

Repeatedly, God will state his threefold promise of land, descendants, and blessing to Abraham. He will tell Abraham to look "to the north and south, to the east and west," with the promise that it was his (Gen. 13:14). Abraham's children would one day be as numerous as "the dust of the earth" (13:16). God takes Abraham outside to look at the stars and shares with him the promise "so shall your offspring be" (15:5). God's generosity is unmatched, and his promises here are undeserved.

Abraham Believed the Lord

Were God's big promises also believable? We can imagine how difficult this might have been for Abraham. He didn't know where these promises would lead him, but he did know what he was leaving behind: everything he knew—his wealth, his family, and his country. God promised Abraham great descendants, but his wife, Sarah, was barren (11:30). And at seventy-five years old, Abraham wasn't getting any younger. He and Sarah laughed privately to themselves at the impossible thought of having children (17:17; 18:12). Would Abraham believe? Were these promises too hard for the Lord?

Upon hearing God's promise, "Abram went, as the LORD had told him" (12:4). Was Abraham a righteous man who would undo what Adam did? Was Abraham's going and leaving everything behind indicative of an obedience greater than Noah's? The story is promising for humanity, but not as we might first think. Under pressure, Abraham tells Sarah to lie to a foreign ruler and say she is his sister (12:13). Abraham would even adopt his own plan B for having a child, seeking one through Sarah's servant, Hagar (16:1–3). Abraham's obedience is not perfect. Yet "Abram believed the LORD, and [God] credited it to him as righteousness" (15:6). Despite his lack of obedience, Abraham took God at his word, a hopeful sign. Yet even though we know God's promise is through Abraham, we still wonder *how* God is going to keep it, given that Abraham himself needs a savior. This question is answered for us as we keep reading the story.

A Smoking Firepot and a Blazing Torch

Abraham pondered God's promises. Concerning the land promise, Abraham even asked, "Sovereign LORD, how can I know that I will gain possession of it?" (15:8). God's answer was more than confirming. It was shocking, and it revealed something very important about *how* God would keep his word.

God answered Abraham's question with a covenant inauguration ceremony. As instructed, Abraham brought and cut in half several animals. Normally in these types of ceremonies both parties to the agreement would walk between the cut animals and swear an oath to each other to keep their promises. If they didn't keep those promises, the curse of the covenant would rest on them. By this event, two people entered into a covenant relationship. We see this kind of ceremony elsewhere in Scripture (Jer. 34:18). But notice something curious about the ceremony God initiated with Abraham.

After the sun went down, Abraham fell into a deep sleep. Then, when a "thick and dreadful darkness came over him," the Lord spoke: "Know for certain that for four hundred years your descendants will be strangers in a country not their own" (15:12–13). While Abraham slept, the Lord outlined how and when all of this would come about: after Abraham was long dead, after four hundred years of affliction for his people, after a marvelous deliverance from that captivity, and after those currently living there grew in iniquity (15:13–16).

Then, instead of *both* God and Abraham walking between the animal pieces (remember, Abraham is asleep), "a smoking firepot with a blazing torch appeared and passed between the pieces" (15:17)—imagery that refers to God. Notice the significance of this: God *alone* walks between the pieces, teaching us that God will keep his promise by *his own commitment to do so.* God binds himself to keep his promise, which entails that ultimately God's saving promise rests on his faithfulness, not on Abraham's obedience or on our obedience. God's covenant with Abraham is unconditional, or unilateral; God alone will fulfill it.

Yet a certain tension grows. God alone saves and keeps his promises, but he still demands complete obedience from us. This latter point is stressed in Genesis 17:1–14, where God expects from Abraham obedience to his covenant commands. And we know from earlier promises that God will save the world through a man, the seed of the woman, and now we know that he will do it through one of Abraham's offspring. But where will God find a truly obedient seed/son to accomplish all of God's saving purposes and to undo the work of Adam? Keep that question in mind as we continue the story.

A New Name and a New Sign

Abraham's encounters with God spanned many years, and over those years God repeated his promises of *descendants*, *land*, and *blessing*. But in Genesis 17, when Abraham was ninety-nine years old, the Lord further cemented these promises into his life and lineage. First, God changed Abram's name to Abraham, which means "father of many nations," because he would become just that (17:5). At that time God promised, "I will make you very fruitful; I will make nations of you, and kings will come from you" (17:6). This promise of *kings* is like a bread crumb, as we will see, leading us both backward and forward in the story.

In addition to a new name, God also gave Abraham a sign. God required Abraham to keep the covenant by the sign of circumcision. God's covenant is unconditional since God alone will fulfill it, but he still demands perfect obedience from Abraham—and from us as well. This creates some tension in the outworking of the covenants. "This is my covenant with you and your descendants after you, the covenant you are to keep: Every male among you shall be circumcised. You are to undergo circumcision, and it will be the sign of the covenant between me and you . . . Any uncircumcised male, who has not been circumcised in the flesh, will be cut off from his people; he has broken my covenant" (17:10–14).

Circumcision marked Abraham's children outwardly from among

the nations as a sign of priestly devotion. Circumcision was how God reminded his people daily that they belonged to him. As Scripture unfolds, we see circumcision also reminded the people that God wanted more than merely a cutting of the flesh. He wanted an internal "circumcision of the heart" (Deut. 30:6; Jer. 4:1–4; 9:25–26; Ezek. 36:25–27).

A Laugh, a Son, and a Lamb

God spoke his promise to Abraham and Sarah repeatedly, and still they laughed. They were one hundred and ninety-nine years old, respectively (17:17; 18:12). Yet God promised that the world's hope was in Abraham and Sarah's son, Isaac, and not Ishmael, who was born to Hagar (17:19–21). When Isaac came, they laughed again, this time out of sheer joy and wonder at God's amazing provision (21:6–7). God did the unthinkable: he provided a son to barren Sarah and old father Abraham.

Many years later, however, Abraham was no longer laughing. God now said to him, "Take your son, your only son, whom you love—Isaac—and go to the region of Moriah. Sacrifice him there as a burnt offering" (22:2). We can only imagine the turmoil in Abraham's heart. He likely wondered to himself, *What is God commanding?* He knew that God's promise would come through Isaac, but how would God keep it if Isaac was dead? Abraham's trust and obedience were put to the test (22:1). As Abraham lifted his hand to slay his son, an angel of the Lord commanded him to stop, saying, "Now I know that you fear God" (22:12). God spared Isaac, but the lesson remained for Abraham. God provided an alternative sacrifice as he spared Isaac's life: "Abraham looked up and there in a thicket he saw a ram caught by its horns. He went over and took the ram and sacrificed it as a burnt offering instead of his son. So Abraham called that place The LORD Will Provide. And to this day it is said, 'On the mountain of the LORD it will be provided'" (22:13–14).

Abraham believed and obeyed God, and the Lord repeated his promise to him: "Through your offspring all nations on earth will be blessed" (22:18).

The story of Isaac makes a subtle and important point. Yes, it is *through* Isaac, the promised seed, that God's salvation will come to the world. But God is also revealing that Isaac *is not enough*. Isaac, too, is a sinner in need of a savior. God's promise will come *through* Isaac, but ultimately Isaac cannot save. The Savior must come *outside* of Isaac, by God's own provision. This is the meaning of the ram that God provides. In sparing Isaac, a substitute must still take his place.

LOOKING BACK: GOD'S PROMISE FOCUSED IN A FAMILY

From Abraham onward, the Bible's story expounds God's promises to and through this man. Still, the Abrahamic promises only make sense in light of what *preceded* him. Let us reflect on God's promises of *land*, *descendants*, and *blessing* against the backdrop of God's previous dealing with Adam.

Returning to Eden

At first glance, the idea of *land* may seem inconsequential. What could Abraham's land have to do with you and me today, where we live? It turns out, everything.

When the Bible's story began, Adam and Eve were together in God's presence in a place—a land—where things between God and people were at rest. The first couple's expulsion from Eden was terrible, but it was right; God's covenantal presence and human sin cannot dwell together unless atonement is made.

East of Eden the ground is hard, as is everything else. God vomited Noah's generation from the land they occupied, covering it over and wiping it clean. Now God comes to Abraham, and instead of rejecting him from this world, he promises that Abraham can have a piece of it—a place where Abraham can go and know the Creator-covenant God. The land promise is God's commitment to his creation purposes, established at creation to Adam. The land promise is also God working out his promise to turn back the curse through a son of Eve, and it will eventually reach fulfillment in a new creation, something Abraham himself longed to see (Rom. 4:13; Heb. 11:10).

Restoring Humanity

God's promise of *descendants* for Abraham was a promise of restoration for humanity. Even more than returning humanity to Eden, through Abraham God restores humanity itself. Ever since God promised that Eve's son and seed would destroy the serpent, we have been eagerly looking for *who* this man will be. In God's promise of offspring to Abraham, we now have a clue where to look: Abraham's lineage. The Lord promised that kings would come from Abraham (Gen. 17:6). Kingship is an institution that expresses the royal Adamic role of humanity, showing most fully what it means to be God's image-bearers in the world.

God is restoring humanity through Abraham, but this doesn't mean all of humanity will be restored. From Genesis 3 onward, we know that the offspring of the serpent and woman will be at odds with one another. Two different groups represent the world's population: those of the serpent and those of the promise. When the world was filled with violence in Noah's day, Noah found favor with God against the world. This conflict would also manifest itself in a painful way in the life of Abraham's children. The Lord said to Abraham, "For four hundred years your descendants will be strangers in a country not their own and that they will be enslaved and mistreated there" (15:13). We aren't told the reason for Israel's enslavement, but this is a signal that God has more to tell us. Thankfully, when her enslavement ends, the waiting will be short. God goes on to promise, "I will punish the nation they serve as slaves, and afterward they will come out with great possessions . . . In the fourth generation your descendants will come back here, for the sin of the Amorites has not yet reached its full measure" (15:14–16).

This somewhat odd statement serves as a reminder of God's amazing patience with human sin. Will he ignore the sin of Abraham's children? Certainly not. God will bless his people as he promised, but he will do so as they trust and obey him. God stresses this point in his words to Israel: "Now if you obey me fully and keep my covenant, then out of all nations you will be my treasured possession. Although the whole earth is mine, you will be for me a kingdom of priests and a holy nation" (Ex. 19:5–6).

Surely, we think, Abraham's children will become the restored humanity, the corporate expression of all that God intended for Adam's race. It remains to be seen how this all will happen, given the people's sin and God's requirement of obedience.

Realizing God's Blessing

God's promise of *blessing* to Abraham has deep roots. God made Adam and Eve and he blessed them. Then he told them to multiply and fill the earth. Noah left the ark and God blessed him. Then he told Noah to multiply and fill the earth. There is a theme here, a pattern of genealogy and geography. Having children and land isn't meaningful to Abraham or good for the world unless Abraham also has God's blessing. Now he has it, and God emphasizes his blessing to Abraham five times in his initial promise: "I will make you into a great nation, and I will *bless* you; I will make your name great, and you will be a *blessing*. I will *bless* those who *bless* you, and whoever curses you I will curse; and all peoples on earth will be *blessed* through you" (Gen. 12:2–3, emphases added).

God blesses Abraham, and through him God will bless the nations. Yet not everyone from among the nations will know God's blessing through God's chosen man. God will bless those who bless Abraham, and God will be the one who curses Abraham. But in an important way yet undisclosed, we are told that through Abraham God will bless *all* of the nations of the earth, all ethnic people groups.

LOOKING AHEAD: THE GOSPEL IN THE TRUE SEED

Abraham's significance grows as the Bible's story continues to unfold. The rest of Genesis, the remainder of the Old Testament, and the entire Bible to come is the story of Abraham's children. While spanning only fourteen chapters in Genesis, Abraham's story contains a hint of nearly every element of the gospel story that follows. Many of the central ideas and even the vocabulary for comprehending the gospel bring us back here, to Abraham. Here are six themes that resurface later in the story.

1. Election by Grace

Why should God choose Abraham? Abraham, a sinner, was chosen by God's grace. Later, Scripture has this to say on this point: "Long ago your ancestors, including Terah the father of Abraham and Nahor, lived beyond the Euphrates River and worshiped other gods. But I took your father Abraham from the land beyond the Euphrates and led him throughout Canaan and gave him many descendants" (Josh. 24:2–3).

There is that crucial phrase, "but I took." Nothing in Abraham's heritage or religious practice merited the Lord's call on his life. He was just another man living as his father before him had lived, worshiping other gods. Abraham was not a righteous man or uniquely inclined toward love for God. And even after receiving God's promises, Abraham sinned in profound ways: leading his wife in a lie and listening to her suggestion—contrary to the promise of God—to impregnate her servant. Abraham reminds us that salvation is all of grace—undeserved and unmerited by our actions, lifestyle, or obedience. In grace, God chose Noah and Abraham, as he does when he chooses each of us.

Furthermore, God elected, or chose, Abraham to receive his gracious promises. Consider how Paul speaks about God's calling of Abraham in the later writings of the New Testament: "Therefore, the promise comes by faith, so that it may be by grace and may be guaranteed to all Abraham's offspring—not only to those who are of the law but also to those who have the faith of Abraham. He is the father of us all. As it is written: 'I have made you a father of many nations.' He is our father in the sight of God, in whom he believed—the God who gives life to the dead and calls into being things that were not" (Rom. 4:16–17).

God gives life to the dead and calls into existence what did not exist. He's the kind of God that calls to himself a man like Abraham.

God's electing grace is seen in the story of his children who follow him. Going against human tradition and human wisdom and intention, God extends his covenant to Isaac, not to Ishmael. Similarly, going against human intuition, God extends his covenant to Jacob, not to the firstborn son, Esau. Despite their human folly and sin, God sovereignly accomplishes his redemptive plan through fallen people he has chosen by grace!

2. Righteousness through Faith

As we have seen, our holy, righteous Creator requires perfect obedience from us. Yet we are disobedient and unrighteous. How, then, can we stand before God, who is just and righteous? Scripture has given us hints at the answer, but the story of Abraham gets more specific on this point: we stand righteous before God by grace *through faith* in his promises. Abraham's story reveals that a right standing before God is attained not based on our own works but because God declares us to be just by faith. Paul makes this exact point in the New Testament, using Abraham as his example: "What then shall we say that Abraham, our forefather according to the flesh, discovered in this matter? If, in fact, Abraham was justified by works, he had something to boast about—but not before God. What does Scripture say? 'Abraham believed God, and it was credited to him as righteousness.'" Now to the one who works, wages are not credited as a gift but as an obligation. However, to the one who does not work but trusts God who justifies the ungodly, their faith is credited as righteousness" (Rom. 4:1–5).

Scripture teaches that God declares us just before him when we take him at his word and believe his promises. This message of acceptance based on faith goes all the way back to Abraham and is the "good news" message at the heart of the Bible's salvation story. Consider how Paul points us to Christ *through* Abraham:

Against all hope, Abraham in hope believed and so became the father of many nations, just as it had been said to him, "So shall your offspring be." Without weakening in his faith, he faced the fact that his body was as good as dead—since he was about a hundred years old—and that Sarah's womb was also dead. Yet he did not waver through unbelief regarding the promise of God, but was strengthened in his faith and gave glory to God, being fully persuaded that God had power to do what he had promised. This is why "it was credited to him as righteousness." The words "it was credited to him" were written not for him alone, but also for us, to whom God will credit righteousness—for us who believe in him who raised

Jesus our Lord from the dead. He was delivered over to death for our sins and was raised to life for our justification.

—ROMANS 4:18–25

3. Salvation through Substitution

God declares us just by grace *though faith*, but a question remains: How exactly can God do this, given our sin? God demands from us perfect obedience, but we don't obey perfectly! Is God merely forgetting our sin, letting it go unpunished? Scripture doesn't ignore the serious problem of human sin. But we will get a fuller answer to that question as the Bible's story unfolds. At this point, Abraham's story simply offers us a hint.

God's command to Abraham to sacrifice Isaac created multiple difficulties. First, it tested Abraham's confidence in God's promise of children as numerous as the stars. Second, it caused Abraham to wonder how, if Isaac died, salvation would come to the world through him. And how would Abraham explain to Isaac what was occurring? As Abraham climbs the mountain, we aren't told everything he's thinking, but Abraham does speak at times. His son asks about the offering, and Abraham answers, "God himself will provide the lamb for the burnt offering, my son" (Gen. 22:8).

Did Abraham expect a substitute for Isaac? It's difficult to know for sure, but the author of Hebrews gives us some insight on this: "By faith Abraham, when God tested him, offered Isaac as a sacrifice. He who had embraced the promises was about to sacrifice his one and only son, even though God had said to him, 'It is through Isaac that your offspring will be reckoned.' Abraham reasoned that God could even raise the dead, and so in a manner of speaking he did receive Isaac back from death" (Heb. 11:17–19).

Whatever Abraham had in mind in saying, "God himself will provide the lamb," he spoke better than he knew. In truth, God did provide a substitute for Isaac, hinting that God himself must ultimately provide the proper substitute to pardon human sin.

Abraham's walk with his son to Mount Moriah foreshadows the journey of another Father and Son on another mountain many years later. God declares us just by grace *through faith*, yet the basis of our righteousness is found not in our righteous deeds but in the righteousness of God's own provided substitute for us, our Lord Jesus Christ. Isaac needed a substitute to die in his place, and God provided. Abraham hears the voice from heaven say, "Stop! There is another to take his place." Yet when the Father and Son walk to Calvary, there is no voice saying, "Stop. Here is another." The types and patterns of the Old Testament give way to fulfillment in the New, and no person can act as our substitute other than Jesus, God's own Son. With echoes back to Genesis 22, Paul states this glorious truth this way: "[The Father] who did not spare his own Son, but gave him up for us all—how will he not also, along with him, graciously give us all things?" (Rom. 8:32).

4. Circumcision for a New Heart

Circumcision was given to Abraham and his children to distinguish them from the surrounding nations. Circumcision said visibly and graphically, "We belong to the LORD!" Yet while circumcision was for "the flesh of your foreskins," it also pointed to the need for something greater. Whole devotion to God requires more than a mere outward cutting of the flesh. Given the depravity and pollution of sin, our Covenant Creator requires total devotion by a transformed person. Moses reminded a circumcised-in-the-flesh people of this truth when he commanded them, "Circumcise your hearts, therefore, and do not be stiff-necked any longer" (Deut. 10:16). But this was precisely the problem. The people needed God to transform them. Later Moses says this very thing, something the prophets will later emphasize as well: "The LORD your God will circumcise your hearts and the hearts of your descendants, so that you may love him with all your heart and with all your soul, and live" (Deut. 30:5–6; see also Ezek. 36:25–27).

How will God do this for his people? He will do this for his people in Jesus Christ! With the dawning of the new covenant in Christ, God will circumcise the hearts of all his people: "In him you were also circumcised with a circumcision not performed by human hands. Your whole self ruled by the flesh was put off when you were circumcised by Christ" (Col. 2:11).

The topic of circumcision raises the question of the identity of Abraham's children. Who are Abraham's "seed"? Follow carefully with four crucial distinctions. This will have surprising payoff for understanding the Bible's story. The first sense in which we follow the "seed" of Abraham is by looking at Abraham's children by natural birth. But we later learn that not all of Abraham's natural children belong to God's covenant people. God divinely elects some and not others. The second type of Abraham's "seed" hints at this. Isaac and Ishmael are both Abraham's natural children, but only Isaac is the promised seed. We see this again when God chooses Jacob over Esau.

We also find a third "seed," even among the chosen covenant people: the believers within the nation descended from the patriarchs. This is why Paul will later say, "A person is not a Jew who is one only outwardly, nor is circumcision merely outward and physical. No, a person is a Jew who is one inwardly; and circumcision is circumcision of the heart, by the Spirit, not by the written code" (Rom. 2:28–29; cf. Rom. 9:6). Outward circumcision set Abraham's children apart, but to God, that was not enough for a true, saving relationship. God required inward circumcision, fully realized only in Christ when the Spirit performs it.

Finally, there is a fourth sense in which we should understand Abraham's seed: the true, singular seed who is Jesus, the fulfillment of the "seed" promise first given to Adam and Eve in Genesis 3:15 (Gal. 3:16). As the Bible's story unfolds, we learn that it is only through the true "seed" of Abraham, Christ Jesus, that believers from all nations become children of Abraham (Gal. 3:9). Jesus circumcises the hearts of those whose faith is in him.

5. Abraham's Sons for God's Global Purpose

God has focused his commitment to humanity in one man—Abraham—and his family. Through Abraham, God works to bring salvation to the nations. The scope of God's plan through Abraham is not local but global. This makes sense if we locate Abraham's story in the context of what *preceded* him in Genesis 1–11. In creation and in Adam, God made his universal purposes plain: Abraham and his seed are now the means God will use to restore what was lost in Adam for the entire world.

Consider Paul's words from the New Testament, which explain how and why salvation is for gentiles (non-Jews), just as it was for Abraham's family (Jews): "Understand, then, that those who have faith are children of Abraham. Scripture foresaw that God would justify the Gentiles by faith, and announced the gospel in advance to Abraham: 'All nations will be blessed through you.' So those who rely on faith are blessed along with Abraham, the man of faith" (Gal. 3:7–9).

And we cannot miss Paul's crucial paragraph that follows and unpacks the relationship of Abraham to Jesus and then to us who believe, whether we are Jews or gentiles:

> The promises were spoken to Abraham and to his seed. Scripture does not say "and to seeds," meaning many people, but "and to your seed," meaning one person, who is Christ . . . in Christ Jesus you are all children of God through faith, for all of you who were baptized into Christ have clothed yourselves with Christ. There is neither Jew nor Gentile, neither slave nor free, nor is there male and female, for you are all one in Christ Jesus. If you belong to Christ, then you are Abraham's seed, and heirs according to the promise.
>
> —GALATIANS 3:16, 26–29

Here we see Paul speaking of Abraham's "seed" in that fourth sense we looked at earlier. Christ is one, true offspring of Abraham who inherits the promises, and all who are united to him by faith, whether Jew or gentile, are counted as the offspring of Abraham and heirs to the promises.

6. *Waiting for a Heavenly City*

The promise of land in Canaan was a first installment on something even better—an entirely new creation. Abraham seems to have some sense that God was doing something new and of cosmic importance through him. "By faith he made his home in the promised land like a stranger in a foreign country; he lived in tents, as did Isaac and Jacob, who were heirs with him of the same promise. For he was looking forward to the city with foundations, whose architect and builder is God" (Heb. 11:9–10).

We must remember that God isn't a territorial deity. His people will fill his earth. The author of Hebrews describes the kind of city Abraham looked forward to: "a better country—a heavenly one" (Heb. 11:16). This was Abraham's hope. He was not looking forward to another land like where he had come from. He looked forward to a land far better, new and different. This is why the writer of Hebrews says that Abraham looked forward to more than just Canaan but expected that he "would be heir of the world" (Rom. 4:13). The land of Canaan functions as a type, a pattern hinting at something greater. God designed it to lead Abraham, his children, and you and me to its fulfillment in an entirely new creation.

Chapter 10

MOSES

A Mountain Full of Smoke

EXODUS

As Genesis closes, all eyes are fixed on Abraham's children. In God's providence, a grandson of Abraham's named Joseph finds favor in Egypt and provides advantages and blessings for his people. At this point Abraham's family is only about seventy strong, hardly the sprawling nation that God had promised.

As the next book, Exodus, opens, the situation has changed. Abraham's children are now a populous nation. The description is communicated to us using the language of the Abrahamic promise: "The Israelites were exceedingly fruitful; they multiplied greatly, increased in numbers and became so numerous that the land was filled with them" (Ex. 1:7). Notice the repetition from the earlier promises, using words like *multiply* and *fruitful* and references to land and people. But things have changed in less happy ways as well. Their multiplication has led to the fulfillment of the promise that Abraham's offspring would be "enslaved" and "mistreated" for four hundred years in a foreign land (Gen. 15:13). Given the promised conflict between the woman's and the serpent's offspring, we shouldn't be surprised to find Abraham's children enslaved to Egypt's king.

Nor should we be surprised to learn that God acts to redeem his people. We're not told why Israel is enslaved, and it doesn't seem to be directly tied to their sin. Yet repeatedly God tells us why he will redeem them from slavery. He will redeem them to display his glory and demonstrate to Israel *and* Egypt that he alone is God, the one who is faithful to all his promises (Ex. 6:7; 7:5, 17; 8:10, 22; 9:14–16, 29; 10:2; 11:7; 14:4, 18).

When reading Old Testament narratives, it's helpful to compare how a book begins with how it ends. Exodus opens with God's people in servitude in Egypt, and it ends with them in service to God. It opens with God's people building cities for an oppressor, and it closes with the building of a tabernacle for God's glorious presence. It opens with the drowning of Israel's children, and it ends with Pharaoh's army drowned under the waters of the Red Sea.

The story is mingled with magicians, the clashing of nations, and miraculous feats—all elements of a profound drama. But it's by grasping *how* God achieves these changes that we gain insight into his saving plan. At the story's center is Moses and the covenant that God inaugurates *through Moses* with the nation of Israel. This covenant does *not* replace God's covenant with Abraham; rather, it carries it forward, bringing focus and structure to Israel's relationship with God now that Abraham's family has become a nation. God's covenant through Moses is God's Law, his *Torah* for Israel, and we'll refer to it as the Law-covenant, what the New Testament refers to as the old covenant.

Just as God's promise of a nation from Abraham seemed impossible, so does God's promise of rescue from slavery. Yet the Creator-covenant God is never thwarted. Moses' rise to leadership over Israel proves this, and the story of God's covenant with Israel—mediated through Moses—spotlights the covenant faithfulness of God.

LOOKING DOWN: THE STORY OF ISRAEL, GOD'S TREASURED POSSESSION

Israel's covenant has a profound purpose: she will become God's "treasured possession . . . a kingdom of priests and a holy nation" (Ex. 19:5–6). In Israel, the world was supposed to witness humanity living in rightly ordered relationship to God, one another, and the rest of the world. This is how God's treasure would look. This is how a kingdom of priests—those mediating God's presence and fulfilling Adam's role—was to live before the world. This is how a holy nation is to reflect God's holiness back to him.

The book of Exodus is structured in three parts. First, God *delivers* his people from Egyptian bondage through Moses (1–15). Second, God *speaks* through Moses to his people in the giving of the Law on Mount Sinai (16–31). Third, God *dwells* with his people in the tabernacle that Moses built (32–40).

At each stage, Moses is prominent in God's plan, highlighting his status as the mediator of God's covenant. At each stage, we also witness a shocking display of sin by the people, a sad reminder of the serious nature of our heart problem, a theme central to the Bible's story.

The Law-covenant can't be understood apart from Moses' story, and the book of Exodus tells that story.

Through the Sea

Moses' rise and rescuing of Israel reveals the incomparable power and greatness of God. In due time, Moses will miraculously deliver his people through the Red Sea by stretching out his hand (14:21). But his story begins with a very different, although similarly incredible, watery scene.

Intimidated by the growing number of Hebrews, Egypt's king orders every Hebrew-born son to be thrown into the Nile River. Moses' parents, sharing Abraham's faith, refuse to comply. They put Moses in the Nile but place him in a basket where, by God's providence, Pharaoh's daughter finds and adopts him. Pharaoh ordered his death, but Moses ends up as his grandson! Like his Hebrew mother, Moses shared more than Israel's blood; he shared Israel's faith. When Moses killed an Egyptian oppressor to save the life of a Hebrew slave—a fellow countryman—he became Pharaoh's target once again.

Moses' actions to save one Hebrew led him away from Egypt. God's action to save his people brought Moses back. God heard his people's cry for rescue, so he chose Moses for an important task: "I am the God of your father, the God of Abraham, the God of Isaac and the God of Jacob . . . So now, go. I am sending you to Pharaoh to bring my people the Israelites out of Egypt" (3:6–10). God, the covenant-maker, is the always-faithful covenant-keeper.

This was good news. Pharaoh enslaved God's people (1:13), but now they were called to know and serve a new Lord. Moses fled Egypt by faith, and by faith he would return, a servant of God to rescue servants for God.

This good news is also terrifying; Moses is to confront Egypt's king and demand the impossible. "Who am I?" Moses asks, adding many reasons why he is unfit for the job (3:11). In one sense, Moses is correct, but God's work of salvation never depends on human greatness. God made abundantly clear to Moses whose mission this was: *God* would be with Moses (3:12); Moses would bear *God's* name (3:14); *God* would perform miracles through Moses (4:1–9); *the Lord* would tell Moses what to say (4:10–12); and *the Lord* would provide Moses with Aaron for his aide (4:13–17). From the beginning to the end, Moses' success would be *God's* doing.

If Moses considered God's calling both wonderful and terrifying, perhaps the people felt the same. Here's what Moses said to his oppressed people:

> Therefore, say to the Israelites: "I am the LORD, and I will bring you out from under the yoke of the Egyptians. I will free you from being slaves to them, and I will redeem you with an outstretched arm and with mighty acts of judgment. I will take you as my own people, and I will be your God. Then you will know that I am the LORD your God, who brought you out from under the yoke of the Egyptians. And I will bring you to the land I swore with uplifted hand to give to Abraham, to Isaac and to Jacob. I will give it to you as a possession. I am the LORD."
>
> —EXODUS 6:6–8

What great and frightening news! Thankfully, God is a perfect match for his promises. Seven times in this promise he says, "I will." Three times he reminds them, "I am the LORD." What God promised to Abraham and now through Moses, God will accomplish. But how will God rescue his people? How will God transfer his people from the service of Pharaoh to his service? Israel's exit from Egypt happened in three steps.

First, God judged Egypt. Through a series of plagues, God demonstrated his power over Egypt's non-gods and brought the nation to her economic knees. The Nile turned to blood, ruining the water supply. Frogs, gnats, flies, and locusts overran the countryside in waves and terrified people in their homes. Even hail pounded the fields. Nothing remained. All of this showed that Israel's God alone was God, but Pharaoh defiantly asked, "Who is the LORD, that I should obey him and let Israel go? I do not know the LORD" (5:2). Moses warned Pharaoh to let Israel go, but every time Pharaoh only hardened his heart in response. The final plague, the death of Egypt's firstborn, crippled Pharaoh and finally won Israel's release.

Israel's rescue from Egypt, though, required more than God's judgment on Egypt. That night the angel of death was non-discriminatory in his work of killing. He passed through the land and brought judgment upon *every* firstborn, regardless of who they were, whether Egyptian or Israelite. There was nothing special to save Israel. They would need more to escape the judgment that had fallen upon Egypt. They also needed deliverance from God's judgment on their own sin.

Yet just as God had provided for Isaac on the mountain, he now provides for Israel. That very night God instructs Moses to tell the Israelites to slay lambs and mark each household's doorposts with the lambs' blood. The angel of death would "pass over" the homes whose doorposts were marked, not because they were Israelites, but because of the blood. Why the blood? This blood represented both the death of a lamb in the place of the firstborn and the faith of those who marked their homes, trusting God's promise. In this way, God's judgment came upon Egypt, but God's salvation came to Israel—to all those who took God at his word. That night the Lord saved his people from death, through death, by his own gracious provision. This event was called the Passover.

Finally, God led his people in an escape from Egypt during the night.

That night Israel ate in haste, their sandals tied, ready at God's command to flee. When Pharaoh gave the word of their release, they made their exit. Yet as Israel approached the Red Sea, they faced two obstacles: the sea ahead and Pharaoh's army behind, coming to destroy them. What was Israel to do?

Nothing.

Which is God's design. God will deliver his people by demonstrating his own incomparably great power. God settled a cloud between Pharaoh's army and Israel and commanded Moses to stretch out his hand. The Lord split the sea in two, and Israel crossed safely on dry ground between the walls of water. Pharaoh's army foolishly followed, and God brought the waters down on them.

All of this shows that God's power is unrivaled! Israel not only escaped from Egypt but also brought with them much wealth (12:35–36). They plundered the Egyptians just as God promised Abraham: "I will punish the nation they serve as slaves, and afterward they will come out with great possessions" (Gen. 15:14; cf. Ex. 6:6). Such was God's marvelous plan. He rescued Israel and displayed his glory.

Through three feats, God accomplished the impossible: the plagues overcame Pharaoh's rebellious will, the Passover overcame Israel's sin, and the parting of the Red Sea overcame Pharaoh's rage. Looking at Pharaoh's army dead on the shore, "the people feared the LORD and put their trust in him and in Moses his servant" (Ex. 14:31). The Lord did it all through his man, Moses, and so this glory extended to Moses as well. Moses, God's servant, led God's people in song: "I will sing to the LORD, for he is highly exalted. Both horse and driver he has hurled into the sea. The LORD is my strength and my defense; he has become my salvation" (15:1–2).

We should add a word here about Israel's sin—a theme that we'll return to at the end of each part of this exodus story. If God has demonstrated to us his power and glory, Israel has displayed her pervasive depravity. Delivered from Egypt, Israel is on the road to the promised land to enjoy God's presence and the fulfillment of his promises. Yet in the desert, with only food on her mind, "the whole community grumbled against Moses and Aaron" (16:2). Some complained that it had been better in Egypt when they "sat around pots of meat and ate all the food [they] wanted" (16:3). Of course, to say such things not only ignored their previous slavery but also questioned God's love, goodness, and grace. Still, God mercifully and graciously met their needs with "bread from heaven" (16:4).

Did this satisfy their complaints? Would they now trust and obey the Lord? Sadly, the answer is no, as we'll see time after time in this story. For now, we want to note that we have learned something further about God and our human problem: God is glorious in power and patient, and our problem runs deeper than geography or slavery (16:10–12).

Up and Down the Mountain

God's intent in redeeming Israel wasn't merely to save her *from* Egyptian servitude but also to call her *into* divine service. God wanted more for Israel than to inherit the promised land; *he* was to be their portion, delight, and inheritance. At the center of life in Eden was God himself, and the same is true in Canaan. The Lord said to Pharaoh: "Let my people go, so that they may worship me" (8:1), and the Lord said to Moses, "When you have brought the people out of Egypt, you will worship God on this mountain" (3:12). That mountain was Mount Sinai. There God would enter into a covenant relationship with Israel and give them his Law to instruct them how to relate to him in love and service. They would become his treasured possession.

The experience of receiving the Law was terrifying. When the Lord called out to Moses from a bush that wouldn't stop burning, Moses looked away in terror (3:6). But that was nothing compared to the giving of the Law! When God gave Moses his Law, he did so from a mountain that shook from thunder, flashed with lightning, and was shrouded in smoke. This intense sensory experience was a reminder that despite Israel's redemption and deliverance from the bonds of slavery, there remained an enduring conflict: the one between God's holiness and human sin going all the way back to Adam.

As if he were standing on the edge of a volcano, Moses gave the priests careful instructions for how they should approach the mountain, going only so far "or [God would] break out against them" (19:24). The people said to Moses, "Speak to us yourself and we will listen. But do not have God speak to us or we will die" (20:19). Moses was already a towering figure, but his role as a mediator between God and the people only increased his stature among the people. As the people stood far off, "Moses approached the thick darkness where God was" (20:21). There, in that cloud of smoke, God spoke to Moses, Moses received the Law, and through Moses, God met with his people. At Mount Sinai, we witness God's commitment to restore the broken relationship first brought about by Adam.

What did Moses receive on the mountain? We can summarize it briefly by thinking about five aspects of the Law: its *context, center, content, consequences,* and *culmination.*

First, the Law's *context* is expressed before any word of command is uttered: "And God spoke all these words: 'I am the LORD your God, who brought you out of Egypt, out of the land of slavery'" (Ex. 20:1–2).

God rescued Israel from slavery, and the context of the Law is a relationship. That relationship wasn't earned by obedience to God's commandments. God had already chosen and delivered the nation. Neither would Israel's obedience serve as a payment for her redemption. No, Israel was delivered from a harsh master *by* and *for* a holy Lord. God relates to his people as the God who first redeems them, and his people relate to him as those redeemed by God's grace.

Second, if we consider the first of the commandments God gives, we see that it expresses the Law's *center:* "You shall have no other gods before me" (20:3). The Law's main concern is the Lord and his people. In Deuteronomy 6:4–5, the Lord says, "Hear, O Israel: The LORD our God, the LORD is one. Love the LORD your God with all your heart and with all your soul and with all your strength." The Law, then, directs the life and love of God's people to her Lord.

Third, we find that the Law's *content* is diverse. Specifically and practically, the Law tells Israel *how* to live as a nation—as a kingdom of priests, God's servant-kings, in relation to him. Frontloading the most important things first, God begins with what are popularly known as the Ten Commandments (Ex. 20:1–17).

The first four commandments deal with Israel's relationship to God: they are to worship God alone; they are not to make a carved image after God's likeness; they are to treat as holy God's name; and they are to keep the Sabbath day as holy. The final six commandments deal with the Israelites' relationships to one another: they're to honor their father and mother, highlighting the importance of the family unit tied to creation, and they are not to murder, commit adultery, steal, bear false witness, or covet, underscoring the value and worth of humans created in God's image.

The fourth commandment has roots in the seventh day of creation, when God rested (Ex. 20:11), and his redemption of Israel from Egypt (Deut. 5:15). It commands Israel to rest on every seventh day as a Sabbath, to cease from their work, to enjoy God and one another, and ultimately to anticipate the full recovery of rest lost by Adam's rebellious choice. At the heart of the Law is a concern to order humanity first in relation to the glorious Creator-covenant God, and then to one another and to the world.

When we think of the Law-covenant, we're tempted to think only of the Ten Commandments. While these commands are given first to highlight their importance, the Law as an entire covenant package includes far more. For example, the Law includes commands concerning how members of the community are to relate with one another in their daily life together, laws for the priesthood and a system of sacrifices, and laws concerning Israel's civil life. People often divide the Law into three parts: civil laws that govern Israel's life as a nation, ceremonial laws that regulate Israel's religious life tied to the sacrificial system, and moral laws such as the Ten Commandments. This is a helpful way to think of how different laws functioned in the nation's life, but ultimately it is best to think of the Law as a single covenant unit or package.

Fourth, the Law comes with blessings and curses. And the blessings and curses of the Law reveal its *consequences*. "See, I am setting before you today a blessing and a curse—the blessing if you obey the commands of the LORD your God that I am giving you today; the curse if you disobey the commands of the LORD your God and turn from the way that I command you today by following other gods, which you have not known" (Deut. 11:26–28).

It is crucial to see how the Law's consequences functioned in Israel's life as a people. The blessings and curses govern how God relates with and responds to his people. When God created Adam and Eve, he blessed them, and he did the same with Noah. When God called Abraham, he promised to bless the world through him. Those who blessed Abraham would be blessed, and those who cursed him would be cursed (Gen. 27:29). In his relationship to Israel, God's blessing comes through Israel's obedience. Obedience will yield long life in the promised land, but disobedience will result in exile from the land.

The commands and the consequences are as straightforward for Israel as they were for Adam. The only question, at this point, is whether Israel will obey and receive life or disobey like Adam and receive death. Israel, like Adam, now faces a momentous choice: "Now what I am commanding you today is not too difficult for you or beyond your reach . . . See, I set before you today life and prosperity, death and destruction . . . Now choose life, so that you and your children may live and that you may love the LORD your God, listen to his voice, and hold fast to him. For the LORD is your life, and he will give you many years in the land he swore to give to your fathers, Abraham, Isaac and Jacob" (Deut. 30:11, 15, 19–20).

God's promises are sure, but will Israel obey? If they don't, then what hope is there for the world? At this point in the story, we know that it is *through Israel*, Abraham's offspring, that God's promise to save will come. How will God keep his promise to save if Israel, like Adam, does not obey him?

Fifth, we should note that the *culmination* of the Law is "rest"—the rest that was first introduced on the seventh day of creation. Rhythms of Sabbath rest were built into Israel's life, every seventh day, every seventh month, and every seventh year (Ex. 16:23; 23:12; 34:21; 35:2; Lev. 23:39; 25:4). Rest was the great goal anticipated by entry into the land (Ex. 33:14; Deut. 3:20; 12:9; 25:19; Josh. 1:13). When Joshua leads

Israel into the land and divides the inheritance among the people, we read this amazing summary statement: "So the LORD gave Israel all the land he had sworn to give their ancestors, and they took possession of it and settled there. The LORD gave them rest on every side, just as he had sworn to their ancestors. Not one of their enemies withstood them; the LORD gave all their enemies into their hands. Not one of all the LORD's good promises to Israel failed; every one was fulfilled" (Josh. 21:43–45).

Sin would complicate things, but this summary reflects a high point in the nation's life under Joshua, a taste of God's rest that they were intended to enjoy. Rest was the goal of the Law, a recovery of what was lost in creation because of sin, and something, as we'll see, that anticipated a far greater rest than was promised in the Law.

But before we develop these points, we must once again focus our attention on the presence of sin in the story. While Moses was still on the mountain speaking with God, the nation of Israel, in less than forty days, committed spiritual adultery—at the very base of the mountain where God and Moses were meeting. They were quick "to turn away from what [God] commanded them and . . . made themselves an idol cast in the shape of a calf" (Ex. 32:8). Led by Aaron, Israel broke every command they swore to obey! In holy wrath, the Lord told Moses to go to the people with a word of judgment. Indignant at the people, Moses broke the tablets the Lord had given him, proof that God's gracious covenant was already smashed to smithereens by Israel's sin. What this episode reveals is that if God's salvation promises are in Israel alone, then there is not much hope for the world. God deserves and demands a faithful covenant partner, but Israel, like Adam before them, does not fit the bill.

Moses interceded for the nation, God graciously restored Israel, and Moses returned to the mountain for another set of tablets. God's glory was displayed not only in a mountain filled with smoke (24:14–18) but also in Moses' face when he came down from speaking with God: "When Moses came down from Mount Sinai with the two tablets of the covenant law in his hands, he was not aware that his face was radiant because he had spoken with the LORD" (34:29).

On that mountain, when Moses pleaded with the Lord to restore the nation, he also pleaded to see the Lord's glory. The Lord granted both, but he gave Moses only a glimpse of his glory. While Moses was positioned in the cleft of the mountain, the Lord showed Moses the trailing edge of his glory. Having found favor with God, Moses saw more than any other Old Testament figure would see, but the problem still remained: what would God do with the sin of Israel? In graphic language, the people are described as "stiff-necked" (33:3–6)—just like all of Adam's descendants. How does the God of glory and holiness dwell with a sinful, rebellious people? How will salvation come to this world through Israel? Even more, will we ever be restored to the place where we know, see, and experience God's glory in undiminished splendor, the very reason we were created?

Into the Tent

Moses is famous for his leadership in Israel's exodus from Egypt. He is also famous for his reception of God's Law and the Ten Commandments on Mount Sinai. What is often neglected is his role in the establishment of the tabernacle and the inauguration of the entire priesthood in the third part of Exodus and the opening chapters of Leviticus.

In the giving of the Law, God included instructions for a traveling, tent-like structure. The Lord expressed its purpose simply and beautifully: "[There] I will dwell among them" (25:8). This is not something the gods of the nations did. The false gods were far off, manipulated by means of carved statues. Not the Lord! Though God seemed far off when Moses' story began at the start of Exodus, by the end of the book God is dwelling near his people.

In its pattern and furniture, the tabernacle's design is exacting and elaborate (25:9). Approaching from the outside, we enter from the east into the courtyard. This is where common people present their offerings and worship. From the courtyard, we enter the tent from the east as well and proceed into the first of two rooms. The first room is the "Holy Place." In this room are three pieces of furniture: the lampstand, the table for the showbread, and the incense altar. Before us hangs a large and stunning pair of curtains decorated with blue, purple, and scarlet and embroidered with cherubim—a kind of portrait of a heavenly sky with angelic beings soaring about. These curtains form a barrier between the Holy Place and the innermost part of the tabernacle, the holy of holies—the place of direct encounter with God. Several pieces of furniture are in view. The ark of the covenant is a box containing the tablets of the Law, and it serves as the Lord's footstool on earth. In front of the ark are reminders of God's saving deeds: an urn of manna, Moses' incense, and Aaron's rod. On its top is a mercy seat for the blood of sacrifices, with two golden cherubim looking over it.

This is ground zero for God's presence on earth. The closer one gets to the tabernacle's epicenter, the greater the holiness and the steeper the requirements for access. The garments, the rituals, and the furniture heighten with each space.

Once constructed, the glory of God filled the tabernacle. When that glory lifted, the people knew to move.

Though God did dwell with his people in this way, clearly it was no return to Eden. The covering of human sin required an elaborate, ongoing system. Only one man entered beyond the curtains to the inner presence of God, and only once each year (Lev. 16). On the Day of Atonement, the high priest made sacrifices for the purification of his own sins and for that place. He also made atonement for the people's sins, placing the sins on a goat and sending it out of the camp. It took with it the guilt of the people.

God's mercy is great, yet as we've come to expect, human sin remains. The people grumbled as they wandered in the wilderness, and they overwhelmed Moses with litigation against one another (Ex. 18:13–26). At the end of his life, Moses knew that Israel would enter the land but that their hearts would lead them away from the Lord and into exile (Deut. 31:21, 27, 29). Long before Israel's history as a nation unfolds, Moses had already predicted what will happen to them as the result of their sin. Moses knew the problem of sin in his own heart. His anger was the reason he couldn't enter the promised land. The Law-covenant was needed, and it was glorious and good, but it was not enough. In God's plan, the Law-covenant did many things for the nation, but it also pointed beyond itself to something—Someone—greater who would deal finally and definitively with the problem of sin.

LOOKING BACK: GOD'S PROMISE FOCUSED IN A NATION

As we consider how the Law-covenant fits into God's plan, we first need to look back to what *preceded* it. Specifically, how does the Law-covenant relate with the Abrahamic covenant and then, before that, to God's covenant with creation?

Abraham's Children Become a Nation

God promised Abraham a nation from his offspring, and Israel *is* that nation. The Law-covenant gives structure to the life of God's people now that they are a nation. Under the Law, Israel is how God's blessing will come to all nations. Repeatedly, God appeals to his promises to Abraham and the patriarchs as the grounds for his continuing faithfulness to Israel. Deuteronomy 7:7–9 is a prime example:

> The LORD did not set his affection on you and choose you because you were more numerous than other peoples, for you were the fewest of all peoples. But it was because the LORD loved you and kept the oath he swore to your ancestors that he brought you out with a mighty hand and redeemed you from the land of slavery, from the power of Pharaoh king of Egypt. Know therefore that the LORD your God is God; he is the faithful God, keeping his covenant of love to a thousand generations of those who love him and keep his commandments.

A Son of God, like Adam

While it's not difficult to miss the close connection of Israel to Abraham, it's easy to miss the connection between Israel and Adam. Recall that God's covenant with Abraham was a reestablishment of God's relationship to humanity to bring about his original purposes for humanity. This means that Israel functions in a similar role to Adam in relationship to God and God's global purposes. As a nation, the people are to image and represent God. Furthermore, as a son is to a father, so Israel is to God. This relationship shapes Moses' appeal to Pharaoh: "This is what the LORD says: 'Israel is my firstborn son, and I told you, "Let my son go, so he may worship me"'" (Ex. 4:22–23). In her life as a nation, Israel's special relationship takes on special shape institutionally in the assignment of prophets, priests, and kings. These institutions express the various roles that Adam held as God's image and son (Luke 3:38), and they indicate what we are to look like as rightly ordered humanity.

The tabernacle points back to Eden as well—its construction in seven steps, ending with rest, echo the seven days of creation. The menorah reminiscent of the tree of life and the embroidered cherubim representing the cherubim remind us that the way back to Eden is guarded because of sin. Even as we approach from the east, we must be protected from God's holy presence—or we die.

LOOKING AHEAD: FROM SHADOWS TO SUBSTANCE

Christ and his covenant are so much better! This is exactly what the Law-covenant was given to help us see. Everything about the Law-covenant was needed, yet it wasn't enough. Built into the Law-covenant were carefully designed limitations. The author of Hebrews says, "The Holy Spirit was showing by this that the way into the Most Holy Place had not yet been disclosed as long as the first tabernacle was still functioning" (Heb. 9:8). The Holy Spirit designed the old covenant to teach God's people about what they really needed and to point beyond itself to something greater: a solution to sin and access to God.

Repeated sacrifices cried out for a once-for-all sacrifice: "When Christ came as high priest of the good things that are now already here, he went through the greater and more perfect tabernacle that is not made with human hands, that is to say, is not part of this creation. He did not enter by means of the blood of goats and calves; but he entered the Most Holy Place once for all by his own blood, thus obtaining eternal redemption" (9:11–12). A once-for-all sacrifice for an eternal redemption.

The Law-covenant could not deliver this kind of salvation. Yet it was not a failed project. In God's overall plan, it serves an important purpose: to prophetically reveal our great need and show the world that hope is found in God alone.

The story of Exodus is a dramatization of this point: God alone saves. Moses was not Israel's hope as a nation. Moses himself was barred from entering the promised land because of his disobedience and sin. The covenant didn't give the people the life they needed, but it did anticipate someone greater. It anticipated someone who would obey perfectly and bring life (Gal. 3:21, 24).

Toward that end, several divinely designed types and patterns are embedded in God's dealings with Israel through Moses—patterns that beautifully point us to Christ.

1. We Participate in a Greater Exodus

God made sure Israel would never forget the exodus. He even built plans for its remembrance into the event itself. With instructions for the Passover meal, he included instructions for what fathers would tell their children down through the ages. Israel's exodus from Egypt was more than a one-time event. It became the paradigm for all of God's redeeming acts to follow, with an important addition, a twist.

The prophets that follow Moses will speak of *another* exodus yet to come. When Israel is later exiled from the land of promise, they speak of a return to the land in language similar to the first exodus story, yet their interest is no longer on deliverance from a foreign power and getting back into the land. Their focus is God's deliverance of his people from what led them there in the first place—their sin. Israel was exiled because of the covenant curses and the people's hardness of heart. No political or national deliverance under the Persian king, Cyrus, could fix *that* problem. Isaiah speaks of a greater redemption, tied to a greater exodus, brought about by the Servant of the Lord, who comes as our substitute and pays for our sin (Isa. 52:13–53:12). What is needed ultimately for God's people is their liberation and redemption from sin.

God will eventually address this problem. With the coming of Jesus, the divine Son becomes a man to fulfill the meaning of his name and to "save his people from their sins" (Matt. 1:21). In Christ, God cures our problem of sin by Christ's life and redemptive death. Jesus speaks of his death as an *exodus* or "departure" (Luke 9:31) because his death is the event to which the exodus, as a type and pattern, ultimately pointed. In Jesus' cross and resurrection, redemption from sin has finally come in its complete sense. In Christ, an even greater exodus from slavery has occurred.

In Christ, you and I experience an exodus more miraculous than Israel knew as she walked between walls of water.

2. We Experience a Greater Rest

Jesus says to us, "Come to me, all you who are weary and burdened, and I will give you rest" (Matt. 11:28). This stands on its own as a gracious invitation. But we'll explore depths to this offer for all eternity. Remember, God's goal in creation was covenantal rest, and Adam abandoned that rest when he sinned. The Bible is a story of God restoring rest for his people, and the Law-covenant is an important step in that story.

Through the Law-covenant, God structured foretastes of ultimate rest into the life of the nation. Every seventh day they rested from their work, a sign of dependence upon God, the one to whom they belonged. Even the promised land held promise for a great life because it was in the land that they enjoyed rest, a place free of sin and its effects, and a place for the free enjoyment of God and his presence. But the Law-covenant could not deal with sin, and so the rest they experienced was only a foretaste of a greater rest yet to come.

Rest has always been about more than the land. Consider two passages with us. In Psalm 95, David warns the people of God this way: "Today, if only you would hear his voice, 'Do not harden your hearts . . . as you did that day . . . where your ancestors tested me; they tried me, though they had seen what I did . . . So I declared on oath in my anger,

"They shall never enter my rest"'" (Ps. 95:7–11). Interestingly, Psalm 95 was written many years *after* Israel entered the promised land under Joshua. The author of Hebrews reasons, "If Joshua had given them rest, God would not have spoken later about another day. There remains, then, a Sabbath-rest for the people of God; for anyone who enters God's rest also rests from their works, just as God did from his" (Heb. 4:8–10).

Jesus offers this rest to us. A rest found in him, and a rest from our works. This is good news for restless people.

3. We Hope in a Greater Israel

God's promise has widened to encompass the nation of Israel, and it will widen further to encompass the nations. Yet God's promise will also come through one man, a son and seed of Eve who will crush the serpent's head. We also know that this son will be a son of Abraham and from the tribe of Judah: "The scepter will not depart from Judah" (Gen. 49:10). This man will succeed where Adam, Abraham, Moses, and Israel all failed.

If our hope, as with the previous covenant heads, is in Israel as a nation to save, we are in serious trouble. Israel, in God's plan, serves many purposes, but a crucial one is to demonstrate that they too need a savior—a savior who comes from them. This is exactly who Jesus is, the true Israelite. Consider how the very events of Jesus' life reflect that he is the Promised One from Israel, who fulfills what Israel failed to do and be. In many ways, Jesus' life mirrors the life of Israel, but in his case, he obeys where Israel did not. For example, like Israel, Jesus, as God's Son, comes out of Egypt (Matt. 2:15). At his baptism, we hear these words from his Father: "This is my Son, whom I love; with him I am well pleased" (3:17). And then Jesus is driven into the wilderness for forty days, where he is tempted just like Israel and Adam were. Yet in contrast to Israel and Adam, Jesus prevails (4:1–11). To those who follow him, Jesus offers himself as the bread of life, the true bread from heaven (John 6:32), and as living water that wells up to eternal life (John 4:14). When Jesus said that he is the true vine, he was referring to himself as the true Israelite. He is the light of the world, fulfilling the role assigned to Israel (8:12).

The point is this: Jesus succeeds where Adam, Abraham, Moses, *and Israel* all failed. Given that you and I are great failures, this is tremendous news. "If you are Christ's," Paul writes, "then you are Abraham's offspring, heirs according to promise" (Gal. 3:29 ESV). Jesus, the true offspring of Abraham, the true Israelite, obeys in his life for us and in his death wins for us our salvation (Gal. 3:13–14).

4. We Hear a Greater Prophet

Moses was a great prophet, but Jesus is far greater. Moses agrees: "The LORD your God will raise up for you a prophet like me from among you, from your fellow Israelites. You must listen to him" (Deut. 18:15). Moses' obituary hints at the expectation this promise built: "Since then, no prophet has risen in Israel like Moses, whom the LORD knew face to face" (34:10). People were still looking for this prophet when Jesus arrived on the scene hundreds of years later.

When Jesus came, he exceeded all expectations. He was the very Word made flesh, the one who not only obeyed but also revealed God perfectly. This is why the author of Hebrews opens his letter by exalting Jesus above Moses: "In the past God spoke to our ancestors through the prophets at many times and in various ways, but in these last days he has spoken to us by his Son" (1:1–2).

Consider this incredible scene. Jesus takes Peter, John, and James up on a mountain to pray. Then something amazing and mind-blowing happens: "As [Jesus] was praying, the appearance of his face changed, and his clothes became as bright as a flash of lightning. Two men, Moses and Elijah, appeared in glorious splendor, talking with Jesus" (Luke 9:28–30). It's one thing to read about history and to talk about the lives of men like Moses and Elijah, great prophets of the Old Testament. It's another thing to see them in person, talking with someone you know!

And what did they speak about? They spoke of Jesus' "departure," the exodus to come, an exodus greater than that led by Moses. Peter offered to make a tent for each of the three, but we're told, "[Peter] did not know what he was saying" (9:33). And then this happened: "While he was speaking, a cloud appeared and covered them, and they were afraid as they entered the cloud. A voice came from the cloud, saying, 'This is my Son, whom I have chosen; listen to him.' When the voice had spoken, they found that Jesus was alone" (9:34–36). This should seem like a familiar scene to you by this point: the mountain, the cloud, and the voice of the Lord. Jesus stands alone on the mountain because he is the greater prophet about whom Moses spoke.

5. We Receive a Greater Law

Moses on Sinai represents the Law in Israel's life. This Law was good in its commands and its purposes, yet a law written on stone could only further harden the heart (2 Cor. 3:7). In deeper slavery to her own sin, Israel either ignored the Law or manipulated it in the service of self-righteousness (Rom. 7:7–9). The Law was holy, but it did not bring Israel to holiness, only condemnation (2 Cor. 3:9). In both its instruction and its inadequacy, it was a tutor for God's people, teaching and leading them to the one who could write the law of God on their hearts (Gal. 3:24).

When Jesus delivered the Sermon on the Mount, he didn't speak merely as a new Moses; he spoke as the one to whom the Law pointed. In Christ, the Law-covenant has not been abolished—it has been fulfilled in the sense that it has reached its God-intended end (Matt. 5:17–20). In Christ, our new covenant head and substitute, our sin is fully paid for and the Spirit's work of new creation is secured. What the Law could not do for us, our Lord Jesus Christ has done by his life, death, and resurrection.

What happened to the curse of the Law? As Paul so beautifully states in the New Testament letter to the Galatian church, "Christ redeemed us from the curse of the law by becoming a curse for us, for it is written: 'Cursed is everyone who is hung on a pole [or tree].' He redeemed us in order that the blessing given to Abraham might come to the Gentiles through Christ Jesus, so that by faith we might receive the promise of the Spirit" (Gal. 3:13–14).

6. We Trust a Greater Mediator

Moses was a great mediator between God and the people. In the exodus story, Moses is present everywhere. God saved him from execution, called out to him, sent him to speak to Pharaoh, gave him instructions for the Passover, and told him to stretch out his hand for the waters to part. What God could have done by his own direct, divine action he did through a man: a mediator.

This is how God worked through Abraham, and this is how God would work through David, as we will see in the next chapter. In an even greater way, this is also true with Jesus. God mediates all his blessings through him. Paul says this as he writes to Timothy: "There is one God and one mediator between God and mankind, the man Christ Jesus, who gave himself as a ransom for all people" (1 Tim. 2:5–6).

Moses and the covenant he mediates cannot compare to Christ and his new covenant. Consider the comparison. Here, the author of Hebrews puts this contrast in beautiful and personal terms:

> You have not come to a mountain that can be touched and that is burning with fire; to darkness, gloom and storm; to a trumpet blast or to such a voice speaking words that those who heard it begged that no further word be spoken to them, because they could not bear what was commanded: "If even an animal touches the mountain, it must be stoned to death." The sight was so terrifying that Moses said, "I am trembling with fear." But you have come to Mount Zion, to the city of the living God, the heavenly Jerusalem. You have come to thousands upon thousands of angels in joyful assembly, to the church of the firstborn, whose names are written in heaven. You have come to God, the Judge of all, to the spirits of the righteous made perfect, to Jesus the mediator of a new covenant, and to the sprinkled blood that speaks a better word than the blood of Abel.
>
> —HEBREWS 12:18–24

Jesus, the mediator of a new covenant, is *our* mediator.

7. We Enter a Greater Tabernacle

The tabernacle was reminiscent of Eden, but it was not a return to the days of unobstructed access to God in the garden. Repeated sacrifices were a reminder of ongoing sin. But the tabernacle did not fail in its job. The tabernacle, and by extension the later temple, was "a copy and shadow of what is in heaven" (Heb. 8:5). And just as the tabernacle symbolized God's greater presence in heaven, so its priesthood and sacrifices symbolized the greater salvation to come. One day Jesus Christ, God the Son in the flesh, would dwell among us—that word for "dwell" being the very word for "tabernacle" (John 1:14).

Jesus tabernacled among us in two senses. First, he tabernacled among us in his life. He lived and walked among us. But we need more than this. And so Jesus tabernacled among us as he hung on the cross, a perfect and final sacrifice for sin, shedding his blood for us, putting away the need for blood altogether. For "when Christ came as high priest of the good things that are now already here, he went through the greater and more perfect tabernacle that is not made with human hands, that is to say, is not part of this creation. He did not enter by means of the blood of goats and calves; but he entered the Most Holy Place once for all by his own blood, thus obtaining eternal redemption" (Heb. 9:11–12).

Jesus' death makes possible the meeting of man with God in the very holy of holies, a way back to Eden. This is why, at Jesus' death, "the curtain of the temple was torn in two from top to bottom," representing "a new and living way opened for us" into the very perfect presence of God (Mark 15:38; Heb. 10:20; cf. Heb. 6:19; 9:3).

8. We Shine with a Greater Glory

The Bible tells us that when Moses came down from meeting with God, his face was shining, or radiant (Ex. 34:29–35). What must that have looked like? What must it have felt like to speak directly with God? By God's design, Moses' face shone for the people and for us so that we might know what it means to speak with God. Under Moses, this glory was dangerous. Moses had to cover his face with a veil to protect his people because they were stiff-necked. Moses himself saw only the tail end of the trail of God's glory, but the people could not survive longer than a glance at the glow left on Moses' face. How wonderful, then, to read these words about Jesus and his work for us:

> Therefore, since we have such a hope, we are very bold. We are not like Moses, who would put a veil over his face to prevent the Israelites from seeing the end of what was passing away. But their minds were made dull. . . . whenever anyone turns to the Lord, the veil is taken away. Now the Lord is the Spirit, and where the Spirit of the Lord is, there is freedom. And we all, who with unveiled faces contemplate the Lord's glory, are being transformed into his image with ever-increasing glory, which comes from the Lord, who is the Spirit . . . For God, who said, "Let light shine out of darkness," made his light shine in our hearts to give us the light of the knowledge of God's glory displayed in the face of Christ.
>
> —2 CORINTHIANS 3:12–14A, 16–18; 4:6

When we believe the gospel, we are in a better position than Moses was speaking with God on the mountain. He could see the afterglow of God's glory; we can stare into its center. Incredibly, this total exposure to the glory of God not only preserves us but transforms us into the image of Christ.

9. We Sing a Greater Song

God's exodus deliverance inspires awe. So does his judgment at that event. That's why Moses sang a song at the destruction of Egypt's army. And we're told that we too will sing Moses' song again on the day when God puts down all his enemies in judgment. Judgment is not our first desire for our enemies, since Jesus teaches us to love them. But because we love God and long to see evil defeated, we will rejoice when rebellion against God ceases. Here's what that rejoicing sounds like:

> I saw what looked like a sea of glass glowing with fire and, standing beside the sea, those who had been victorious over the beast and its

image and over the number of its name. They held harps given them
by God and sang the song of God's servant Moses and of the Lamb:

> "Great and marvelous are your deeds,
>> Lord God Almighty.
> Just and true are your ways,
>> King of the nations.
> Who will not fear you, Lord,
>> and bring glory to your name?
> For you alone are holy.
> All nations will come
>> and worship before you,
> for your righteous acts have been revealed."
>
> —REVELATION 15:1–4

Some unusual images are in this passage, but the cause for rejoicing
is plain enough.

Just as God rescued his people from their hardened enemies at the
Red Sea, so he will one day drown all of our enemies in his wrath. Other
armies would arise in this world long after God punished Egypt's army.
The salvation we read about in Revelation is a salvation a thousand times
more secure and sure than what Moses experienced with his people, and
so our rejoicing will be that much greater on the day God's enemies are
finally defeated, for the last time.

Chapter 11

DAVID

A Throne Full of Hope

1–2 SAMUEL, 1–2 CHRONICLES, AND PSALMS

T wo men have unlawful sex with women who serve at the entrance to the tent of meeting (1 Sam. 2:22–25). The men's names are Hophni and Phinehas, and they are God's priests. Israel's leaders are wicked, and awful things are occurring in the promised land under God's Law. It's *not* supposed to be this way! We immediately know that the serpent's offspring is alive and well, even holding some of the highest positions of leadership in Israel. This early scene in 1 Samuel sets the stage for the next covenant-mediator we will meet.

First, some backstory. After Moses died, Joshua led Israel into the promised land with great success—at first. We even caught hints of the inclusion of believing gentiles into God's people. Rahab, a gentile prostitute from behind the walls of Jericho, believed, and Caleb, a former gentile, was the first to inherit land along with God's people. The Lord blessed obedience with victory in battle, but Israel's success faltered because she did not fully obey. After Joshua, the book of Judges records Israel's descent into spiritual anarchy. The story of Joshua is mostly positive, but the story of Judges is mostly negative. We see that spiritual idolatry has social consequences as well, including the rise of gang rape and murder. False gods are proxies for the serpent's God-hating designs, and the message we hear in this section of Scripture is repeated and clear: "In those days Israel had no king; everyone did as they saw fit" (Judg. 17:6; cf. 18:1; 19:1; 21:25). The Law-covenant has not brought life. Israel needs a dramatic spiritual reversal and a heart transformation. Even more, we hear a new cry from the people. Israel needs a king.

Thankfully, a king was always part of God's plan. God made Adam to function like a "king" and rule over creation, but Adam failed. God promised Abraham, "Kings will come from you," and even specified his tribal origin: "The scepter will not depart from Judah" (Gen. 49:10; cf. Gen. 17:6; Num. 24:7–19). Even before Israel entered the promised land, God outlined the profile and job description of the king (Deut. 17:14–20). Although Moses and Joshua were "king-like," they were not *this* king.

But in the story of Ruth, located between Judges and 1–2 Samuel, our anticipation for the king grows. Ruth, a gentile woman, worshiped the God of Israel and then married into an Israelite family from a small town of Bethlehem. According to the genealogy at the end of her story, this lowly woman would be the great-grandmother of Israel's great king. First and Second Samuel tell the story of God's installation of David, his true king.

Abraham, Moses, and Joshua are all towering figures in the Bible's story, but David brings the storyline of the Bible to a high point with his life. God's previous covenants are all brought to a head, culminating in the covenant God cuts with David and his sons. God's answer to sin and its curse is becoming clearer with every step in the Bible's story. The promised son of Eve who will crush the serpent's head will also be a son of David.

In 1–2 Samuel, Israel goes from having no king to having a great king. More than that, the nation transitions from a mobile people to a people planted in Jerusalem with plans in hand to build God a house—the temple. Israel's hope, indeed the world's hope, now rests upon David's throne.

LOOKING DOWN: A STORY OF GREAT REVERSALS

David's story will ultimately lead to blessings that are universal and eternal. It begins, however, with the tears of a lowly and barren Israelite woman named Hannah. Hannah's womb pictured the spiritual barrenness of her people, yet she prayed for a child. The Lord granted her a son, and she named him Samuel. Her great expectations are apparent right away: "As soon as the child is weaned, I will bring him [to the tent of meeting], so that he may appear in the presence of the LORD and dwell there forever" (1 Sam. 1:22 ESV).

Her womb pictured Israel's need, and this great reversal of personal fortune pictures the reversal that will come to the nation and the world. She knows this, and these hopes permeate her prayer:

> My heart rejoices in the LORD;
>> In the LORD my horn is lifted high.
> My mouth boasts over my enemies,
>> for I delight in your deliverance.
> There is no one holy like the LORD;
>> there is no one besides you;
>> there is no Rock like our God.
> Do not keep talking so proudly
>> or let your mouth speak such arrogance . . .
> The bows of the warriors are broken,
>> but those who stumble are armed with strength . . .
> The LORD sends poverty and wealth;
>> he humbles and he exalts . . .
> He will guard the feet of his faithful servants,
>> but the wicked will be silenced in the place of darkness.
> It is not by strength that one prevails;
>> those who oppose the LORD will be broken.
> The Most High will thunder from heaven;
>> the LORD will judge the ends of the earth.
> He will give strength to his king
>> and exalt the horn of his anointed.
>> —1 SAMUEL 2:1–3A, 4, 7, 9–10

"In those days," we're told, "the word of the LORD was rare" (1 Sam. 3:1; cf. 2:12, 22). Hophni and Phinehas, the profane priests introduced at the start of this chapter, were symbolic of their times. Yet Hannah expected her son to bring about the installment of a king for Israel and future hope for the world. Thankfully, she was right.

The reversals Hannah sees in her prayer begin when God speaks his word to young Samuel in the night. As a prophet, Samuel's first job is to declare God's coming judgment on the house of Eli the priest, father of Hophni and Phinehas. God would flatten Eli's proud house, exalt young Samuel, and through Samuel speak his word to Israel (4:1). Israel's priests no longer obeyed God's voice, so God reestablished his word and his priesthood in Samuel. God exalts Hannah and brings wicked leaders low, a first of many reversals to come.

When Hannah sings out her prayer, Israel has no king. But by the end of 2 Samuel, Israel's king, David, sings another song that sounds much like Hannah's prayer (2 Sam. 22), and his song is the Lord's answer to Hannah's prayer. Between the bookends of these two heartfelt prayers, the Lord answers Hannah's prayer by bringing low the proud and exalting the humble. This is the very pattern of David's life story.

A Tall and Handsome Young Man

Israel knows she needs a king. God had already anticipated the coming of the king when he promised that kings would come from Abraham's family (Gen. 17:6), specifically from Judah's line (Gen. 49:8–12). Before his death, Moses anticipated the coming of Israel's king and described specifically the kind of king he should be (Deut. 17:14–20). The book of Judges holds out hope for the nation in the rise of the king (Judg. 21:25). Israel was right to ask for a king, but she was wrong to want a king "such as all the other nations have" (1 Sam. 8:5). As earthly kings go, the kings of the nations did not seek the Lord.

That kind of king, Samuel warns, will only "take" their sons, "take" their daughters, "take" their fields, "take" their servants, and more. Israel will cry out to the Lord, but he will not answer (8:10–18). God intends a king like David, but first he gives the people what they desire. As often happens, the Lord's plan includes a scenic route with a tour of human sin preceding divine grace. The people will get the king of their choosing, and that king is Saul.

Saul was a king like the kings of the nations. He was "as handsome a young man as could be found anywhere in Israel" and "a head taller than anyone else" (9:2). Inwardly, and tragically, Saul didn't trust the Word of the Lord. In his first high-pressure battle, Saul disobeyed God's Word and fabricated his motive when confronted. In response, Samuel said to him, "Your kingdom will not endure; the LORD has sought out a man after his own heart and appointed him ruler of his people, because you have not kept the LORD's command" (13:14). Saul didn't learn from his failure. When commanded to wipe out the Amalekites completely, he instead spared anything of value (15:9).

The Lord gave Israel the king *they* wanted, but God remained faithful to his promises. "Because you have rejected the word of the LORD," Samuel said to Saul, "he has rejected you as king . . . The LORD has torn the kingdom of Israel from you today and has given it to one of your neighbors—to one better than you" (15:23, 28). This tearing marks the rest of Saul's life. As Hannah prayed, the Lord brought low the proud, but by God's grace, the kingship didn't end with Saul.

"The Spirit of the LORD came upon David"

Enter young David. We should not be surprised to find that David doesn't look the part of a king. Even Samuel needed the Lord's gentle reminder to identify him properly: "Do not consider his appearance or his height . . . The LORD does not look at the things people look at. People look at the outward appearance, but the LORD looks at the heart" (1 Sam. 16:7).

Just like Hannah, David is lowly.

Samuel knows the Lord's king will come from the family of Jesse. But when Jesse presents his sons to Samuel, David, who is the youngest, is out tending his sheep. The Lord must clearly show Samuel that David is *his* king.

After Samuel anointed David, a new reversal began, and the Spirit of the Lord "came powerfully upon David" and "departed from Saul" (16:13–14).

David is now anointed and empowered by the Spirit, and God's reversals continue to unfold. Israel meets her enemies, the Philistines, in battle. Humanly speaking, their champion, a giant of a man named Goliath, was invincible. He was exceptionally tall, well-armed, and battle-strong (17:4–7). David, by contrast, was short, practically unarmed, and young. The only time David had spent on the battlefield was delivering lunches to his older brothers! Yet here's what David said to Goliath: "You come against me with sword and spear and javelin, but I come against you in the name of the LORD Almighty, the God of the armies of Israel, whom you have defied. This day the LORD will deliver you into my hands, and I'll strike you down and cut off your head. This very day I will give the carcasses of the Philistine army to the birds and the wild animals" (17:45–46).

David was consumed with God's name and glory. He was also empowered by the Spirit, more powerful than any giant. And David was animated by a twofold purpose more indestructible than his opponent, one that should be familiar to you by now: "the *whole world* will know that there is a God in Israel" and *Israel* "will know that it is not by sword or spear that the LORD saves; for the battle is the LORD's" (17:46-47, emphases added; cf. Ex. 6:7; 7:5). On that day, David felled Goliath with a sling and a stone. More accurately, we should say that the Lord felled Goliath through *his* king.

The contrast between David and Goliath is clear, but there is a sharper contrast to make here. Saul—the people's king—was tall and well-armed. David—the Lord's king—was short and unarmed. Saul, with the rest of Israel, was "dismayed and terrified" (17:11). David feared no man. Whether it was the Philistines or the opinion of his own people, Saul "feared the people," a fear that was at the root of his life of sin (15:24 ESV). As the kingdom is torn from his hands, Saul proudly seeks David's life. David, by contrast, humbly refuses to take Saul's life. At Saul's death, David is overwhelmed with sorrow and stands against those who seek revenge against Saul's house. He trusts the Lord wholeheartedly.

Saul's downfall brings David's exaltation as David establishes his reign in Jerusalem, which becomes known as "the City of David" (2 Sam. 5:9). There, we're told, "[David] became more and more powerful, because the

LORD God Almighty was with him" (5:10). At news of David's move into Jerusalem as king, the Philistines attack, but they cannot prevail.

When the ark of the covenant enters Jerusalem, David's devotion to the Lord is seen with shocking expression. Wearing a linen ephod, "David was dancing before the LORD with all his might" (6:14). The spiritual intensity of this moment was plain to all, and David's wife Michal despised David for it, for she was also a daughter of Saul and, like her father, her heart was hard. Further highlighting the Lord's reversal between the house of Saul and the house of David, the narrator notes that Michal "had no children to the day of her death" (6:23). Here again, the Lord exalts the humble and brings low the proud.

An Eternal Throne and Hope for the World

David's story climaxes in 2 Samuel 7, one of the Bible's weightiest chapters. Here, we learn *how* all of God's promises to this point converge in the person of David. The chapter is like many roads of promise merging into one massive superhighway of promise. It is worth careful attention.

As 2 Samuel 7 opens, David's devotion to the Lord overflows into action: "Here I am, living in a house of cedar, while the ark of God remains in a tent" (7:2). Building the Lord a house sounds like a noble desire, until we hear the Lord's response: "I have not dwelt in a house from the day I brought the Israelites up out of Egypt to this day. I have been moving from place to place with a tent as my dwelling. Wherever I have moved with all the Israelites, did I ever say to any of their rulers whom I commanded to shepherd my people Israel, 'Why have you not built me a house of cedar?'" (2 Sam. 7:6–7).

That's what God thinks about *needing* a house. It's easy for us to think that God needs our service. Yet, in truth, we need him—not the other way around. The Lord reminds David of this fact: "I took you from the pasture, from tending the flock, and appointed you ruler over my people Israel. I have been with you wherever you have gone, and I have cut off all your enemies from before you" (2 Sam. 7:8–9).

God has done much for David, yet he has even greater plans in store:

"Now I will make your name great, like the names of the greatest men on earth. And I will provide a place for my people Israel and will plant them so that they can have a home of their own and no longer be disturbed. Wicked people will not oppress them anymore, as they did at the beginning and have done ever since the time I appointed leaders over my people Israel. I will also give you rest from all your enemies. The LORD declares to you that the LORD himself will establish a house for you" (2 Sam. 7:9b–11).

A house for *David*? That's what he said, and here's what it entails: "When your days are over and you rest with your ancestors, I will raise up your offspring to succeed you, your own flesh and blood, and I will establish his kingdom. He is the one who will build a house for my Name, and I will establish the throne of his kingdom forever. I will be to him a father, and he will be my son" (2 Sam. 7:12–14).

David was filled with emotion as the ark entered Jerusalem, but now he is overwhelmed. "Who am I?" he asks, that God would favor him (7:18). But it's vital to note that David isn't merely overwhelmed because God has promised that his family will rule forever over Israel. No, David is overwhelmed because he realizes that God's promise is that he and his sons will rule forever over the entire world. Notice what David says: "Who am I, O Lord God, and what is my house, that you have brought me thus far? . . . You have spoken also of your servant's house for a great while to come, *and this is instruction for mankind*, O Lord God!" (2 Sam. 7:18–19 ESV, emphasis added).

David gets it right: God's promise entails not only hope for Israel *but also hope for the world*. God's promise, begun in Genesis 3:15, narrowed through Abraham's seed, is narrowed further through David's line. God's plan for all of humanity is now wholly tied to David and his sons. It's through the Davidic king that salvation will come and the horrible effects of Adam's sin will be reversed!

When you hear a promise like this, praise is in order, and that's what David does. God's greatness and grace overwhelm him: "How great you are, Sovereign LORD. There is no one like you, and there is no God but you, as we have heard with our own ears" (2 Sam. 7:22).

After God established the Davidic covenant, David's reign expanded widely. David's greatness was seen in his military victory, for "the LORD gave David victory wherever he went" (8:14), and David did "what was just and right for all his people" (8:15). He secured Jerusalem, and he initiated the construction of the temple there for a permanent place of meeting between God and his people.

Adultery and Displeasure

David was a great king, but he was *not* God's final king. That becomes clear in short order. After a flurry of military victories, chapter 11 opens with this ominous note: "In the spring, at the time when kings go off to war, David sent Joab out with the king's men and the whole Israelite army. They destroyed the Ammonites and besieged Rabbah. But David remained in Jerusalem" (11:1). As king, David belongs with his men, but he is home. From his roof he "saw a woman bathing," and then he "took her" (11:4 ESV). The scene is brisk. David takes what he wants. The scene ends with the words, "I am pregnant" (11:5). It gets worse. To cover his tracks, David plots the death of Bathsheba's husband. Uriah, a friend of David's, was out to war with the men. David had him murdered to cover up his adultery. "The thing David had done displeased the LORD" (11:27).

In his sin, David looks just like Saul—until he is confronted. In that revealing moment, David replies straightforwardly, "I have sinned against the LORD" (12:13). He's *not* like Saul after all. Yet David still reaps the consequences of his sin. The remainder of 2 Samuel is given to David's chastisement. David's reign is never the same, and, in truth, David is never the same. David's son, Amnon, rapes his sister, Tamar. In calculated rage, another son, Absalom, murders his rapist brother. Later, Absalom plots and executes an overthrow of David's throne in Jerusalem. David is on the run once again, but this time from his own son. In due time and dependence upon the Lord, David will regain his throne, but he will die a weak man—a shadow of who he was to be for his people.

LOOKING BACK: GOD'S PROMISE
FOCUSED IN A KING

In King David, all of God's previous promises converge. If God has promised it, he will do it *through his king*. Starting from the vantage point of God's promises to David, let's look back to his promises to Moses, then to Abraham, and then to Adam.

The King of Israel

David is the king the nation needed. In Deuteronomy, Moses spoke about a king "the LORD your God is giving you" (17:14). God promised to Abraham that "kings" would come from his line (Gen. 17:6), and Moses prepared his people for the day when they would choose their king. This king would come from Israel (Deut. 17:15), and he would wholly depend on the Lord. He wasn't to "acquire great numbers of horses" (17:16) since his power was to be found in the Lord. He wasn't to "take many wives, or his heart will be led astray. He must not accumulate large amounts of silver and gold" (17:17) since he was to treasure the Lord above all else.

The king also was to love and obey God's Word, what the Israelites called the *Torah*. Moses instructs, "When he takes the throne of his kingdom, he is to write for himself on a scroll a copy of this law, taken from that of the Levitical priests. It is to be with him, and he is to read it all the days of his life so that he may learn to revere the LORD his God and follow carefully all the words of this law and these decrees" (17:18–19). When the king's heart is the Lord's, the people flourish (17:20), and this was true in David's life. David wasn't the perfect embodiment of all that Moses promised, but in a provisional way he was God's chosen man to rule his people.

A King from Abraham's Line

When God promised Abraham that "kings" would come from him, it wasn't immediately clear just how crucial the king would be in God's plan (Gen. 17:6). But in Genesis 49:10 a glimpse is given of *how* God's promises to Abraham will be fulfilled through the king:

> The scepter will not depart from Judah,
>> nor the ruler's staff from between his feet,
> until he to whom it belongs shall come
>> and the obedience of the nations shall be his.
>
> —GENESIS 49:10

This promise helps make sense of why David's rule is understood through the lens of the Abrahamic promises. God's king would come from the tribe of Judah, and his rule would be eternal and universal over all people. The Bible continually hints that this rule would include gentiles. For example, God included Ruth, a believing gentile, in the king's line.

God promised Abraham a great name, and in 2 Samuel 7:9, the Lord promises David, "I will make your name great, like the names of the greatest men on earth" (cf. 1 Chron. 17:8). God promised blessing to the nations through Abraham, and in Psalm 72:17, Solomon, David's son, shows us how he sees David's royal line:

> May his name endure forever;
>> may it continue as long as the sun.
> Then all nations will be blessed through him,
>> and they will call him blessed!

All of this indicates that the Abrahamic blessing for the world will come to the world *through the king*.

The King Who Is God's Son

David was to be all that Adam was supposed to be—a faithful son/king. As we saw previously, Adam's role as image/son pervades the storyline to this point. Collectively as a nation, Israel was intended to embody all that God had planned Adam to do and to be. At her deliverance from

Egypt, Israel was corporately identified as God's son (Ex. 4:22–23). Now David is identified as God's individual son (2 Sam. 7:14), and he takes on Israel's role as her representative. Israel remains God's corporate son, but in the Davidic covenant, the king assumes Israel's roles and functions as God's representative to the world. In his entire life, the king is to act like God—his Father—as a faithful, obedient son, and ultimately bring God's saving rule to this world. All of God's promises and purposes are now centered on the Davidic king.

It should not surprise us that previous offices within Israel begin to coalesce in David and the kings. Solomon, David's son, is the temple builder—constructing and planning the place where the priests serve. David himself is instrumental in returning the ark of the Lord to the people and establishing the city of Jerusalem. And as the prophets speak of the Messiah, the office of king and priest begin to unite, as we see in passages like Psalm 110. In this famous Davidic psalm, David speaks of *his* Lord as distinct from *the* Lord, yet as one who is equal with God since he sits on the Lord's throne and shares his rule. David also identifies *his* Lord as a king-priest in the order of Melchizedek (Ps. 110:1–4).

Passages like this underscore the groundbreaking importance of the Davidic covenant in God's unfolding plan, and serve as the basis for the Old Testament's anticipation of the coming of King Jesus.

In David, we begin to see a confluence of offices—prophet, priest, and king—signaling the reestablishment of what God intended for humanity in Adam.

LOOKING AHEAD: THE KING IS COMING!

We have much to look forward to. Like the prior representatives of God—Adam, Abraham, and Israel—David also fails. For a time things are positive under King Solomon, but that time of peace and prosperity doesn't last long. Still, there is hope because God's promise of a Davidic king who will rule forever will never fail.

Psalm 72, written by Solomon, not only helps us see how Solomon viewed God's promise but also is a key text that helps us look ahead to a "greater" David, a future king. We'll look at four parts of Psalm 72 to identify four dimensions of this future king's reign. His rule will be *righteous*, *eternal*, *universal*, and *compassionate*.

1. Royalty with Righteousness

The first dimension of the future rule of David's son is *righteousness*.

> Endow the king with your justice, O God,
>   the royal son with your righteousness.
> May he judge your people in righteousness,
>   your afflicted ones with justice.
> May the mountains bring prosperity to the people,
>   the hills the fruit of righteousness.
> May he defend the afflicted among the people
>   and save the children of the needy;
>   may he crush the oppressor.
>
> —PSALM 72:1–4

This is the king our world needs. Our world cries out for justice, but because of sin, even our best leaders are dangerous if we give them too much power. A truly righteous kingdom awaits God's righteous king.

We can hear Solomon's anticipation of this kind of kingdom in his prayers. When he looked back at David's life, he remembered the Lord's favor for David: "You have shown great kindness to your servant, my father David, because he was faithful to you and righteous and upright in heart. You have continued this great kindness to him and have given him a son to sit on his throne this very day" (1 Kings 3:6).

Of course, David wasn't righteous in himself, yet the Lord declared him just because he believed God's Word of promise (Ps. 32:1–2). David loved the glory of the Lord and at times demonstrated great obedience, yet he wasn't fully obedient. As we have seen in previous chapters, this creates a tension in the Bible's story. God demands perfect obedience from us, but we don't perfectly obey. Of his king, God demands and Scripture anticipates a righteous, obedient king.

But where is he? As Solomon dedicates the temple, he reiterates God's promise: "Now, LORD, the God of Israel, keep for your servant David my father the promises you made to him when you said, 'You shall never fail to have a successor to sit before me on the throne of Israel, if only your descendants are careful in all they do to walk before me according to my law, as you have done'" (2 Chron. 6:16). But notice the emphasis Solomon puts on the obedience of the king. The future righteous kingdom only comes with the arrival of a future righteous, obedient Davidic king.

Again, we ask: Where is this king?

In Psalm 24, David reminds us of the kind of person who can dwell in God's presence: the "one who has clean hands and a pure heart, who does not trust in an idol or swear by a false god" (Ps. 24:4). But who is that? David hints at *who* this person is when he tells us that the "King of glory" is the King who is also "the LORD" (Ps. 24:7–10). We will develop this point further in the next chapter. For now, remember this: the hope of the world rests in the coming of this righteous, obedient king.

2. As Long as the Sun Rises

The only thing better than a righteous king is a righteous king who rules without end. God promises us that David's righteous rule will be *an eternal rule.*

> May he endure as long as the sun,
> as long as the moon, through all generations.
> May he be like rain falling on a mown field,
> like showers watering the earth.
> In his days may the righteous flourish
> and prosperity abound till the moon is no more.
>
> —PSALM 72:5–7

Till the moon is no more! This king's rule will last forever.

Grounded in the Davidic covenant, God's sure promises to David are repeated throughout Old Testament history, which David himself recognizes (2 Sam. 23:1–7), regardless of how unrighteous David's sons are (and they fail catastrophically). When Solomon follows "other gods" and his "heart had turned away from the LORD," the Lord promised to "tear the kingdom" from him, but not without this qualification: "Nevertheless, for the sake of David your father, I will not do it during your lifetime. I will tear it out of the hand of your son . . . I will give one tribe to his son so that David my servant may always have a lamp before me in Jerusalem, the city where I chose to put my Name" (1 Kings 11:9–12, 36). Likewise, when Abijah reigned over Judah and "committed all the sins his father had done before him" because "his heart was not fully devoted to the LORD his God, as the heart of David his forefather had been," then "for David's sake the LORD his God gave him a lamp in Jerusalem by raising up a son to succeed him" (15:3–4). And when Jehoram was king of Judah, "he did evil in the eyes of the LORD. Nevertheless, for the sake of his servant David, the LORD was not willing to destroy Judah. He had promised to maintain a lamp for David and his descendants forever" (2 Kings 8:18–19).

The story of Israel, Judah, and her kings after David is long and difficult. Yet a certain theme sticks: despite the faithlessness of David's sons, God's promise of an eternal king through David is going to happen. The Lord will see to it. Yet we wait to see *who* this king will be.

3. A King for Everyone Everywhere

This righteous and eternal kingdom is also *a universal kingdom*.

> May he rule from sea to sea
> and from the River to the ends of the earth.
> May the desert tribes bow down before him
> and his enemies lick the dust.
> May the kings of Tarshish and of distant shores
> bring tribute to him.
> May the kings of Sheba and Seba present him gifts.
> May all kings bow down to him
> and all nations serve him.
>
> —PSALM 72:8–11

This is a picture of total dominion over the world. In this kingdom, there are no rival forces. As we noticed in the establishment of the Davidic covenant, David recognized that the Lord's promises to him had universal implications because the covenant was for the "instruction of mankind" (2 Sam. 7:19 ESV), or it served as "the charter for humanity." This king's rule will achieve the universal rule that God first intended for humanity.

This universal expectation of the future Davidic king is everywhere in the Old Testament *after* David. For example, Psalm 2 raises the question, "Why do the nations conspire and the peoples plot in vain?" (2:1). The whole earth, it seems, is set against God and his king. Yet "the One enthroned in heaven laughs; the Lord scoffs at them," for he says to his king, "You are my son; today I have become your father. Ask me, and I will make the nations your inheritance, the ends of the earth your possession" (2:4, 7–8). Or in Psalm 110, David writes concerning his future descendant, "The LORD says to my lord: 'Sit at my right hand until I make your enemies a footstool for your feet'" (110:1). Given the Davidic promise, Scripture tells us to look *ahead* to the coming of the Davidic son/king who will fully bring God's rule to the entire world.

4. A Heart of Compassion

The rule of David's future son would not conform to the patterns of this world's rulers. He would not *take* from his people. He would only give! This righteous, eternal, universal king would himself come out of lowly Bethlehem, the smallest of Judah's clans (Mic. 5:2). The reversals we witnessed in the story of 1–2 Samuel will extend to this kingdom in *a rule of untold compassion.*

> For he will deliver the needy who cry out,
> the afflicted who have no one to help.
> He will take pity on the weak and the needy
> and save the needy from death.
> He will rescue them from oppression and violence,
> for precious is their blood in his sight.
>
> —PSALM 72:12–14

This king brings reversals, but at great cost to himself.

As David did, he will suffer on his way to exaltation. He will bring about great reversals for others by means of a great reversal of his own. He will be on the run. He will be anointed. He will be exiled. He will suffer outside the gate. He will give himself completely for the good of his people. It's interesting that when Solomon builds the temple, he does so on Mount Moriah (2 Chron. 3:1), where the Lord appeared to David and where Abraham was told to sacrifice Isaac (Gen. 22:2) hundreds of years earlier. In a similar yet greater way, the future Davidic king will also be offered up, but now as the perfect sacrifice for his people.

Psalm 72 projects a future of incredible hope, and it ends with a prayer that rightly concludes our chapter on David.

> Praise be to the LORD God, the God of Israel,
>   who alone does marvelous deeds.
> Praise be to his glorious name forever;
>   may the whole earth be filled with his glory.
>   —PSALM 72:18–19

As the psalm ends, so we say, "Amen and Amen" (v. 19).

Chapter 12

THE PROPHETS

A Message Full of Tension

ISAIAH–MALACHI

What would it be like if God kept a diary? Diaries can be intriguing because they hold a person's inner thoughts and feelings. Reading through a diary helps us understand how they see themselves and their relationships with others. So what does a diary written by God look like?

Hosea 11 is akin to a diary entry from the Lord. And the entry we read in this chapter is full of tension: "When Israel was a child, I loved him, and out of Egypt I called my son" (11:1). We start with these tender words of love and affection, a reminder of God's love for Israel in the exodus from Egypt. Plagues were dispatched, waters were parted, and food fell from heaven. In all this, the Lord tenderly called his son, Israel. But the next line of the diary is not so nice and tender: "The more they were called, the more they went away; they kept sacrificing to the Baals and burning offerings to idols" (11:2 ESV). Israel had a good childhood, but soon she stopped listening to the Lord, and she did the exact opposite of what God commanded. Her problem is now greater than her previous slavery in Egypt. She needs a solution greater than another exodus from Egypt.

Throughout Israel's history, an inverse relationship has existed between the faithfulness of God and the faithfulness of Israel. The Lord graciously gave Moses the Law, while at the same time the people rebelliously constructed a golden calf and worshiped it. The Lord mercifully provided manna from heaven while the people reminisced about their meat pots back in Egypt. The promise-making Lord kept his covenant word by bringing Israel safely to Canaan, but once there Israel violated her covenant promises with a hardness of heart reminiscent of her forefathers.

Then came David, the long-awaited king—or so we had hoped. The Lord promised David an eternal kingdom by which God would rule the world and restore humanity. But as wonderful as David was—God called him a "man after my own heart" (Acts 13:22)—the great king's life ended coldly, in the company of concubines lying with him to keep him warm. David, the man in whom the hope of the entire world resided, died not by ruling over the earth but, like all of us, with the earth ruling over him.

David's son, Solomon, started out strikingly well, exceeding David in wisdom, wealth, and rule. But it was short-lived. For a time, it looked like all of God's promises to David were being fulfilled in David's "greater" son. Maybe Solomon was the final king God had promised long ago! Although the nations gathered to him, Solomon accumulated horses and wives—the opposite of the Lord's command (cf. Deut. 17:14–20). The kingdom rose and fell under David; it rose higher and fell harder under Solomon.

After Solomon, Israel was never the same: the kingdom divided and wicked kings ruled. Only a small number ruled well in the south. And just as Adam was banished from Eden, Israel too was eventually exiled from her land. It is not a promising story.

This context provides the backdrop for what the Lord says in his diary entry, written through Hosea. The nation of Israel, corporately identified as God's son, had proved to be no more faithful than Adam. Even more significant, God's individual son, the Davidic king, had now failed as well. As we walk through biblical history and see God's promise unfold, an astounding tension develops between God's promise to redeem and how God will keep his promises. Given the disobedience of his people, especially as it is centered in the life of the kings, how will God save and restore this fallen world?

The tension is significant. It matters because it raises several questions. Is God's plan for redeeming humanity just a nice theory or mere words? Can God really be trusted given such dismal results? Is God like so many people who make a promise but, in the end, break it? Or maybe he is powerful enough to keep his promise, but he doesn't care enough to do so. Perhaps you've thought this about God at times and cried, "How long, O Lord?" And, "Will you keep your promises, and when?"

We wouldn't be the first to ask these questions. We read them in the Old Testament and especially in the Prophets. For example, the prophet Habakkuk looked at the wickedness of God's people and pleaded, "How long, LORD, must I call for help, but you do not listen? Or cry out to you, 'Violence!' but you do not save?" (Hab. 1:2). The words "How long?" might sound like a cry for personal vindication, but that's not quite what they mean. In Scripture, they are a cry for the realization of God's promises, a plea for God's word of salvation to come to this world through the Davidic king.

Habakkuk doesn't see God's promises taking place, and he is understandably distraught.

Asaph, the author of Psalm 73, was similarly distressed. "Surely God is good to Israel," he wrote (Ps. 73:1). "But as for me, my feet had almost slipped; I had nearly lost my foothold. For I envied the arrogant when I saw the prosperity of the wicked. They have no struggles; their bodies are healthy and strong" (73:2–4). Psalm 72, building on the promises of the Davidic covenant, speaks of a king who will reign in righteousness, "from sea to sea and from the River to the ends of the earth" (72:8). In the structure of the Psalter, Psalm 73 was placed next to Psalm 72 for a significant reason. What Israel expected and what she experienced were at odds with each other. There is tension in the story between the promises of God, the spiritual poverty of the people, and the failure of the Davidic kings. The prophets acknowledge this tension and cry out to the God of sovereign grace for its resolution.

But the Prophets also reveal an even deeper tension, one that is found in the Lord's diary entry in Hosea as well. Here we discover a tension in the very heart of God. Responding to Israel's sin, the Lord wrote, "Will they not return to Egypt and will not Assyria rule over them because they refuse to repent? A sword will flash in their cities; it will devour their false prophets and put an end to their plans. My people are determined to turn from me. Even though they call me God Most High, I will by no means exalt them" (Hos. 11:5–7).

It doesn't get more hopeless than this—God himself seems to have given up on his people. But then it doesn't get more hopeful than what the Lord says next:

> How can I give you up, Ephraim?
>   How can I hand you over, Israel? . . .
> My heart is changed within me;
>   all my compassion is aroused.
> I will not carry out my fierce anger,
>   nor will I devastate Ephraim again.
> For I am God, and not a man—
>   the Holy One among you.
>   I will not come against their cities.
>
> —HOSEA 11:8–9

Here we place our ear beside the heartbeat of the Covenant Lord. He wants more than justice for Israel. He wants *her*! God declares his love and his wrath, his affection and his anger. There is tension in the heart of the Lord when his just and holy character collides with his tender love, mercy, and grace. Thankfully, this tension is resolved in the Bible's story. Through the writings of the prophets, it becomes clearer to us *how* what God promised in Genesis 3:15 will come about. The tension between God's holiness and justice *and* his love and grace pervades the Prophets. Much to our amazement and blessing, we learn that the Lord will act to satisfy his own justice, to display his holy love, and to keep his promises to his undeserving people.

LOOKING DOWN: THE TWO-BEAT RHYTHM OF THE PROPHETS

Like a drum cadence, the prophets pound home a dual message. We'll get to that message shortly. Before we do, let's think about who the prophets were. We can start by locating them in our Bibles. Seventeen prophetic books record the message and ministry of the prophets. In our

English Bibles, these books are organized into two divisions: the Major and Minor Prophets. These labels refer to their book length and *not* their relative importance. The Major Prophets include Isaiah, Jeremiah, Lamentations, Ezekiel, and Daniel. The Minor Prophets are a collection of twelve shorter writings, including Hosea, Joel, Amos, Obadiah, Jonah, Micah, Nahum, Habakkuk, Zephaniah, Haggai, Zechariah, and Malachi.

Admittedly, we might find these books intimidating. They assume knowledge of historical events that are often left unexplained in the text itself. They can be harsh-sounding in ways that make us wince. And at first glance they appear strange, repetitive, and cryptic. For example, in Ezekiel we read that the Lord told Ezekiel, "Eat this scroll; then go and speak to the people of Israel." Ezekiel ate it and it "tasted as sweet as honey" (Ezek. 3:1–3). This is a strange command, but it's standard fare among the Prophets. God is making his point to and through his prophets in shocking ways that use all our senses.

But the Prophets don't have to be so difficult to grasp! To see what unites them, we must also understand what drives the prophets to communicate their message. Seven features unite them:

1. *The prophets share the same authority.* Prophets speak for God. Under the Law-covenant, Moses was the first prophet, who set a pattern for later prophets (Deut. 18:15–18). God's people need his word, and the prophets bring God's word to the people. The prophets are God's authorized spokesmen.
2. *The prophets share the same covenantal context.* The prophets speak in the context of the Law-covenant, which prescribed blessing for obedience and cursing for disobedience. Although the prophets write at different times in relation to the exile—before, during, or after—the entire prophetic literature is written by men who lived under the old covenant, *after* God's promises to David, but *before* the Lord fulfills his promises in the dawning of a new covenant.
3. *The prophets share the same assignment.* Prophets showed up when the people were practically begging God to come and make

good on his promises to curse them. As God's spokesmen during this period, Israel's prophets are the Lord's lawyers—covenant prosecutors—litigating the covenant established through Moses. Working off texts such as Leviticus 26 and Deuteronomy 28, they warn of judgment for sin in the form of exile, and they promise blessing for obedience and repentance.

4. *The prophets share the same perspective on the future.* The prophets speak with a hope informed by God's promises to David and all of God's promises given through the biblical covenants. They warn of a future that is worse *and* better than anyone can imagine. They look forward to the "Day of the LORD," when God will act to save and bring about his promises, though they most likely view it as a single event tied to the coming of the Lord. As the prophetic word is later fulfilled, we'll discover that God's promises come to fruition in two stages: first, as they are inaugurated at Jesus' coming, and ultimately, as they are consummated at his return. The prophets aren't thinking of God's promises being fulfilled in two stages, as we see them today, but more in terms of one cataclysmic event.

5. *The prophets share the same diverse methods for communicating their message.* They speak their message by words, but they are not limited to words. Hosea marries a prostitute and names his daughter "Unloved" to make his point (Hos. 1:6). Jeremiah places his underwear under a rock and returns a long time later to get it (Jer. 13:1–7). Ezekiel uses crayons, eats a scroll, and lies on his side for 390 days, and then on the other side for 390 days (Ezek. 3–4). Isaiah walks around naked and barefoot for three years (Isa. 20). Yet in all their words and actions, they communicate God's word to the people.

6. *The prophets share the same tension.* How will God fulfill his great promises through such hardhearted people? Israel suffers under the consequences of her chronic sin, but this also reflects the chronic sin of her leaders, Israel's shepherds, specifically the prophets, priests, and kings.

7. *The prophets share the same message of judgment and salvation.* We will pull from the various prophets to get a sampling of what these messages sound like through different voices. While they share a common context and message, each prophetic voice is like a different ride in an amusement park, with its own turns and twists, scenes and surprises.

Let's take a closer look at the prophets' crucial message of judgment *and* salvation.

Message 1: Searing Judgment

Earlier we mentioned that the prophets were covenant lawyers, arguing the merits of God's case before the people. But the prophets were also artists and actors. It might be better to say that their prophetic ministry expressed itself in a variety of forms. They creatively dramatized the horror of sin and its awful implications. We can summarize the prophets' message of judgment in four different ways: *deportation*, *divorce*, *desertion*, and *destruction*.

First, *the prophets promised deportation in exile*. They spoke frequently of Israel's coming exile from the land. The land, like the garden of Eden and the tabernacle, was seen to be a holy place. In Leviticus 20:22, the Lord said through Moses, "Keep all my decrees and laws and follow them, so that the land where I am bringing you to live may not vomit you out." The Lord uses this violent imagery to describe what the land will do to his people, a reminder that human sin not only arouses God's holy anger but also violates the relationship human beings have with God's good earth. "I was angry with that generation," said the Lord of those who grumbled in the wilderness (Ps. 95:10), an anger that resulted in judgment by deportation from the land.

The picture of vomiting instructs us as we consider the effects of sin. We know that certain foods can be at odds—in tension—with the human stomach, and so the body rejects them. A person who is lactose intolerant, for example, cannot tolerate drinking milk. It stirs up an involuntary, allergic reaction. In a similar way, some things are fundamentally at odds with the Lord. The Lord is holy, and because of his holiness he is incompatible with human sin. Holiness and sin may seem like odd concepts today, unfamiliar to us apart from the Bible. We might consider instead that every person has things that he or she finds objectionable, things that are incompatible with their moral constitution.

Every culture and every religion has its set of objectionable behaviors or beliefs. The same is true of human behavior that is odious and evil. God, by his very nature, is fundamentally incompatible with human sin. And because God cannot tolerate sin, the land he created will vomit up his people into exile—their sin makes the Lord sick. This threat of exile from the land is the main warning the prophets announce, but other images of judgment also orbit around the theme of exile.

Second, *the prophets promised divorce*. The Lord gave the prophet Hosea an unenviable job: "Go, marry a promiscuous woman and have children with her" (1:2). This sad assignment portrayed an even sadder reality: "for like an adulterous wife this land is guilty of unfaithfulness to the LORD" (1:2). Hosea offers a clear message: Israel is a spiritual adulterer, and the Lord is an enraged, heart-torn lover. What should Hosea and his wife name their children? The Lord made that easy for them. "Jezreel" was his name for the firstborn, a name that calls to mind a slaughter. And the second child would be called "No Mercy" (1:4, 6)—a lovely reminder of inevitable punishment.

To put this in context today, it would be like calling your children "Twin Towers" and "Hitler."

The third child had an even more striking name given to him: "Call him Lo-Ammi (which means 'not my people'), for you are not my people, and I am not your God" (1:9). The progression of these names represents God's certificate of divorce. The book of Jeremiah even uses the word *divorce:* "Have you seen what faithless Israel has done? She has gone up on every high hill and under every spreading tree and has committed adultery there. I thought that after she had done all this she would return to me but she did not . . . I gave faithless Israel her certificate of divorce and sent her away because of all her adulteries" (Jer. 3:6–8).

Perhaps you have experienced the pain of a divorce or have been close to someone going through one. Whatever the circumstances, a divorce always brings tremendous sadness. It indicates the end of the relationship and devastates those involved. Certainly, this is the last thing the Lord wanted to do. But Israel's persistent unfaithfulness had left him with no other options.

Third, *the prophets promised desertion from the Lord.* It's hard to imagine a more dramatic portrayal of the Lord's departure from his people than the vision given to Ezekiel. Ezekiel sees a storm, and in the storm are four flashing, flaming, flying creatures, each with four faces, and each darting about like lightning. For each creature, Ezekiel sees a wheel, but these aren't your standard wheels: "Their rims were high and awesome, and all four rims were full of eyes all around. When the living creatures moved, the wheels beside them moved; and when the living creatures rose from the ground, the wheels also rose" (Ezek. 1:18–19). Ezekiel sees a vehicle, a transportation device. But who is its driver? And where is it going? We'll answer those questions in just a moment.

God intends Ezekiel's vision to convey the depth of Israel's sin. The Lord gives Ezekiel a visionary tour of the temple, that holiest of places, where God uniquely dwells with his people. Ezekiel sees an idol at the temple gate, a little statue of a human intended to protect the city from attack. In the vision the statue is called the "idol that provokes to jealousy," for we know that God will not share his worship with anyone or anything (8:3). Then, as Ezekiel recounts, "he brought me to the entrance to the court. I looked, and I saw a hole in the wall" (8:7). The Lord said to Ezekiel: "Go in and see the wicked and detestable things they are doing here" (8:9). Ezekiel enters, and on the wall he sees carvings of other gods.

It gets even worse. In the inner court, Israel's leaders are worshiping the sun. Ninety-three times Ezekiel uses the words "detestable things" or the word "abominations" to depict what's occurring in his vision. His point is that idolatry and all that flows from it—injustice to widows and the fatherless, child sacrifice—are abominable to God. This is why the Lord says, "I will deal with them in anger; I will not look on them with pity or spare them. Although they shout in my ears, I will not listen to them" (8:18). Can we blame him for responding this way?

So back to our earlier questions. Who was the one driving that flaming, all-seeing vehicle we see at the start of Ezekiel's vision? Here is what we're told:

> Now the cherubim were standing on the south side of the temple when the man went in, and a cloud filled the inner court. Then the glory of the LORD rose from above the cherubim and moved to the threshold of the temple. The cloud filled the temple, and the court was full of the radiance of the glory of the LORD. The sound of the wings of the cherubim could be heard as far away as the outer court, like the voice of God Almighty when he speaks . . . Then the glory of the LORD departed from over the threshold of the temple and stopped above the cherubim.
>
> —EZEKIEL 10:3–5, 18

At the Lord's command, that cherubim guarded the way back to Eden. They were later embroidered on the curtains leading into the holy of holies in the tabernacle and temple. Now we see them here. This is the Lord in this vehicle, and Ezekiel is witnessing him *pulling out*. God's packing up and leaving the temple. Nothing could be worse. What the Lord threatened the exodus generation—*not* to dwell amid his people (Ex. 33:3)—has now become a reality.

Finally, *the prophets promised the destruction of Jerusalem and the temple*. Ezekiel portrays this as well. He builds a small diorama, a model intended to illustrate Babylon's siege of Jerusalem. He takes a brick and engraves a city on it. Then he mounts a siege on that brick using little ramps, army camps, and battering rams. Joel teaches this same truth with another devastating picture: a locust plague. The picture he gives is one of total devastation: "What the locust swarm has left the great locusts have eaten; what the great locusts have left the young locusts have eaten; what the young locusts have left other locusts have eaten" (Joel 1:4). Today, we know some of the science behind how locust swarms happen. As locusts multiply, they rub against each other, causing stimulation and elevated serotonin levels. This, in turn, causes the locusts to eat more and breed more, which causes more stimulation and even more eating and breeding. Multiplying into the billions, locusts can eat their own weight in a day and, with the help of the wind, travel hundreds of miles.

What is the impact of a locust storm? Imagine a bride on her wedding day, dressed up and beaming in anticipation of her groom. Everything is perfect, but then terrible news comes: the groom has died. That is what Joel means when he says, "Mourn like a virgin in sackcloth grieving for the betrothed of her youth" (1:8). Everything seemed wonderful, and then suddenly everything was horrible. The impact of God's judgment was more than physical; it affected everything—the economic, social, and emotional.

The judgment coming is worse than locusts, of course. Locusts are but a picture of the coming armies that the Lord will unleash on his people. Jeremiah describes the destruction of Jerusalem using the language of de-creation, a reversal of the original creation process. It's the most awful destruction imaginable.

> I looked at the earth, and it was formless and empty;
> and at the heavens, and their light was gone. . . .
> I looked, and there were no people;
> every bird in the sky had flown away.
> I looked, and the fruitful land was a desert;
> and all its towns lay in ruins
> before the LORD, before his fierce anger.
> —JEREMIAH 4:23–26

What good are God's covenantal promises if it all ends like this?

Israel's only hope—indeed our only hope—is that the Creator-covenant Lord will act to redeem us from his own judgment on our sin. That's one of the major points of the Prophets! Given how bad our sin problem is, as represented by Israel, *God must act in sovereign grace to save.*

If this section feels like a hard punch to the gut, then you've heard the prophets correctly. If you see in Israel's life a microcosm of your own human sin, you've understood them accurately. If you feel the utter hopelessness of your situation apart from God acting in grace to save and make all things right, then you've truly begun to grasp the prophetic message of judgment and hope. Thankfully, the Lord and his prophets have more to announce than a message of judgment. They also bring "good news."

Message 2: Stunning Salvation

Either God will act to save us or there will be no salvation. As Jonah reminds us and as all the prophets teach, "Salvation is of the Lord" (Jonah 2:9). This truth is clearly seen in the unfolding of the biblical covenants.

For Adam and Eve, God acted to save them, and he promised a serpent-crushing savior. For Noah, God initiated by providing plans for a boat. As Abraham slept, God walked between the pieces of the sacrificial animal and agreed to take the covenant curses upon himself. For Isaac, God initiated his salvation by providing a ram in his place. For Israel, God not only rescued them from Egypt; he also provided the means for his people to draw near to him through the priesthood. In each covenant, the story of salvation advances a step further as the Lord takes the initiative to save. The prophets continue this message, carrying it forward.

And yet, as we have seen, as the story advances, tension increases. Alongside God's promise to save is another promise that God will save *through* an obedient human seed/son, one who is ultimately identified with the Davidic king. Since the kings are nothing but disasters, we wonder, How will God keep his promise to save? How will God bring his people back from *deportation*, *divorce*, *desertion*, and *destruction*? Where will God's redemption come from?

A careful reading of the Prophets reveals the glorious answer. It's an answer, not just for Israel, but for all nations, just as God had promised to Abraham (Gen. 12:1–3). Let's look at what the prophets say about God's redemption by answering three questions:

- Question 1: *Who* will come to save?
- Question 2: *What* kind of salvation will he bring?
- Question 3: *How* will he bring this salvation to pass?

The Prophets communicate two expectations in answer to the first question, *Who will come to save?* First, *the Lord himself and the Lord alone is the one who saves his people.* To a people devastated by the Babylonian exile, the Lord speaks a needed word through Isaiah: "Comfort, comfort my people, says your God. Speak tenderly to Jerusalem . . . In the wilderness prepare the way for the LORD; make straight in the desert a highway for our God . . . say to the towns of Judah, 'Here is your God!'" (Isa. 40:1–9).

To the generation who returned from exile to a temple absent God's glory, the Lord says through Malachi, "I will send my messenger, who will prepare the way before me. Then suddenly the Lord you are seeking will come to his temple; the messenger of the covenant, whom you desire, will come" (Mal. 3:1).

To a people ravaged by wicked shepherds, the Lord says through Ezekiel, "*I myself will* tend my sheep and have them lie down, declares the Sovereign LORD. *I will* search for the lost and bring back the strays. *I will* bind up the injured and strengthen the weak, but the sleek and the strong *I will* destroy. *I will* shepherd the flock with justice" (Ezek. 34:15–16, emphases added). Yes, the Lord will come in judgment, yet after judgment the Lord himself will redeem his people.

But as developed through the covenants, there is a second expectation for *who* will come to save: God will save *through an obedient seed/ son, uniquely identified with the Davidic king.* Ezekiel, for example, beautifully portrays this truth. After repeatedly saying that the Lord is coming to save, we read this: "I will place over them one shepherd, my servant David, and he will tend them; he will tend them and be their shepherd. I the LORD will be their God, and my servant David will be prince among them. I the LORD have spoken. 'I will make a covenant of peace with them" (34:23–25). So the Lord will save, but *he* will save *through* the Davidic king.

Isaiah teaches the same truth. Israel's hope is found in the Lord, "high and exalted" (6:1–2). Yet her hope is *in the Davidic king,* who will be virgin-born (7:14), who will sit on David's throne forever (9:7), a king who will bear the very names of God—Immanuel (7:14), Wonderful

Counselor, Mighty God, Everlasting Father, and the Prince of Peace (9:6). In Isaiah 11, Isaiah pictures the Davidic house as a mighty tree reduced to a mere stump. Yet "a shoot will come up from the stump of Jesse; from his roots a Branch will bear fruit. The Spirit of the LORD will rest on him" (11:1–2).

In these passages, we see the Lord who saves and alongside him the Davidic king who will rule the world in righteousness, and who stands in the closest of relationship to the covenant God of Israel. The relationship between the Lord and the king is described as a Father-son relationship (2 Sam. 7:14; cf. Ps. 2). This means that in the coming of the Lord to save, we also have the coming of the king who will perfectly obey as a son and do his Father's will, unlike those who preceded him.

That's the *who* of salvation. Now let's look at the *what: What kind of salvation is this?* Built on the previous covenants, the prophets announce that *the Lord, through his son-king, will bring a new, better, and final covenant.* When the prophets speak of a "covenant of peace" or an "everlasting covenant," this is what they have in mind. Jeremiah's promise is the most comprehensive among the prophets. Consider all that *God* promises he "will" do:

> "The days are coming," declares the LORD, "when *I will* make a new covenant with the people of Israel and with the people of Judah. It will not be like the covenant I made with their ancestors when I took them by the hand to lead them out of Egypt, because they broke my covenant, though I was a husband to them," declares the LORD. "This is the covenant *I will* make with the people of Israel after that time," declares the LORD. "*I will* put my law in their minds and write it on their hearts. *I will* be their God, and they will be my people. No longer will they teach their neighbor, or say to one another, 'Know the LORD,' because they will all know me, from the least of them to the greatest," declares the LORD. "For *I will* forgive their wickedness and will remember their sins no more."
>
> —JEREMIAH 31:31–34, EMPHASES ADDED

This covenant is *new* in all the right ways. Similar to the covenant made at Sinai, the new covenant's purpose is to bring the Abrahamic blessings to Israel and the nations. The difference? This new covenant is effective. It will bring that about, unlike the old. The newness of this covenant is best seen in how it fulfills the previous covenants.

That's the *who* and the *what* of salvation. Now the *how: How will the Lord bring this salvation about? The Lord's salvation is made possible through a sinless sufferer.* This question brings us back to a key question raised by the Bible's story: Given human sin and the holiness of God, *how* can God and humans be reconciled?

To this point, the biblical story has been filled with hints and shadows leading us toward an answer. In the exodus redemption, we remember the Passover lamb. Through the blood of a lamb, judgment passed over Israelite homes. The Lord gave Moses instructions for an elaborate system of sacrifices. The amount of blood spilled in the temple was simply incredible—sacrifices were repeatedly made for sin. Embedded deep in the story is a profound truth: human sin requires the judgment of death, and that judgment is only averted by a substitute who takes our place and bears our sin. Leviticus 17:11 reminds us that God gave the sacrificial system to Israel to teach them this lesson: "The life of a creature is in the blood, and I have given it to you to make atonement for yourselves on the altar; it is the blood that makes atonement for one's life."

The prophets speak of a future substitute—one cast in terms of the previous patterns, but who now, in himself, solves the problem of sin fully and forever. Isaiah speaks of the servant yet to come. Like a good preacher, Isaiah shocks and awes us, but first he confuses us a bit. Speaking to the world, Isaiah describes Israel as "a light for the Gentiles, to open eyes that are blind, to free captives from prison and to release from the dungeon those who sit in darkness" (Isa. 42:6–7). This is good news for a world that has known only darkness since Adam. And Isaiah reminds us that, as promised, Israel, Abraham's children, will bless the nations. But Isaiah has even more to say about Israel.

Speaking of Israel as a nation, he asks, "Who is blind but my servant?" (42:19). Israel was a corporate servant, functioning as a "savior" by serving as an example to the nations of what God wanted his image-sons to look like. Yet instead of being a good example, Israel as God's servant-son was disobedient and himself in need of redemption from his sin. The people of God were called to be a light to the nations—a redeemed humanity, obeying God's Word and showing the world how glorious the Lord is by keeping his glorious Law—but they themselves couldn't even see! How would they help others to see?

Here we have two portraits of the servant: a substitute and a light for others. But what is the point—what hope is there for humanity—if God's servant, Israel and her kings, fail?

Isaiah answers these questions for us. He speaks of *another* servant, one who is from Israel but who is also distinct from Israel. A servant who represents Israel because he is Israel's king and a truly obedient son. This Messiah, as the servant, will "bring back the preserved of Israel," and to him the Lord says, "I will make you a light for the nations, that my salvation may reach to the end of the earth" (49:6 ESV). But—and consider this carefully—this glorious servant who brings salvation is also "despised" and "abhorred by the nation" (49:7 ESV).

How strange and how surprising! Remember the question at the heart of the Bible: How can sinful humans be reconciled with a holy God? Cast in the imagery of Isaiah, we might ask it this way: How can God's people move from darkness to light? Isaiah reveals the answer in what is the darkest and brightest moment in the biblical story. He tells us that the Lord will accomplish a substitutionary sacrifice for sin. He will do it through the suffering of his obedient servant.

This servant's appearance will not be lovely but be "marred, beyond human likeness," and he will have "no beauty or majesty to attract us to him, nothing in his appearance that we should desire him" (52:14 ESV; 53:2). He will be "despised and rejected by mankind, a man of suffering, and familiar with pain," and people will hide their faces from him (53:3).

This truth is akin to staring into the sun during a solar eclipse. When we look, we see both the brightness of the love of God and the darkness of human sin. Consider what this servant will do and for whom he will do it. Note the pronouns *he* and *our*.

Surely he took up our pain
    and bore our suffering,
yet we considered him punished by God,
    stricken by him, and afflicted.
But he was pierced for our transgressions,
    he was crushed for our iniquities;
the punishment that brought us peace was on him,
    and by his wounds we are healed.
We all, like sheep, have gone astray,
    each of us has turned to our own way;
and the LORD has laid on him
    the iniquity of us all.

—ISAIAH 53:4–6

What did he—the servant—do to deserve this?

He was oppressed and afflicted,
    yet he did not open not his mouth;
he was led like a lamb to the slaughter,
    and as a sheep before its shearers is silent,
    so he did not open his mouth.
By oppression and judgment he was taken away.
    Yet who of his generation protested?
For he was cut off from the land of the living;
    for the transgression of my people he was punished.
He was assigned a grave with the wicked,
    and with the rich in his death,
though he had done no violence,
    nor was any deceit in his mouth.

—ISAIAH 53:7–9

So then why is he subjected to this?

Yet it was the LORD's will to crush him and cause him to
suffer,
and though the LORD makes his life an offering for sin,
he will see his offspring and prolong his days,
and the will of the LORD will prosper in his hand.
After he has suffered,
he will see the light of life and be satisfied;
by his knowledge my righteous servant will justify many,
and he will bear their iniquities.
Therefore I will give him a portion among the great,
and he will divide the spoils with the strong,
because he poured out his life unto death,
and was numbered with the transgressors.
For he bore the sin of many,
and made intercession for the transgressors.

—ISAIAH 53:10–12

The servant who is our Savior is God's answer to the tension we have highlighted time and again. This individual is how God will keep his promise. This is how the Lord will bring salvation.

Isaiah gives layers of images and words here. But verse 11 focuses them into a laser beam to draw our attention: "By his knowledge my righteous servant will justify many, and he will bear their iniquities." The Messiah-Servant will do two things in his death. First, he will take what is ours—our iniquities. And second, he will give us what is his—his righteousness. He will provide an obedient covenant partner.

All of this points us ahead to the future death of Messiah Jesus. The crowd at the cross sees a bloody, weak man who must die. With Isaiah's prophetic insight, we see the Lord of glory, Immanuel, God with us, the divine Son become man on the cross, dying to take our sin and to give us his righteousness. As the New Testament will say, "God made him who had no sin to be sin for us, so that in him we might become the righteousness of God" (2 Cor. 5:21). On the cross, the black hole of the human heart devoured the light of the world, but as John wrote, "The light shines in the darkness, and the darkness has not overcome it" (John 1:5).

LOOKING BACK: NEWER IS BETTER

What's new about the new covenant? For our answer, let's return to the new covenant promise we looked at earlier in Jeremiah 31. The Lord called this covenant *new* for several good reasons. It's better than the old covenant made with Israel at Sinai, the covenant Israel broke. Even more, the new covenant is new in its unique ability to fulfill the Adamic, Abrahamic, and Davidic expectations. To put this another way, the new covenant eclipses each previous covenant *because it fulfills them.* This covenant resolves the tension we've felt in the Bible's story to this point.

In at least four profoundly hope-giving ways, this new covenant is *new* and *better*, ultimately bringing about what God had always planned and purposed. As in previous chapters, we'll begin by comparing this covenant to the previous covenants, working our way back to Adam.

An Obedient Mediator

In relation to the Davidic covenant, the new covenant *clarifies* how God will fulfill his promises. In contrast to the Davidic kings, the mediator of the new covenant is *a new and obedient mediator.* A righteous Davidic king is coming, and he will be God's obedient son. In him, the Davidic promise has reached its fulfillment. The mediator of this covenant is the one who brings God's saving rule and reign to this world. Out of the chopped-down tree of David's line comes "The LORD Our Righteous Savior" (Jer. 33:16), who is the righteous Savior-King we need.

A Real Solution to Sin

In relation to the Law-covenant, the new covenant brings fulfillment by way of *contrast.* This covenant will do what God's covenant through Moses could not do. It will bring *a new and effective solution to sin.* The Law-covenant gave us the sacrificial system and the priesthood. The failure of that covenant was its inability to make people right with God.

As Paul will later say, the Law never brought the righteousness of God, but it, along with the prophets, testified to it by pointing forward to the coming of Christ and his salvation work (Rom. 3:21–26).

By contrast, this new covenant will deal with the problem of human sin and guilt in relation to God. This covenant will bring the full forgiveness of sins. God says, "I will forgive their wickedness and will remember their sins no more" (Jer. 31:34). A new and effective priesthood will bring a new and effective sacrifice, leading to full and direct access to God.

A Universal Scope

The Abrahamic covenant gave us the promise of blessing for the nations through Abraham's seed and offspring. But the Abrahamic covenant on its own was not enough to bring about the universal blessing it promised because Abraham's offspring themselves needed a redeemer. The new covenant has *a new and universal scope.*

This new covenant is universal in several ways. First, it is universal in the sense that everyone in this covenant knows the Lord: "No longer will they teach their neighbor, or say to one another, 'Know the LORD,' because they will all know me, from the least of them to the greatest" (31:34). God's covenant through Moses included those who savingly knew the Lord and many who did not. Infant children circumcised at birth, for example, did not know the Lord in a saving way at their circumcision. The boundaries for the Abrahamic covenant were ethnic, tied to Abraham's physical descendants. The new covenant will be composed of those who savingly know the Lord, people born of the Spirit who are circumcised in heart.

This covenant is also universal in its fulfillment of the international intentions of the Abrahamic covenant. Through the prophet Joel the Lord says, "I will pour out my Spirit on all people. Your sons and daughters will prophesy, your old men will dream dreams, your young men will see visions. Even on my servants, both men and women, I will pour out my Spirit in those days" (Joel 2:28–29). Notice the universal language: *all* people, sons and daughters, male and female, young and old. This universality does not entail universal*ism*. Instead it is universal in that *all those in the covenant* know God in a saving way.

Joel makes this point clear as he continues: "Everyone who calls on the name of the LORD will be saved" (2:32). The glory of the promise is that those who call on the Lord's name will come from every tribe, nation, people, and tongue. In the new covenant, the Abrahamic promise is realized as Jews and gentiles both receive the promise and experience salvation in Christ alone, the new and better mediator.

The international scope of the new covenant is emphasized in many places in the prophets. Incredibly, Isaiah speaks of Assyria and Egypt worshiping alongside Israel as a new worshiping community that fills the earth with God's blessing (Isa. 19:23–24). Amos envisions a day when the Lord will restore Israel to glory, incorporating "the remnant of Edom and all the nations that bear my name" (Amos 9:12). When Amos uses the term *Edom*, it's shorthand for the entire gentile world. His statement speaks to an entirely new situation, one brought about by a new covenant with a new and universal scope.

A Regenerated Heart

Reaching all the way back to Adam, the centerpiece of God's covenant with creation was humanity, the crown of God's creation, and it was mediated through Adam. When Adam fell, he took humanity and the creation with him in his sin and rebellion. God's new covenant reverses this, including the effects of the curse God has placed on humanity and the world because of Adam's sin. This new covenant creates *a new and regenerated heart*.

This new covenant community will be a truly new people, a regenerated people. That is what the Lord means when he says, "I will put my law in their minds and write it on their hearts" (Jer. 31:33). This people will truly love and obey the Lord. They will be made new *from the inside out*. The fundamental problem of humanity's rejection of the Lord will be reversed in the life of his people. Ezekiel puts it this way: "I will give you a new heart and put a new spirit in you; I will remove from you your heart of stone and give you a heart of flesh. And I will put my Spirit in you and move you to follow my decrees and be careful to keep my laws" (Ezek. 36:26–27; cf. 11:19–20).

Ezekiel gives us a vision of what this means in a vivid picture of God's regenerating work. Ezekiel sees a large valley filled with dry bones, representing how dead Israel had become. They weren't just bone dead— they were as dead as a valley *filled* with dry bones. At God's command, Ezekiel prophesied into this valley: "Dry bones, hear the word of the LORD! This is what the Sovereign LORD says to these bones: 'I will make breath enter you, and you will come to life. I will attach tendons to you and make flesh come upon you and cover you with skin; I will put breath in you, and you will come to life. Then you will know that I am the LORD'" (37:4–6). Adam and his race had died, but with the new covenant, the Lord would "swallow up death forever" (Isa. 25:8) and bring resurrection life.

LOOKING AHEAD: THE FUTURE
IN SURROUND SOUND

In the Prophets, we have surround-sound imagery to portray the future age, drawing on all the Old Testament's typological threads to reveal how marvelous the fulfillment of God's promises will be. Earlier we summarized the prophets' message of judgment in four ways: the Lord will *deport* his people, *divorce* them, *desert* his temple, and *destroy* their city. Thankfully, for each aspect of judgment there is a corresponding aspect of salvation.

1. A New Exodus Will Save

The Israelites faced a powerful, hardened enemy in the pharaoh of Egypt. It's difficult to imagine a more powerful deliverance than the exodus—freedom from slavery to an oppressive king. Yet a greater exodus will come. The prophets draw on the pattern and memory of the exodus to project into the future a greater exodus from a problem even greater than slavery in Egypt: human sin and death. The Lord would "extend his hand yet a second time" to gather his people from exile (Isa. 11:11 ESV). This greater deliverance is described with the visual spectacle and imagery of the original exodus. The Lord will "utterly destroy the tongue of the Sea of Egypt," "wave his hand over the River with his scorching breath," and "lead people across in sandals" (11:15 ESV). "Singing" and "everlasting joy" will replace "sorrow and sighing" (51:11).

For this kind of change, deliverance from captivity is not enough. Only the sacrificial work of the Servant can address the heart problem that plagues Israel.

2. A New Marriage Will Flourish

The Lord's response to whoring Israel is both dramatic and dynamic. The Lord is an enraged, heart-torn, betrayed lover. He will not settle for divorce. And while he spoke in the language of divorce in naming one of Hosea's children "Not My People" (Hos. 1:9), these dramatized divorce papers were not his final word. God also gave Hosea a promise concerning the ultimate future of Abraham's children: "Yet the number of the children of Israel shall be like the sand of the sea . . . and I will say to Not My People, 'You are my people'; and he shall say, 'You are my God'" (1:10; 2:23 ESV). A faithless people will become a faithful people, and a broken marriage will be renewed.

Hosea's message does more than help us grasp the nature of sin as spiritual adultery. It goes even farther than showing us that God loves us despite our spiritual adultery. Hosea's message is about the love of God that *removes* our spiritual adultery and makes us faithful.

How will this happen? We know the answer by now: the sovereign promise-making and promise-keeping God will graciously do it himself! The Lord says, "I am now going to allure her; I will lead her into the wilderness and speak tenderly to her" (2:14). He will woo his bride, and then he will purify her: "I will heal their waywardness and love them freely, for my anger has turned away from them" (14:4). Freely loved, God's people flourish! "I am like a flourishing juniper; your fruitfulness comes from me" (14:8). The imagery of marriage stretches back to the first pages and forward to the last pages of the Bible. These final pages give us the text for the announcement of a marriage celebration—a marriage uniting Jesus Christ to his people:

> Hallelujah!
>> For our Lord God Almighty reigns.
> Let us rejoice and be glad
>> and give him glory!
> For the wedding of the Lamb has come,
>> and his bride has made herself ready.
> Fine linen, bright and clean,
>> was given her to wear.
>
> —REVELATION 19:6B–8

This is the people the new covenant creates: God's people—radiant, righteous, and united to her Lord in marriage. The love of a husband for his bride in our earthly experience cannot compare to God's love for his people. We may rightly think of ourselves in relation to God as subjects relating to a king or as citizens relating to a sovereign. But we should also think of ourselves as a bride relating to a groom.

3. A New Temple Where God Will Live

The Lord deserted his people, but he would return. Ezekiel was given a horrifying vision of the Lord leaving his temple, but he was given a heavenly vision as well.

In visions of God he took me to the land of Israel and set me on a very high mountain, on whose south side were some buildings that looked like a city . . . The glory of the LORD entered the temple through the gate facing east. Then the Spirit lifted me up and brought me into the inner court, and the glory of the LORD filled the temple . . . He said: "Son of man, this is the place of my throne and the place for the soles of my feet. This is where I will live among the Israelites forever. The people of Israel will never again defile my holy name—neither they nor their kings—by their prostitution and the funeral offerings for their kings at their death."

—EZEKIEL 40:2; 43:3–7

Ezekiel toured the temple, and it was in spiritual shambles. Then Ezekiel toured a new and future temple, a structure that looks like a city, on the Lord's move-in day. Adam and Eve were banished from Eden to the east, the Lord left his temple to the east, and now from the east the Lord returns!

Ezekiel was to "describe the temple to the people of Israel, that they may be ashamed of their sins. Let them consider its perfection, and if they are ashamed of all they have done, make known to them the design of the temple—its arrangement, its exits and entrances—its whole design and all its regulations and laws" (43:10–11). So what design did Ezekiel convey to the exiles? Let's consider a few of its features.

First, take note of the entrances. There are twelve city gates, three at each point of the compass, each gate named after one of the tribes of Israel. In terms of its shape, the temple has precise measurements. A man measuring with a measuring rod took Ezekiel all through the temple and measured everything out loud (40:3). He measured each gate, the vestibules, every room, chambers for priests, the inner temple. The temple has a four-cornered shape measured by length and width. It's perfectly square (45:2).

Now let's check out the lighting: "I saw the glory of the God of Israel coming from the east . . . and the land was radiant with his glory . . . and the glory of the LORD filled the temple" (43:2–5). God is the light for the temple, and he lights up the whole world.

Finally, let's consider the influence of the temple. A river flows out from the temple, beginning as a trickle but growing wider and deeper with every mile. Eventually it is so wide that you can't pass it. It becomes a source of life for the entire world. "Swarms of living creatures will live wherever the river flows . . . Fruit trees of all kinds will grow on both banks of the river. Their leaves will not wither, nor will their fruit fail. Every month they will bear fruit, because the water from the sanctuary flows to them. Their fruit will serve for food and their leaves for healing" (47:9, 12).

The details of this structure are designed to communicate the sheer holiness of God. But the very best part is the reason why the structure itself exists: "This is the place of my throne and the place for the soles of my feet. This is where I will live among the Israelites forever" (43:7).

The temple's design communicates God's presence, and so the climax of this vision is also the last line of the book of Ezekiel: "And the name of the city from that time on will be: The LORD Is There" (48:35). God creates a new people to gather them into his presence. This is *the purpose* the new covenant fulfills. God intended this from creation in Eden, but he fulfills it through the work of Jesus as our Savior.

4. A New Creation Will Dawn

The Lord's devastation was great to show us the extent of our problem. His restoration is also great to show the extent of *his* steadfast love and mercy. Through Isaiah, the Lord gave his people a picture of the cosmic scope of the new covenant's impact. Recall that Isaiah promised a child born of a virgin, whose name would be "Wonderful Counselor, Mighty God," someone who would sit on David's throne, a "shoot from the stump of Jesse." Here's the new creation this Messiah will usher in:

> The wolf will live with the lamb,
>> the leopard will lie down with the goat,
> the calf and the lion and the yearling together;
>> and a little child will lead them.
> The cow will feed with the bear,
>> their young will lie down together,
>> and the lion will eat straw like the ox.
> The infant will play near the cobra's den,
>> And the young child will put its hand into the viper's nest.
> They will neither harm nor destroy
>> on all my holy mountain,
> for the earth will be filled with the knowledge of the LORD
>> as the waters cover the sea.
>
> —ISAIAH 11:6–9

This is a most unusual place—certainly not like any place we know in the world as it currently exists. Amos describes a place that is similarly intriguing, where "the reaper will be overtaken by the plowman and the planter by the one treading grapes" and "new wine will drip from the mountains and flow from all the hills," when the Lord "will bring [his] people Israel back from exile" (Amos 9:13–14). This incredible place, where seedtime and harvest run right over each other, is what Isaiah calls "new heavens and a new earth" (Isa. 65:17). There, "the former things will not be remembered, nor will they come to mind" (65:17). There, "the wolf and the lamb will feed together" and "dust will be the serpent's food" (65:25). The new covenant will bring about an entirely new creation.

This new creation is good, not primarily because it includes upgrades to the current created order, but because it's a totally renewed creation that includes our eternal rest in the presence of our triune Covenant Lord. That's why one of the best things about this new creation is that it doesn't have a sun. It doesn't need one! For "the LORD will be your everlasting light, and your God will be your glory" (60:19). There, in the perfect presence of the Lord, every tragedy will be wiped out, for "he will swallow up death forever. The Sovereign LORD will wipe away the tears from all faces; he will remove his people's disgrace from all the earth" (25:8).

Three great tragedies: death, pain, and guilt. As sure as the Lord has spoken, each of these will be vanquished forever. Living in the undiluted presence of God with these tragedies removed—this is the glory of the new creation.

Chapter 13

JESUS

A Cup Full of Blood

THE GOSPELS

S ilence.

We all know the sound. Silence can be excruciating. It was painful for Israel. For four hundred years, God was silent.

This had happened before. God was also silent when Israel was in Egypt. Then, when Pharaoh ordered her sons killed, Israel cried to God. The Lord heard, and he lit up a bush and called to Moses, "Moses! Moses! . . . I am the God of your father, the God of Abraham . . . I am sending you to Pharaoh to bring my people the Israelites out of Egypt" (Ex. 3:4, 6, 10). The Lord spoke, he judged, and he saved.

The Lord was silent yet again during the spiritually dark years following Israel's settlement in the land (1 Sam. 3:1). Everyone did as they saw fit, the priesthood was corrupt, and Israel had no king. Yet the Lord heard people like Hannah, who called to the Lord in prayer (1 Sam. 2:1–10), and he raised up Samuel to speak his word to the people (1 Sam. 3:21–4:1) and established his Davidic king. The Lord spoke, he judged, and he installed his king.

Fast-forward to first-century Palestine, and four hundred years have elapsed since Israel has last heard a word from God. Some things have changed, and some things remain the same. The empire of Assyria has come and gone, along with Babylon after her, followed by the Persians and Greeks. Rome is the new superpower, and Israel is an oppressed and occupied people, living out their existence in a small corner of the Roman

Empire. Her throne is empty, and God's promises seem forgotten. Israel has plenty of religious leaders, but none of them is the righteous king promised by the prophets.

Pharisees make up one branch of Israel's elite ruling class. Respected middle-class priests, Pharisees esteemed the Scriptures highly, but also their tradition, which they claimed went back to Moses. Yet many of them elevated their tradition over the teaching of God's Word, although some longed to see God provide deliverance through the promised coming king. Another branch, the Sadducees, were wealthy aristocrats, chief priests who held seats of honor among the local government. They didn't believe in the resurrection of the dead, nor any Scripture beyond Moses. Both groups tended to love the honor of men, gave money to be praised, prayed to be heard, and dressed to be seen. Some of the Pharisees were scribes—those who copied and taught the Old Testament Law. Scribes were meticulous when it came to the letter of the Law, but many of them didn't follow its intention.

These were Israel's proud shepherds. Most of them regarded themselves highly, but not their Lord, as evidenced in their later confrontation with Jesus (John 5:39–47). Those who added to and subtracted from his Word made it null and void (Mark 7:1–13). Other than a few exceptions, while they didn't always get along, in due time they would come together around a common cause—a common enemy. Much has changed over the last four hundred years, yet at a deeper level not much has changed at all. Israel still needs a word from God, a new heart, and an obedient Messiah-King.

Into this, God spoke. But this time his word to the people would be different; it would be better. As Scripture says, "In the past God spoke to our ancestors through the prophets at many times and in various ways, but in these last days he has spoken to us by his Son (Heb. 1:1–2).

In our Bibles, we have four book-length accounts of the life, death, and resurrection of Jesus of Nazareth, also called the Christ or the Messiah. These four accounts are Matthew, Mark, Luke, and John. Named for their authors, the church has historically called these the "Gospels"—a word derived from a Greek word meaning "good news." These are not four competing accounts but four complementary portraits of who Jesus is. That's why early Christians called them the fourfold Gospel; one Gospel with four accounts.

These Gospels are more than mere biographical or historical records, although they record both history and the basic content of Christ's life. They are *theological* history that accurately describes and interprets *who* Jesus is and *what* he has come to do according to God's eternal plan. When Winston Churchill wrote his famous history of World War II, he was writing not merely to convey facts but to make sense of the origin, unfolding, and ultimate outcome of the war. Similarly, and in a completely truthful way, the triune God through the Gospel authors interprets for us the significance of Jesus' person and work so that we may know him who is life eternal (John 17:3). The Gospel accounts are written to answer these fundamental questions:

1. Question 1: *Who* was Jesus the Christ?
2. Question 2: *What* kind of salvation did he bring?
3. Question 3: *How* did he secure that salvation?

These three questions will shape the three divisions of this chapter. You might also recognize these questions from the previous chapter, where we explored the nature of the stunning salvation promised by the prophets. The New Testament announces that Jesus is the one who brings that stunning salvation.

At times, we may want to know more about Jesus than we find in these books, given that the Gospels are not exhaustive accounts of his life. Yet we should recognize that everything God wants us to know about Jesus is found in the Gospels. Consider John's stated purpose in writing his Gospel: "Jesus performed many other signs in the presence of his disciples, which are not recorded in this book. But these are written that you may believe that Jesus is the Messiah, the Son of God, and that by believing you may have life in his name" (John 20:30–31).

So although we could say much more about Jesus, here we will cover the answers to the most important questions we can ask about Jesus— apart from whom all of God's promises are empty.

THE TIME HAS COME; THE SON IS HERE

Our New Testament bursts open with God's speaking and sending activity. Angels appear and speak. But they do not speak to Israel's proud leaders. They speak to the lowly who are eagerly waiting to hear God's voice and know something of their need for God's forgiveness of sins. If we listen closely to what the angels say, we'll hear the answer to the first question, *Who was Jesus the Christ?*

The first angel came to a faithful priest whose wife, Elizabeth, was aged and barren—a sadness familiar to the storyline of the Bible. "'Do not be afraid, Zechariah; your prayer has been heard,' the angel said. 'Elizabeth will bear you a son, and you are to call him John . . . he will be filled with the Holy Spirit . . . he will go on before the Lord, in the spirit and power of Elijah . . . [he will] make ready a people prepared for the Lord'" (Luke 1:13–17).

A second angel appeared to a young engaged woman in Nazareth. Nazareth was on the outskirts of a rural community called Galilee. No one special had ever come from there until the Lord spoke through an angel: "Do not be afraid, Mary; you have found favor with God. You will conceive and give birth to a son, and you are to call him Jesus. He will be great and will be called the Son of the Most High. The Lord God will give him the throne of his father David, and he will reign over Jacob's descendants forever; his kingdom will never end" (1:30–33).

The fact that Mary was a virgin was not a problem, because the Creator-covenant God was at work. Matthew reminds us that the virgin conception was not unexpected: "All this took place to fulfill what the Lord had said through the prophet: 'The virgin will conceive and give birth to a son, and they will call him Immanuel' (which means, 'God with us')" (Matt. 1:22–23; cf. Isa. 7:14). It's all part of the promise, as God reminded Abraham long ago: "For no word from God will ever fail" (Luke 1:37; cf. Gen. 18:14). Mary's heart overflowed in rejoicing with a song whose themes of promise and reversal echoed Hannah's prayer before her (Luke 1:46–55).

A third angel appeared to Mary's soon-to-be husband, Joseph. How else could he properly receive the news that his virgin fiancée was pregnant? The angel said to him, "Joseph son of David, do not be afraid to take Mary home as your wife, because what is conceived in her is from the Holy Spirit. She will give birth to a son, and you are to give him the name Jesus, because he will save his people from their sins" (Matt. 1:20–21). Months later, Jesus would be born in David's city, Bethlehem (2:1–6).

God was silent, and then he spoke. These angels announced the coming of the stunning salvation the prophets foretold. Jesus would deliver his people from their sins. The Spirit conceived him—the same Holy Spirit the prophets promised would uniquely act in the future age. Jesus' name means "the LORD saves," a fitting name because in him the new covenant age has dawned and with it the forgiveness of sins. As Paul later writes, "When the set time had fully come, God sent his Son, born of a woman, born under the law, to redeem those under the law, that we might receive adoption to sonship" (Gal. 4:4–5). Adam, Abraham, and David had all awaited a son, and now that son has finally arrived. The prophets expected *the Lord himself to come* to save his people, and for a *son of David* to come to reign. This child is simultaneously the Lord and the messianic king. He is here!

The arrival of Jesus signals the fulfillment of the ages and the beginning of the culmination of history. On every page of the Gospels, the weight of this arrival is felt, yet in slightly different ways in each Gospel portrait.

Matthew begins his account with "This is the genealogy of Jesus the Messiah the son of David, the son of Abraham" (Matt. 1:1), and then traces Jesus' genealogy back through David to Abraham. This genealogy is more than record keeping. It's the record of God keeping his promises, something to marvel at for eternity. Matthew's Gospel emphasizes the arrival of God's kingdom, whose saving rule is known in the ministry of Jesus. Matthew 5–7 is often referred to as "the Sermon on the Mount." Just as Moses ascended a mountain to receive the Law, in this section we see Jesus ascending a mountain to proclaim that the Law has reached its fulfillment in him (5:17). Jesus' entire self-understanding is that he is greater than Moses and the Law because in him the entire Old

Testament—all of God's plans and promises—have reached their God-intended end: "Do not think that I have come to abolish the Law or the Prophets; I have not come to abolish them but to fulfill them" (Matt. 5:17). This is a profoundly arrogant statement—unless it is true!

Jesus' statement about himself in Matthew 5 is not a one-off incident. In Matthew 11, reflecting on the importance of John the Baptist, Jesus tells his followers that no man ever born among women is greater than John! But why would he say this? Jesus' answer, explaining the greatness of John, points back to himself: John the Baptist had the privilege of finally pointing out who Jesus is (11:13)! Jesus views *himself* as the center of all of God's plans. He alone culminates all prophetic revelation. He alone reveals the Father. He alone ushers in the promised rest lost at Adam's fall. "All things have been committed to me by my Father. No one knows the Son except the Father, and no one knows the Father except the Son and those to whom the Son chooses to reveal him. Come to me, all you who are weary and burdened, and I will give you rest" (11:27–28).

Mark begins his account of the life of Jesus in a way that is characteristic of his entire Gospel—direct and to the point. Mark writes, "The beginning of the good news about Jesus the Messiah, the Son of God" (Mark 1:1). Mark introduces us to Jesus not through a birth narrative but through his baptism, when "a voice came from heaven: 'You are my Son, whom I love; with you I am well pleased" (1:11). From this statement, Mark structures his Gospel to emphasize Jesus' identity as God's Son. He puts the spotlight on those who correctly identify Jesus. Curiously, while others get the identity of Jesus wrong, the demons fall down when they see him and cry out, "You are the Son of God" (3:11).

At the center of Mark's unfolding account, Jesus asks his disciples the big question: "Who do people say that I am?" The disciples reply, "Some say John the Baptist; others say Elijah; and still others, one of the prophets."

"But what about you?" Jesus asks. "Who do you say I am?" Peter answers, "You are the Messiah" (8:27–29).

It is unlikely that Peter understood the full import of what he had said, but he was right. "Messiah" or "Christ" is not Jesus' last name but a title derived from the Old Testament. Peter is saying that Jesus is the "Christ"—the anointed Savior and the Davidic king. Later in the story, a Roman soldier witnesses Jesus' last breath and becomes the first human besides John to get Jesus' identity right: "Surely this man was the Son of God!" (15:39). The divine Son has become the incarnate Son to fulfill all of God's promises and to inaugurate the long-awaited new covenant age.

Similar to Matthew's account, Luke gives us a genealogy, but he traces Jesus' line back to the very beginning, to "Adam, the son of God" (Luke 3:38). Jesus is the human son of Eve who will undo what Adam did by crushing the head of the serpent. Luke goes to great lengths to demonstrate that Jesus fulfills the Old Testament Scriptures, from the announcement of his birth to his conception, in his life and ministry, and ultimately in his death and resurrection. Luke's content likely matches what Jesus explained in his famous Emmaus road appearance, when "beginning with Moses and all the Prophets, he explained to them what was said in all the Scriptures concerning himself" (24:27).

John begins his own account of the life of Jesus in a different but complementary way. Beginning in eternity past and echoing the very first words of the Bible, John identifies Jesus as the Word or Son from eternity, who has always existed in relation to God the Father: "In the beginning was the Word, and the Word was with God, and the Word was God" (John 1:1). This Word is none other than God the Son, the one through whom the Father created the world. The Son is the agent of creation, the maker of the world, its life and its light. The Son did not come into existence a long time ago; he has always existed in eternal relationship, fellowship, and communion with the Father and the Spirit.

Then we read this staggering statement about what has now happened in history: "The Word became flesh and made his dwelling among us. We have seen his glory, the glory of the one and only Son, who came from the Father, full of grace and truth" (1:14).

John's words here should remind us of what God did for Moses in Exodus 33–34. After the golden calf incident, when the Israelites sinned in the worship of an idol, Moses pleaded with God to show him his glory. After placing Moses in the cleft of the mountain, God passes by and reveals his glory by announcing his name: "The LORD, the LORD, the compassionate and gracious God, slow to anger, abounding in love and faithfulness, maintaining love to thousands, and forgiving wickedness, rebellion and sin" (Ex. 34:6–7). What Moses only saw dimly, John announces has fully come in Christ! In the Word made flesh, "we have seen his glory . . . full of grace and truth" (1:14), and we have the revelation of God that far surpasses anything given to Moses. As John goes on to say, "The law was given through Moses; grace and truth came through Jesus Christ. No one has ever seen God, but the one and only Son, who is himself God and is in closest relationship with the Father, has made him known" (1:17–18). In Jesus the Messiah, the divine Son has fully disclosed God's glory because he is one with the Father, and he has done so by adding to himself our human nature.

The Gospels unite in affirming that in Jesus, God the Son has become man. In so doing, they merge the twin expectations of the Old Testament story: the one who saves is ultimately the Lord himself in and through his king. *Who is Jesus the Christ?* Jesus is indeed the Davidic son and king, God the Son incarnate, the Lord of glory now taking up residence with us and bringing to pass all the Father's glorious plans and purposes to save us from our sins (Matt. 1:21).

IN HIM THE NEW COVENANT AGE HAS DAWNED

Many claim Jesus as an important part of their spiritual lives, even their salvation. But *what kind of salvation does he bring?* The Bible tells us that the salvation Jesus brings is the salvation the Old Testament anticipated and predicted. Yet in the Gospel accounts, we have more than a mere retelling of what the prophets promised. In Jesus' life and teaching, these promises break into the world.

In this section, we will listen in on four conversations revealing Jesus' establishment of the new covenant. Taken together, these conversations indicate that the new age promised by the prophets has now arrived in Jesus' incarnation, life, death, and resurrection.

Four Conversations for a New Covenant Age

The first conversation is recorded in Matthew, Mark, and Luke. It's a conversation between Jesus and Satan during Jesus' temptation in the wilderness. At Jesus' baptism, a voice from heaven says, "This is my Son, whom I love; with him I am well pleased" (Matt. 3:17). As soon as the Spirit descends on him, the Spirit leads Jesus into the wilderness, where his claim to be God's obedient Son is tested. There he remains alone and without food for forty days. Physically speaking, this would have been a difficult trial. And we know from experience that when our bodies are physically weak, we are also vulnerable to many other temptations. These temptations fully press Jesus' trust in his Father.

Appealing to Jesus' profound physical hunger, the devil tempts him to doubt the *goodness* of his Father. Jesus, instead of trusting his Father, is tempted to turn stones into bread, act independently of his Father, and depart from the path set out for him that will ultimately lead to the cross. He is also tempted by Satan's misuse of Scripture (Matt. 4:6) to doubt his Father's *protection and care* for him. If Jesus threw himself off the temple in a grandiose act (Ps. 91:11–12), would not his Father rescue him?

Finally, the devil tempts Jesus to doubt his Father's *authority* and the way the kingdom would come to this world. Satan offers Jesus all the kingdoms of the world. Of course, they were not his to give. Satan is a counterfeit ruler, and as Satan did with Adam and Eve (and does with all temptations), he adds to, subtracts from, and twists God's words. In his response to each of these temptations, Jesus quotes Scripture, showing his complete trust in his Father's plan for him (Matt. 4:4 [Deut. 8:3]; Matt. 4:7 [Deut. 6:16]; Matt. 4:10 [Deut. 6:13]). In this, he does not sin. This helps us to understand why the Spirit leads the Son into the wilderness to be tempted in the first place. The answer: to show that Jesus succeeds where everyone else—Adam, Noah, Abraham, Moses, Israel, David—has failed.

Jesus' obedience shows us that the salvation he brings is secure. Because of his perfect obedience to his Father, Jesus really can secure salvation for his people. Because Jesus is the faithful, righteous Son of God, he really can save, as he acted on our behalf as our covenant-mediator to "fulfill all righteousness" (3:15).

The prophets spoke of a *new and obedient mediator*—obedient where everyone else failed. This is now him!

The second conversation revealing Jesus' new covenant salvation is connected to his healings. Mark recounts the remarkable episode of a paralytic lowered through the roof of a home filled with people eager to hear Jesus. The man's friends hoped that Jesus would heal him. Jesus' response surprised everyone. Seeing the crippled man, he said, "Son, your sins are forgiven" (Mark 2:5). This offended the scribes: "Who can forgive sins but God alone?" (2:7). But Jesus continued, "Which is easier: to say to this paralyzed man, 'Your sins are forgiven,' or to say, 'Get up, take your mat and walk'?" (2:9).

In inaugurating God's kingdom and the new covenant, Jesus came to do something greater, indeed far more difficult, than merely healing people. He came to forgive us of our sins, the very problem that gave rise to disease and death. In this healing miracle, Jesus reveals that *he* is the one who ends our infirmities by paying for our sin and satisfying God's own righteous demand against us.

What do Jesus' healings show us about the salvation he brings? They reveal a deeper truth about the new covenant's newness—our complete forgiveness and a totally restored relationship with our triune Covenant God. Israel's elaborate system of priests and sacrifices could not do the job, but Jesus can.

The prophets promised a truly *effective solution to sin*, including the end of sickness and death (Matt. 11:4–5; Luke 4:16–21). This is what Jesus brings.

For a third conversation, we turn to Jesus' exchange with a Samaritan woman. This encounter is illustrative of many truths, but it uniquely discloses that in Christ's coming the eras are changing. The story picks up at noon, with Jesus seated by a well where a woman comes for water. Shocked when Jesus asks her for a drink, she responds to him, saying, "You are a Jew and I am a Samaritan woman. How can you ask me for a drink?" (John 4:9). That's a good question!

The fact that Jesus was in Samaria at all is curious. Samaria was the straightest path from Judea to Galilee, but most Jews avoided it. Samaritans were a racial mixture of Jew and gentile—a result of intermarriage many years before and especially repulsive to the "pure-bred" Jew. Added to this racial impurity, the Samaritans had modified the Pentateuch to accommodate their own story, and they built their own temple as a place of worship on their own mountain to rival Jerusalem. So when this woman asks why Jesus would speak to her, it's a good question. But Jesus doesn't bother to answer it. Instead he offers her some water of his own: "Everyone who drinks this water will be thirsty again, but whoever drinks the water I give them will never thirst" (4:13–14).

As the conversation unfolds, we learn additional details about why this woman came to the well in the heat of the day. She's avoiding the company of other women because she's an outcast. She's living with a man who isn't her husband, and she's had five husbands. When Jesus spoke to outsiders like her, his actions angered the Pharisees and perplexed his disciples. They all misunderstood his mission.

The conversation with the woman moves from water, to living water, to her adultery, but it also takes another important step. She discerns that Jesus is from God, and possibly to deflect the conversation, she asks a theological question about the proper place of worship: Jerusalem or her mountain? Jesus' answer is instructive about the salvation he's inaugurating. "Woman . . . believe me, a time is coming when you will worship the Father neither on this mountain nor in Jerusalem. You Samaritans worship what you do not know; we worship what we do know, for salvation is from the Jews. Yet a time is coming and has now come when the true worshipers will worship the Father in the Spirit and in truth, for they are the kind of worshipers the Father seeks. God is spirit, and his worshipers must worship in the Spirit and in truth" (John 4:21–24).

Jesus tells this woman that the temple and its worshiping community are being transformed. Now that Jesus has come, worship won't happen at the temple in Jerusalem, and worship won't be offered externally by those of Abrahamic descent who won't worship him internally, with their hearts. Jesus is bringing a change in eras. He is the true temple

(2:18–22), and true worship is in the Spirit (John 3). Jesus' new covenant brings internal transformation for its members. It's also global in its scope, including worshipers from Israel, Samaria, and all nations.

This global focus pervades Jesus' ministry. The Samaritan woman was an outsider to Judaism, as were the tax collectors and sinners that Jesus engaged regularly in the Gospels. Compare this with Jesus' posture toward the leaders of Israel. It's impossible to miss the meaning of Jesus' sharp words to them: "Do not think you can say to yourselves, 'We have Abraham as our father.' I tell you that out of these stones God can raise up children for Abraham'" (Matt. 3:9). Besides the affirmation of God and the cries of demons, it's a Roman soldier who acknowledges Jesus as the Son of God, as he stands at the foot of the cross (Mark 15:39). These closing words of Matthew's Gospel, Jesus' parting words, also reinforce this global theme: "Go and make disciples of all nations" (Matt. 28:19).

What does Jesus' visit with the Samaritan woman show us about the salvation he brings? It tells us that Jesus' salvation is for all nations. All who enter will enter the same way, for "there is neither Jew nor Gentile, neither slave nor free, nor is there male and female, for you are all one in Christ Jesus." And "if you belong to Christ, then you are Abraham's seed, and heirs according to the promise" (Gal. 3:28–29).

Jesus' new covenant fulfills the *universal scope* of God's promises to Abraham and promises rehearsed by the prophets—promises rooted in God's prior purpose for humanity from all creation.

The fourth conversation is one Jesus had with a man possessed by a demon (Mark 5:2). Anyone who looked at this man would see that he was clearly beyond help. He lived alone among the dead, in the tombs outside of town. The townspeople restrained him with chains, but he broke them repeatedly. He scraped himself with rocks and his clothes were tattered. He cried out day and night. If you weren't looking at him, you could still hear him. And he was strong!

But Jesus was much stronger. At the sight of Jesus, the man ran to him, fell to the ground, and cried out, "What do you want with me, Jesus, Son of the Most High God?" (5:7). The demons inside this man knew that they had met a greater foe than they had ever faced before.

Jesus said to them, "Come out of this man!" (5:8) and sent the demons into a nearby herd of two thousand pigs, which immediately ran into the lake to kill themselves. Humanly speaking, this man was beyond help, but Jesus was no mere human. He is the divine Son become man, our Deliverer and Savior.

What happened to the man after Jesus rescued him? The locals came to see what had happened, and there he was, "sitting there, dressed and in his right mind" (5:15). Incredibly, their response was mixed. While the man himself was thrilled, the villagers, recognizing that Jesus was stronger than this man, feared Jesus and begged him to leave. Jesus disrupted their lives. They would rather have the local monster than *him!*

This remarkable story pictures how Jesus utterly transforms people. It's a picture of conversion, of how Jesus makes completely new people out of the old. In John 3, a man named Nicodemus comes to Jesus at night. As a Pharisee, he fears people seeing him meet with Jesus publicly, but as we soon learn, he is also in the "dark" spiritually. Jesus' word for him? "Very truly I tell you, no one can see the kingdom of God unless they are born again" (John 3:3). Being born is a one-time thing, so Jesus offered him the favor of a clarification: "Very truly I tell you, no one can enter the kingdom of God unless they are born of water and the Spirit" (3:5).

Nicodemus was confused, but as a student of the Scriptures, he shouldn't have been. Jesus was referring to the kind of new life spoken of by the prophet Ezekiel: "I [the Lord] will sprinkle clean water on you, and you will be clean; I will cleanse you from all your impurities and from all your idols. I will give you a new heart and put a new spirit in you; I will remove from you your heart of stone and give you a heart of flesh. And I will put my Spirit in you and move you to follow my decrees and be careful to keep my laws" (Ezek. 36:25–27).

Nicodemus, a good Pharisee, should have been looking forward to this day when the Lord would take a valley of dry bones and raise them to life (Ezek. 37). While Jesus is being a bit cryptic, as he often was, he is also pointing Nicodemus to Scripture—the same Scripture that had anticipated him as the inaugurator of the new age.

What does Jesus' encounter with the demoniac show us about the salvation he brings? That while Adam stands as the head of the human race, Christ stands as the head of a new race, a completely regenerated humanity.

Just as the prophets had promised, Jesus' new covenant brings *a new and regenerated heart*.

Already and Not Yet

The New Testament is clear: Jesus fulfills all that the prophets expected and predicted. Yet he does this in a way that the prophets did not fully expect. We might wonder, *Is this* really *the full exodus from sin, the new marriage, the new temple, and the new creation that they had promised?* The answer is yes and no. Yes, because in Christ what the prophets promised has truly arrived. But no as well, since the fullness of all that God has promised still awaits a future day of consummation. This is what theologians refer to as the "already and not yet"—a crucial truth we must grasp to make sense of Jesus' new covenant salvation work.

The prophets saw the future as a single event consisting in the arrival of the Lord and his Messiah and fulfillment of all of God's promises. They believed that everything would happen at once. But as God's plan unfolds, we discover that there are two comings of the Lord. The first is in his incarnation, consisting of his entire life and ministry. The second is yet to come, his future return when he consummates all things.

When Mark opened his Gospel, he quoted from Isaiah, "a voice of one calling in the wilderness, 'Prepare the way for the Lord, make straight paths for him'" (Mark 1:3). As we saw earlier, that's the promise of a *new exodus*, an exodus from sin and all that it entails. This is the new exodus that Jesus signaled he was bringing. His wilderness temptation repeated Israel's wilderness temptation. He multiplied loaves to feed thousands and said, "I am the bread of life," comparing himself to the bread their ancestors ate (John 6:48). They ate manna, "yet they died," but Jesus is the "living bread" that comes "from heaven" (6:49–51). Has the new exodus now come in Christ? Yes, but not fully.

The prophets spoke of God's people, radiant and purified as a bride for a husband—a *new marriage*. Jesus the bridegroom has come, and the church is now the bride, but we still await the consummation when we will be with the Lord, as his bride, living in the new creation.

Consider the promise of a *new temple*. Jesus said some cryptic things about the temple when he spoke of tearing it down and rebuilding it, which he has done through his work of death and resurrection (2:19–22). In faith-union with Christ, the Spirit has made his church the new temple (Eph. 2:19–22), yet we still await the fullness of our relationship to Christ as his people in the future consummation (Rev. 21–22).

Finally, consider that the prophets spoke of a *new creation*. Isaiah promised, for example, that there would come a day when "he will swallow up death forever. The Sovereign LORD will wipe away the tears from all faces; he will remove his people's disgrace from all the earth" (Isa. 25:8). Isaiah went on to promise that in that day the lame will walk, the blind will see, and the mountains will drip with wine. In his ministry, Jesus gave every indication that this new creation has now arrived with him. John tells us that when Jesus turned water into wine at Cana (John 2:1–11), it was his first sign. But it was also a sign that the new creation is now here! Jesus healed the lame and he gave sight to the blind, just as promised (Luke 4:16–21). He even raised the dead. Jesus not only said that he *brings* resurrection; he said, "I am the resurrection and the life. The one who believes in me will live, even though they die" (John 11:25).

Jesus does not write prescriptions. He *is* the prescription. And yet we still die. Is this—our present experience after Christ's coming—really the new creation? Again, the answer is yes and no.

We will explore further the nature of this tension in the next chapter. For now, it's enough to note that *all* the promises of God reach their fulfillment in these two stages tied to Christ's two advents.

So far we have focused on the question of Jesus' *identity*. He is God the Son, the divine Lord who is also the human royal son of David. We have considered as well the *kind of salvation* that Jesus brings. He brings the new covenant salvation promised by the prophets, with all its glorious facets. But we also need to consider *how* he secured this salvation for us. Or, from a different angle, why it was necessary for God's Son to come in the first place. There is no "good news" or true understanding of the Bible's message apart from the answer to this question.

IT IS FINISHED

Jesus did not come merely to identify with us; he came to do a work that we could not do. He said, "My Father is always at his work to this very day, and I too am working" (5:17), and "My food . . . is to do the will of him who sent me and to finish his work" (John 4:34). He prayed to his Father at the end of his life, "I have brought you glory on earth by finishing the work you gave me to do" (17:4). Before he gave up his Spirit on the cross, he said, "It is finished" (19:30). What was finished? What is the work that Jesus came to do? How does Jesus secure salvation for his people?

A helpful, three-part answer that beautifully summarizes all that Jesus did to accomplish our salvation is that he did the work of our *prophet*, *priest*, and *king*. By fulfilling all these offices, *Jesus has become our all-sufficient Savior,* the only one we need! Jesus brings God's Word as Truth incarnate, God's presence by the payment of our sin as our Great High Priest, and God's rule as the King of Kings and Lord of Lords. The author of Hebrews captures this three-part role with these wonderful words: "In the past God spoke to our ancestors through the prophets at many times and in various ways, but in these last days he has spoken to us by his Son, whom he appointed heir of all things, and through whom also he made the universe. The Son is the radiance of God's glory and the exact representation of his being, sustaining all things by his powerful word. After he had provided purification for sins, he sat down at the right hand of the Majesty in heaven" (Heb. 1:1–3).

As the radiance of God's glory, Jesus is our *great prophet*. As the purification for our sins, he is our *Great High Priest*. As the one who sat down at God's right hand, he is *our King*. We'll turn now to explore each of these facets of Jesus' glorious work. As we do, we want to make plain the deeper human need that Jesus' work addresses. Understanding his threefold work helps us to trust him more completely and praise him more fully.

The Radiance of God's Glory

Without a word from God, humanity is stumbling blindly in the dark. We search for the light of knowledge, wisdom, and understanding in the ideas of this world and in studying the stuff of creation. We turn to books, magazines, and even the social media feeds of our favorite celebrities or athletes. But what we desperately need is to hear from the source and standard of truth. We need God to speak to us about what is ultimate for the world, for us, and for our future.

This is exactly what our gracious triune Creator-Lord has done. In the past, he spoke through the prophets, but now he has definitively spoken in his Son. God has not left us in the dark! *Jesus, the Son, came as the great prophet* who was promised for his people. As the author of Hebrews writes, he is "the radiance of God's glory" (1:3). When Jesus opened his mouth to teach, people knew that something was different: "The people were amazed at his teaching, because he taught them as one who had authority, not as the teachers of the law" (Mark 1:22). When Jesus taught, people heard the very word of God. Jesus said, "I do nothing on my own but speak just what the Father has taught me" (John 8:28). When Jesus taught, he taught as one who knew the content and intent of all previous revelation because he is God the Son (Matt. 11:25–27). *He* is the one about whom *all* the prophets prophesied.

As the true prophet, Jesus not only teaches God's Word like other prophets but *is* God's revelation, the Word become flesh (John 1:14). This is why Jesus could say, "Anyone who has seen me has seen the Father" (14:9). He is the "radiance" of God's glory, the "exact imprint" of his nature (Heb. 1:2–3 ESV). As John writes, "The law was given through Moses; grace and truth came through Jesus Christ. No one has ever seen God, but the one and only Son, who is himself God and is in closest relationship with the Father, has made him known" (John 1:17–18). Moses, the great prophet of the Old Testament, promised a prophet yet to come, one that the people of God would listen to (Deut. 18:15–18). Jesus *is* that prophet (Acts 3:22–26)!

How was Jesus received? Did the people listen to him as God's Son, the final and true prophet? Given the hardness of the human heart,

Jesus, the light of the world, was rejected because "people loved darkness instead of light because their deeds were evil" (John 3:19). We rejected Jesus and in doing this have proven how much we need him!

A Death That Truly Redeems

Without a solution for our sin and guilt, we are condemned, regardless of how much truth we know. The holiness of God and our sinfulness create a huge problem for us. Before God, we are impure and guilty, and our consciences know it. There has always been a market for new religions because we are aware of our problem and we search for some form of relief.

The Bible offers the only answer that can truly address the problem of human sin and guilt. Scripture affirms the utter holiness of God and the horror of our sin, and tells us that *all* people are born with Adam's sin and pollution *and* his guilt and condemnation (Rom. 3:23; 5:12–21; 6:23). When other religious systems suggest that good works can merit God's favor, they minimize divine holiness and human sinfulness. Yet consider these bold words: "Therefore, brothers and sisters, since we have confidence to enter the Most Holy Place by the blood of Jesus, by a new and living way opened for us through the curtain, that is, his body, and since we have a great high priest over the house of God, let us draw near to God with a sincere heart and with the full assurance that faith brings, having our hearts sprinkled to cleanse us from a guilty conscience and having our bodies washed with pure water" (Heb. 10:19–22).

The letter to the Hebrews was an early Christian sermon heralding the total sufficiency of Christ to deal with human sin. Here we have a command *to draw near to God* without reservation or hesitation. The author uses the imagery of the temple and the holy of holies, telling us to go behind the curtain, that barrier that separated the people from God's holy presence, where only Aaron and the high priests could go, and only once a year with blood. The author urges us to enter that place with confidence and a clear conscience. How? "By the blood of Jesus" (10:19).

The mention of blood would have brought back memories—fresh memories!—for the original Jewish Christian readers of this letter.

Blood filled their calendar. Each time they brought an animal to the temple for sacrifice, there was blood. And there was blood on the Day of Atonement each year.

Blood was a visual reminder for every Israelite, basic to their relationship with God. But the remarkable thing about all this blood is that it was never enough. This was probably *the* key point that God sought to teach Israel under the old covenant. It was like "playing pretend." The Bible calls these practices—the offering of sacrifices in the temple—shadows of the real thing. The priests offered sacrifices with blood for their own sins, for the place of sacrifice, and for the sins of the people—and then they did it again and again! When the high priest died, new priests picked up where he left off. The Scriptures taught that the problem of human sin is very great. But this system was like trying to duct tape a breach in Hoover Dam. It could not hold. And that was the point.

The inadequacy of the priesthood and the sacrificial system given through Moses is intentional. As the author of Hebrews reminds us, "The Holy Spirit was showing by this that the way into the Most Holy Place had not yet been disclosed as long as the first tabernacle was still functioning. This is an illustration for the present time, indicating that the gifts and sacrifices being offered were not able to clear the conscience of the worshiper" (Heb. 9:8–9). God *intended* that the old system would teach us this to prepare us for the sufficiency of the priesthood and sacrifice of Jesus the Messiah, our Great High Priest.

So what is different about Jesus' blood that makes it better than animal sacrifices? It *is* enough! Jesus, God the Son incarnate, sinless and fully human, "appeared once for all at the culmination of the ages to do away with sin by the sacrifice of himself" (9:26). His blood was enough because of *who* he is.

Consider how often the New Testament refers to Jesus' blood as shorthand for Jesus' substitutionary death for sins.

- "God presented Christ as a sacrifice of atonement, through the shedding of his blood—to be received by faith. He did this to demonstrate his righteousness" (Rom. 3:25).

- "Since we have now been justified by his blood, how much more shall we be saved from God's wrath through him!" (Rom. 5:9).
- "In him we have redemption through his blood, the forgiveness of sins, in accordance with the riches of God's grace that he lavished on us" (Eph. 1:7–8).
- "But now in Christ Jesus you who once were far away have been brought near by the blood of Christ" (Eph. 2:13).
- "For you know that it was not with perishable things such as silver or gold that you were redeemed from the empty way of life handed down to you from your ancestors, but with the precious blood of Christ, a lamb without blemish or defect" (1 Peter 1:18–19).
- "And they sang a new song, saying: 'You are worthy to take the scroll and to open its seals, because you were slain, and with your blood you purchased for God persons from every tribe and language and people and nation'" (Rev. 5:9).

These passages all affirm a common truth. We can now enter God's presence with confidence because of Jesus' blood. We don't deserve to be there, but Jesus' blood makes it possible. *Jesus is our Great High Priest.* He died in our place to provide "purification for sins," and he takes us with him as he enters the Father's presence (Heb. 1:3). As there is nothing between the Father and Son, so there is nothing between the Father and us, because we stand in faith-union with Christ. Indeed, "in him and through faith in him we may approach God with freedom and confidence" (Eph. 3:12). The blood of animals isn't enough to solve the problem of sin, but Jesus' blood is.

Jesus not only endures temptation in the wilderness, but he obeys his father "by becoming obedient to death—even death on a cross!" (Phil. 2:8). Jesus not only announces to the paralytic, "Your sins are forgiven," but he goes to the cross to pay for that man's sins and to satisfy all of God's righteous requirements for him. Jesus not only offers the woman at the well water leading to eternal life, but he makes that offer good by dying for her sins. Jesus not only sends the demons out of the demoniac, but he dies for the sins of his people to release them from the devil's grip forever.

As we reflect on the sufficiency of Jesus' work, we must never forget its true cost. The cup Jesus had to drink was the cup of God's wrath against our sin. He took our curse by "becoming a curse for us" (Gal. 3:13). There was no other way. Our triune God's righteous demands against our sin required the death of the Son in our place. No other solution would do (Luke 22:42).

This is the center of the Bible and of human history: the cross where Jesus died in our place. The Gospel authors made sure we would not miss this point. Of the thirty-three years of Jesus' life, the Gospels focus nearly half of their writing on the final week of his life. The entire shape of Matthew, Mark, and Luke is structured to move geographically from Galilee to Jerusalem in one long journey toward the cross (see Luke 9:51; Mark 8:31). In John's Gospel, John the Baptist announces Jesus' first appearance with these words: "Look, the Lamb of God, who takes away the sin of the world!" (John 1:29).

At the heart of the Bible is Jesus' saving work. At the heart of Jesus' saving work is his obedient life and sacrificial death. At the heart of Jesus' death is his representative substitution; Jesus died for sinners in our place. And at the heart of all of this is the love of God for sinners. Jesus took what we deserve, and he gives us what he deserves. Jesus obeyed where Adam disobeyed, and then imputes to us the perfect righteousness that is his. This truth can be summarized in a single sentence, as Paul does when he tells us that "God made him who had no sin to be sin for us, so that in him we might become the righteousness of God" (2 Cor. 5:21).

This is the most precious truth of Scripture, but it is not the last thing that Jesus did, for he did not remain dead in the tomb. Jesus is our prophet, who reveals God to us. He is our priest, who brings us to God. And he is our risen and exalted King, who rules for God.

Jesus Sits Down in Triumph

We need more than a prophet and a priest—we also need a king. *Jesus is our King*, the one who "sat down at the right hand of the Majesty in heaven" (Heb. 1:3). As our King, Jesus addresses the human problem of our need for a righteous ruler, an obedient servant-king.

Jesus was King over all of creation as the divine Son. In his incarnation, he was also born a king, although his enthronement as the messianic King did not occur until after his work was done at the cross and in his resurrection (Phil. 2:8–11). On the cross, Jesus was the King even though the crowds did not understand this. Ironically, the sign above the cross—King of the Jews—spoke the truth despite their cries to do away with him. Scripture repeatedly teaches that although Jesus was Son and Lord from birth, it was still necessary for him to do a work to become our Savior and King (Rom. 1:3–4). Why? Because before he takes his throne, he must defeat his enemies—sin, death, and the devil—on a cross as our covenant head (Phil. 2:6–11; Rev. 5:5–10).

No one who looked at Jesus hanging from a cross expected him to sit at God's right hand. Certainly, Satan didn't expect this. While the presence of Satan is relatively quiet after his big scene in Genesis 3, he is still there, working behind the scenes of the story. He stirs Cain's murderous heart, the violence in Noah's day, the design plans for the Tower of Babel, Pharaoh's stubborn will, and Saul's self-absorbed paranoia. He fuels the treachery of Israel's kings and the rise and fall of every nation that stands in opposition "against the LORD and against his anointed [Messiah]" (Ps. 2:2).

Yet from the earliest pages of the Bible, his end is determined, his downfall promised by God:

> I will put enmity between you and the woman,
>   and between your offspring and hers;
> he will crush your head,
>   and you will strike his heel.
>
> —GENESIS 3:15

There is a twist in this ancient conflict when Satan enters Judas to do the work of betraying Christ. While Jesus' disciples called him "Lord," Judas imitated the religious leaders in calling Jesus "Rabbi." What began as subtle disdain grew into something much worse when Judas colluded with the religious authorities to betray Christ. Judas took a bribe, and the religious leaders took Jesus to his cross, manipulating Roman authorities and leveraging the power of the state for their ends.

But things were not all as they appeared. Three days following his violent death, Jesus rose from the grave victorious over sin, death, and the devil himself. It was "by his death he might break the power of him who holds the power of death—that is, the devil—and free those who all their lives were held in slavery by their fear of death" (Heb. 2:14–17). Jesus turned the tables on Satan, using Satan's most wicked weapon against him. As the divine Son, Jesus has all authority, and as the incarnate, crucified, and risen Son, Jesus is granted authority over the unseen world and all demonic powers (Matt. 28:18).

How did Jesus' death win him victory over all of our enemies? Jesus defeated Satan by turning his own murder into our payment for sin, snatching us away from the devil's grip. Because he is the sacrificial priest-king who stands in our place and pays for our sin, he is also the victorious king *in his resurrection and exaltation:* "He forgave us all our sins, having canceled the charge of our legal indebtedness, which stood against us and condemned us; he has taken it away, nailing it to the cross. And having disarmed the powers and authorities, he made a public spectacle of them, triumphing over them by the cross" (Col. 2:13–15).

When Jesus nailed our debt to the cross, he disarmed Satan! The world searches for a solution to sin, guilt, disease, and death. Christians look to a cross. Because of his work, death has no power over him or us. "Do not be afraid. I am the First and the Last. I am the Living One; I was dead, and now look, I am alive for ever and ever! And I hold the keys of death and Hades" (Rev. 1:17–18). Jesus was a king in his birth, a king in his life, *and uniquely a king in his death*.

Of course, we need to remember the already/not yet nature of all that Jesus brings. Jesus has *already* defeated the devil by his death and resurrection. Satan's fate is sealed, yet he awaits a final day of judgment—a day that will certainly come as certain as Jesus' death and resurrection. Paul speaks about the end: "Then the end will come, when he hands over the kingdom to God the Father after he has destroyed all dominion, authority and power. For he must reign until he has put

all his enemies under his feet. The last enemy to be destroyed is death"
(1 Cor. 15:24–26).

This is what Jesus' resurrection and exaltation guarantee for us. The
divine Son who became man does a work that only he can do for us. After
Jesus was raised from the dead, he ascended to the Father's right hand,
and from this royal position he now reigns and rules over his people
and the world. We await his return from heaven as the King of Kings,
knowing that he will complete what he achieved in his first coming in
glorious, consummated fullness. With the church of all ages, we cry with
eager expectation, "Come, Lord Jesus" (Rev. 22:20).

Chapter 14

CHURCH

A People Full of the Spirit

ACTS AND THE NEW TESTAMENT EPISTLES

What comes to mind when you hear the word *church?* Perhaps you think of a building? Hopefully your thoughts about the church are positive. Maybe you had a childhood filled with wonderful experiences. For some people, though, the memories are not positive. Some see the church as an institution committed to good social causes, while others see it as an oppressive and backward organization. Opinions about the church vary widely, but the key question we need to ask is this: What did Jesus have in mind when he said, "I will build my church"? (Matt. 16:18). If this is *his* church, then we want to know what his purpose was in building it.

The identity of the church is directly tied to the identity of Jesus Christ. The church is what the church is because she is related to him. By virtue of Jesus' work as the great prophet, priest, and king, he brings about a new people who are in covenantal union with him. Anything the New Testament says about us is true because it is first said about him.

Here's what that means. If we are a *new humanity*, it's because we are in union with Christ, the last Adam and first man of the new creation. By his incarnation and work, Jesus is now our elder brother, and we have been adopted into God's family (Heb. 2:10–13). If we're a *true temple*, it's because we are in union with him as the true temple, and we are indwelled by the Spirit (Eph. 2:18–20; John 2:19–20). If we're a *royal priesthood*, it's because he is the Great High Priest, who has constituted us a kingdom of priests (1 Peter 2:9; Heb. 5–10). If we will rule and reign with him, it's because he is the king who by his obedient life, death, and resurrection has restored us to our image-bearing royal role (Heb. 2:5–18).

Jesus' identity transforms our identity because his work has transformed our relationship with the triune God. Jesus satisfied God's justice, and now we are justified. Jesus propitiated God's wrath, and now we're no longer enemies but adopted sons and daughters. And what is individually true of us as Christians is also corporately true of us as the church. Christ's work applied to us has both of these dimensions: an individual and corporate application.

In this chapter we'll investigate the creation of the church as God's corporate people by considering what, in God's glorious plan of redemption, the church is as his new covenant people. We'll discover how the work of Christ applies not only to individual believers but also to the church as a whole. We will look at a variety of biblical images that help us better understand the identity of the church—an identity bound up with Christ's identity.

In this period between Christ's two advents, the new creation is present in the church and in the lives of individual believers, but the fullness of the new creation has not yet arrived. We still await its consummated fullness when Christ returns. In this chapter we'll focus on the aspects of the new creation that God has already given, and in the next chapter we'll investigate what is still to come. Another way to think of this is that we will first study who we are as God's *people* before we turn to the *place* God has created for us at Christ's return in glory and power.

WIND AND FIRE

"What does it mean?" This was the question asked by the people in Jerusalem fifty days after Jesus was crucified. As Jews worldwide gathered to celebrate Pentecost, they saw and heard several things they could not explain. Here's how the Bible describes the events that took place: "Suddenly a sound like the blowing of a violent wind came from heaven and filled the whole house where they were sitting. They saw what seemed to be tongues of fire that separated and came to rest on each of them. All of them were filled with the Holy Spirit and began to speak in other tongues as the Spirit enabled them" (Acts 2:2–4).

Some were bewildered "because each one heard their own language being spoken" (2:6). They were amazed and astonished, saying, "Aren't all these who are speaking Galileans? Then how is it that each of us hears them in our native language? . . . we hear them declaring the wonders of God in our own tongues!" (2:7–11). Some mocked, saying they were drunk. But everyone asked the question, "What does this mean?" (2:12). They understood what they heard, but they didn't understand what it meant. People don't normally speak fluently in languages they don't know—especially rural, uneducated Galileans!

The sound of these diverse languages is one of the sounds that characterize the birth of the church. This was Pentecost, the annual festival celebrating the day God gave the Law to Moses at Sinai. Jesus' disciples stayed together in Jerusalem where, days earlier, Jesus had told them to wait for his Spirit. "Do not leave Jerusalem . . . but wait for the gift my Father promised . . . For John baptized with water, but in a few days you will be baptized with the Holy Spirit" (1:4–5).

The disciples were discouraged after Jesus' death, but after his resurrection they were greatly *encouraged*. When Jesus spoke of the Spirit, their sense of encouragement burst with expectation for the arrival of God's kingdom spoken of by the prophets. They asked, "Lord, are you at this time going to restore the kingdom to Israel?" (1:6). Jesus answered, "It is not for you to know the times or dates the Father has set by his own authority. But you will receive power when the Holy Spirit comes on you; and you will be my witnesses in Jerusalem, and in all Judea and Samaria, and to the ends of the earth.' After he said this, he was taken up before their very eyes, and a cloud hid him from their sight" (vv. 7–9).

The Spirit was the subject of Jesus' teaching in the days before his crucifixion. Jesus comforted his disciples with the promise that he would send his Spirit. He said, "It is for your good that I am going away" (John 16:7). Why? Because, "I will send [the Spirit] to you" (16:7). Jesus' departure is by way of the cross, forming the basis for the Spirit's new covenant work, predicted and anticipated by the prophets.

This is what Peter announced on Pentecost.

At the sound of these languages, he rose to explain what it all meant: "These people are not drunk, as you suppose. It's only nine in the morning! No, this is what was spoken by the prophet Joel: 'In the last days, God says, I will pour out my Spirit on all people. Your sons and daughters will prophesy, your young men will see visions, your old men will dream dreams. Even on my servants, both men and women, I will pour out my Spirit in those days, and they will prophesy . . . And everyone who calls on the name of the LORD will be saved'" (Acts 2:15–21).

Peter is telling the people that what they are hearing is the sound of Jesus Christ reigning from his throne! The crucified Jesus is now risen from the dead, seated at the Father's right hand, and from his throne has poured out the Spirit upon his people. This was the sound of God's new creation breaking into the world: first to individuals and then to constitute a new people, the church.

Remember that the word for "Spirit" is the same word for "wind," and in Scripture there is often an interplay with these different meanings. The "Spirit of God was hovering over the waters" at creation (Gen. 1:2). God "sent a wind over the earth" at its recreation after Noah's flood (8:1). Speaking of the Spirit's work to bring new birth, Jesus said, "The wind blows wherever it pleases. You hear its sound, but you cannot tell where it comes from or where it is going. So it is with everyone born of the Spirit" (John 3:8). Now, as the disciples gathered in Jerusalem, a sound "like the blowing of a violent wind" filled the house (Acts 2:2), and the church—God's new creation people—was born. The Spirit had come.

While all of this is good news, it terrified its first hearers. Remember, when Peter spoke, he spoke to those who crucified Jesus—and he didn't hold anything back: "[Jesus] was handed over to you by God's deliberate plan and foreknowledge; and you, with the help of wicked men, put him to death by nailing him to the cross. But God raised him from the dead . . . Exalted to the right hand of God, he has received from the Father the promised Holy Spirit and has poured out what you now see and hear . . . Therefore let all Israel be assured of this: God has made this Jesus, whom you crucified, both Lord and Messiah" (Acts 2:23–36).

We are told that those present were "cut to the heart" and asked, "What shall we do?" (Acts 2:37). Enormous guilt was met with extraordinary grace. Peter had more than an indictment; he also had an invitation: "Repent and be baptized, every one of you, in the name of Jesus Christ for the forgiveness of your sins. And you will receive the gift of the Holy Spirit. The promise is for you and your children and for all who are far off—for all whom the Lord our God will call" (2:38–39). Those who believed were baptized, numbering "three thousand" (2:41).

The description of the life of this earliest church is beautiful: "They devoted themselves to the apostles' teaching and to fellowship, to the breaking of bread and to prayer" (2:42). They "sold property and possessions" to meet one another's needs (2:45). They "broke bread in their homes and ate together with glad and sincere hearts, praising God and enjoying the favor of all the people. And the Lord added to their number daily those who were being saved" (2:46–47). This is the birth of the church—God's new covenant community and new creation people.

What began that day spread from Jerusalem to the ends of the earth as "the word of God spread" (6:7; 11:19; 12:24; 13:49; 19:20) and as the apostles "proclaimed the kingdom of God and taught about the Lord Jesus Christ—with all boldness and without hindrance!" (28:31, speaking of Paul).

A NEW PEOPLE FOR A NEW AGE

The creation of the church is a miracle of incomparable glory. Initially, we might compare it to the transformation of a caterpillar to a butterfly, but this fails to capture the truly miraculous nature of its formation. A more fitting comparison is to the work of God in speaking the universe into existence out of nothing. This is how the Bible describes it: "God, who said, 'Let light shine out of darkness,' made his light shine in our hearts to give us the light of the knowledge of God's glory displayed in the face of Christ" (2 Cor. 4:6). The triune God, who created the universe by his word, now creates new life through the word of the gospel.

What an amazing transformation this is! Humanly speaking, it's impossible to create anything out of nothing, and so the church is an *impossible* people. It is a spiritual community, making visible the invisible reality of God's purposes and promises. To get our minds around what God has done, we'll look at four transformations that make this impossible people possible, followed by two signs that make the invisible church visible.

Out with the Old, In with the New

With the coming of Christ, God's new creation came in *a person*. In the church, Christ's new creation has arrived as *a new people*. As Paul puts it, "If anyone is in Christ, the new creation has come: The old has gone, the new is here!" (2 Cor. 5:17). We know a great change has taken place, but what exactly is that change? Here are four transformations that make the church possible.

1. FROM DEATH IN ADAM TO LIFE IN CHRIST

Death is a tragic evil, an interruption of God's original purpose for humanity. And death is how the Bible describes our spiritual condition: "As for you, you were dead in your transgressions and sins" (Eph. 2:1). This is not a predicament, a pickle, a phase, or a rough patch. This is spiritual death, the root cause of our physical death. Thankfully, Paul tells us that death need not be the final word: "Because of his great love for us, God, who is rich in mercy, made us alive with Christ even when we were dead in transgressions—it is by grace you have been saved" (2:4–5). *In Christ, the church is a spiritually regenerated community.*

As the prophets looked to the future, they spoke of a transformed people—an entire community made new by an internal heart circumcision. Israel of old was God's people, but they were a mixed group. Within the covenant community were both believers and unbelievers—an "Israel within Israel"—but the new covenant community is different. It is *not* a "mixed" people, because in Christ the church is a regenerate community that people enter not by natural birth but by faith in Christ and the Spirit's work of new birth.

Ezekiel described Israel as a valley filled with dry, dead bones. Recall what the Lord said to them through his prophet: "Dry bones, hear the word of the LORD! . . . I will make breath enter you, and you will come to life" (Ezek. 37:4–5). Jesus alone can create this community. When Jesus said, "I am the resurrection and the life" (John 11:25), he was not merely saying that God would use him to raise several people from the dead. God had previously worked through Elijah and other prophets to raise people from the dead. In Christ, however, God now authorizes *all* resurrections. Death is defeated because Christ *alone* gives spiritual life.

Christ stands in complete and total contrast with Adam. Adam, the first man and head of the old creation, represents sin, rebellion, and death. Jesus, God the Son incarnate and the head of the new creation, represents obedience, life, and resurrection power (Rom. 5:18–19). As in Adam all die, so in Christ is life, the forgiveness of sin, righteousness, and the Spirit (Rom. 5:12–21; 8:1–17).

2. FROM ETHNIC HOSTILITY TO INTERNATIONAL UNITY

In addition to giving us new, spiritual life, the gospel neutralizes our toxic relationships, creating peace between diverse peoples. In our sin we turn our differences—education, wealth, physical ability, ethnicity—into reasons for alienation from one another. We don't merely exclude one another; we enslave, reject, and even murder one another based on our differences. Human beings are proud. We have a hard time getting along, and this is what the gospel reverses. The church is a display of God's power to raise the dead, but it is also a display of God's power and wisdom to reconcile alienated people (Eph. 3:1–13). We can say to one another, "As there is nothing between us and God, so there is nothing between us." *In Christ, the church is a new, reconciled humanity.*

Nowhere is this more profoundly seen than in the uniting of Jews and gentiles. Gentiles, according to Paul, were "called 'uncircumcised' by those who call themselves 'the circumcision,'" and "separate from Christ, excluded from citizenship in Israel and foreigners to the covenants of the promise" (Eph. 2:11–12). As such, they were "without hope and without God in the world" (2:12). The Jewish term *uncircumcision* is derogatory. God gave Abraham circumcision to distinguish his covenant people from the nations, but for many Israelites, circumcision became an excuse to harbor deep hatred toward the gentiles. Jews spoke of gentiles as fuel for the fires of hell, they forbade one another even from helping a gentile woman to give birth lest they aid in bringing a gentile into the world, and they held funerals for Jewish children who married into gentile families. The division was profound. The Jews hated gentile nations![4]

Of course, one reason for this was the hostility of the gentiles toward the Jewish people. Pharaoh and the Canaanites fought Israel despite evidence of the Lord's power and favor toward Israel. As Psalm 2 graphically illustrates, the nations and her kings "rage" against God and his Messiah. The Jews, however, were guilty of an additional sin that led to this hostility: their spiritual pride. This is one reason Paul refers to the Mosaic Law as "the dividing wall of hostility" (Eph. 2:14). The Law-covenant was God-given and intended to separate Israel from the nations for her own purity and preservation. The goal of the Law was for Israel to be a light to the gentiles, that through her the Messiah would come to bring salvation to the nations. But in her pride Israel took what was good and misused the Law as a means of justifying herself before God and as an excuse to hate the nations. The Law exposed Israel's sin and revealed in a greater way the hideous nature of the human heart.

Some aspects of the Law-covenant put gentiles at a real disadvantage. They were separated from God's national people and covenant promises. The very construction of the temple reflected this truth.[5] The Jerusalem temple built by Herod consisted of a series of layered spaces representing closeness to and alienation from God. Immediately around the temple was the court of the priests. East was the court of Israel and then the court of women. These three courts were on the same elevation as the temple itself. From here, four steps down, was a walled platform, and then on the other side of that wall were fourteen more steps down to another wall, and beyond that wall was the court of the gentiles. Gentiles could see the temple, but they couldn't approach it. Simply put, as gentiles, they were "without hope" and were "without God in the world" (Eph. 2:12).

But in Christ, all of this is changed. Jews and gentiles are reconciled, and gentiles who were "far away have been brought near by the blood of Christ" (2:13). Christ, who is "our peace," "has made the two groups one and has destroyed the barrier, the dividing wall of hostility, by setting aside in his flesh the law with its commands and regulations" (2:14–15). For what purpose? "His purpose was to create in himself one new humanity out of the two, thus making peace, and in one body to reconcile both of them to God through the cross, by which he put to death their hostility" (2:15–16).

Isaiah promised, "Peace, peace, to those far and near" (Isa. 57:19). He imagined a day when the indescribably opposed people of Egypt, Assyria, and Israel would join in the worship of God (Isa. 19:19–25). Jesus brings that peace, and *he* makes that people.

This work of reconciling Jews and gentiles into one community—the church—raised numerous questions, especially for Jewish believers who had lived their entire lives under the Law. Should gentiles have to keep the Law? One group, the Judaizers, insisted that gentiles, to follow Christ, must be circumcised and obey the entire Law-covenant to be saved (Acts 15:5). But the apostles rejected this view. Based on Scripture, they concluded that the salvation of gentiles was proof that God's promises were now fulfilled in Christ and his new covenant people (13–18). Christians, whether Jew or gentile, are not "under the law" but instead are a *new humanity* "under the law of Christ" (1 Cor. 9:21 ESV). Equally and without distinction, Jewish and gentile believers are one people, inheritors of all of God's promises in Christ Jesus (Gal. 3:26–29).

Under the old covenant, Israel was defined by its genealogical association with Abraham, yet this was not an absolute or enduring principle. It wasn't absolute because the history of Abraham's descendants showcases several gentiles who became Jews, as we see in the case of Rahab and Ruth. And it wasn't an enduring principle because God had originally promised that he intended to bring salvation to the nations through Abraham. As Paul writes, "Those who have faith are children of Abraham" (Gal. 3:7). Is this a reinterpretation of God's original intent in his promises to Abraham? Not at all. Paul continues, explaining God's intention in the promise to Abraham: "Scripture foresaw that God would justify the Gentiles by faith, and announced the gospel in advance to Abraham:

'All nations will be blessed through you.' So those who rely on faith are blessed along with Abraham, the man of faith" (3:8–9).

But weren't God's promises to Abraham *uniquely* for his physical offspring? Again, Paul clarifies God's intention: "The promises were spoken to Abraham and his seed. Scripture does not say 'and to seeds,' meaning many people, but 'and to your seed,' meaning one person, who is Christ . . . There is neither Jew nor Gentile, neither slave nor free, nor is there male and female, for you are all one in Christ Jesus. If you belong to Christ, then you are Abraham's seed, and heirs according to the promise" (3:16, 28–29).

This is instructive for us as we ask the question, Who are the *true* children of Abraham? Paul's answer is that from the very beginning God intended his people to be those who share the faith of Abraham *and* who are united to the *true* seed of Abraham—Christ. The church is God's *new covenant* community, a *new humanity*, *international* in scope, composed of believers who regardless of their ethnicity are Abraham's true children by faith in Jesus.

3. FROM ABOMINATION TO HOLY NATION

The Law-covenant could not cleanse the conscience or secure the full forgiveness of sin. Nor could it make disobedient people obedient. God never intended it to do so. In his plan, the old covenant had multiple purposes: to demonstrate God's grace; to unveil how God would ultimately save; to reveal to Israel the depth of her sin; and to function as a "guardian until Christ came that we might be justified by faith" (Gal. 3:24). Jesus, the one to whom the Law pointed, purifies our consciences by removing our guilt, and he writes the law on our hearts by the Spirit in such a way that we can now obey from the heart. *In Christ, the church is a purified community.*

Consider this description of the church: "You are a chosen people, a royal priesthood, a holy nation, God's special possession, that you may declare the praises of him who called you out of darkness into his wonderful light" (1 Peter 2:9).

Before Christ, disobedience reigned, but now, in Christ, his people are "holy," no longer walking in darkness but in the light. In Peter's description of the church, it now takes on the role of Israel under the old covenant. Previously, it was Israel who was "a kingdom of priests and a holy nation" (Ex. 19:6), but now that same language is applied to the church. Why? Because in Christ we are transformed and can now live as God created Adam and Israel to live. We "no longer live as the Gentiles do," for we are "taught in [Christ]" to "put off [our] old self" and "put on the new self, created to be like God in true righteousness and holiness" (Eph. 4:17, 21–24).

4. FROM COSMIC REBELS TO HEAVENLY ROYALTY

In Adam, humanity is a gang of cosmic rebels. The prophets spoke of a coming kingdom, and in Christ, we have switched kingdoms. Paul describes our salvation in royal terms: "The Father . . . has qualified you to share in the inheritance of his holy people in the kingdom of light. For he has rescued us from the dominion of darkness and brought us into the kingdom of the Son he loves" (Col. 1:12–13). We are joint heirs with Christ, seated with him in the heavenly places. Jesus is seated at God's right hand, and united to him, we now begin to participate in his reign even as we await his return (3:1–3). *In Christ, the church is a royal people.*

In Christ, our royal function is restored, although we still await our glorification. Jesus, God's Son, has come into this world to restore us to what God created us to be in the first place (Heb. 2:5–18). No wonder Paul marvels that God's "intent was that now, through the church, the manifold wisdom of God should be made known to the rulers and authorities in the heavenly realms, according to his eternal purpose that he accomplished in Christ Jesus our Lord" (Eph. 3:10–11).

What Makes the Church Visible?

We have considered four transformations that make the church possible. But these invisible and spiritual transformations need visible expression.

In this section, we will consider the two new signs for God's new covenant salvation: baptism and the Lord's Supper. These signs make the church visible. For a contemporary example, wedding rings don't make two people married; the public vows and promises they make to each other establish the marriage. But the rings serve as visible reminders of those realities and promises. The symbols remind them of *who* they are and tell the world where their allegiance and affections lie.

As covenant signs, baptism and the Lord's Supper are two ways we reenact the gospel.

BAPTISM

Baptism is an initiation sign and rite. In some traditions, walking an aisle or raising a hand can serve as a sign of initial conversion, yet if we're not careful, such visual and public expressions can replace God's ordained sign: baptism.

Baptism is a symbol of our faith-union in Christ and marks our entry into the new covenant community. In much the same way a husband can speak of "that day when I put the ring on her finger" as shorthand for marriage, the New Testament speaks of baptism as shorthand for our conversion.

The word *baptism* is a transliteration of a Greek word, *baptizō*. Baptism first appears when we read of John the Baptist baptizing men and women ahead of Jesus' arrival. In this context, it is a sign of preparation and repentance. Through his own baptism by John, Jesus began his public ministry by identifying with his people as their covenant-mediator (Matt. 3:13–16). After his resurrection, Jesus commissioned his disciples to take the gospel to the ends of the earth. As a sign of union with Christ, under the lordship of the triune God, Jesus commanded his people to "go and make disciples of all nations, baptizing them in the name of the Father and of the Son and of the Holy Spirit" (28:19).

If covenant signs are deliberate, then what does baptism signify? The rainbow is a sign that God has put down his war bow; never again will he judge the earth with a flood as he did in Noah's day (Gen. 9:15). Circumcision was an outward sign to show that Abraham's seed was set apart from the nations as God's holy, priestly people, and that outward symbol pointed toward the inward reality the Lord ultimately required of them. Baptism, as a sign of the new covenant, signifies our *union with Christ*.

We can think of baptism's significance in four directions. First, baptism points *backward* to the death, burial, and resurrection of Jesus. As Paul put it, when we were "baptized into Christ Jesus [we] were baptized into his death," which means we were "buried with him through baptism into death in order that, just as Christ was raised from the dead through the glory of the Father, we too may live a new life" (Rom. 6:3–4).

Second, baptism points *forward* to the day when we stand secure before God's judgment throne. Think about how Noah and his family were saved from the torrents of God's judgment that killed every other living person on earth. Peter tells us that "water symbolizes baptism that now saves you also" (1 Peter 3:21). Unless Jesus returns, every Christian will face death, but Christians will not face negative judgment when they meet God, for Jesus has taken that judgment for them. Baptism pictures the safe passage of Christians from death to new life in a new creation through resurrection.

A third direction explains how this safe passage is possible. Baptism points to an *inward* reality. Peter goes on to tell us that baptism saves "not [by] the removal of dirt from the body but the pledge of a clear conscience toward God. It saves you by the resurrection of Jesus Christ, who has gone into heaven and is at God's right hand" (3:21–22). How does baptism picture the cleansing of our consciences? Paying careful attention to Paul's words, we can see that baptism pictures more than Jesus' death and resurrection. It pictures our own death and resurrection with him—our union with Christ. "We were therefore buried with him," Paul wrote, "into [his] death" (Rom. 6:4). As we are "united with him in a death like his," so too "we will certainly also be united with him in a resurrection like his" (6:5).

Our covenantal union with Christ yields profound *outward* changes in our lives as well. For, as Paul continued, "our old self was crucified with him" so that "we should no longer be slaves to sin" (6:6). Our union with Christ utterly transforms our lives, for "the death he died, he died to sin once for all; but the life he lives, he lives to God. In the same way, count yourselves dead to sin but alive to God in Christ Jesus. Therefore, do not let sin reign in your mortal body so that you obey its evil desires"

(6:10–12). We have passed from one realm of existence to another, from death to life, and it shows.

Baptism is also an outward public witness to one's identification with Christ and his people. It's God's chosen initiation rite whereby Christians are *identified* as Christians. This public component comes with a cost, because being baptized means counting Christ's public humiliation on the cross as our personal hope for eternal life. In the first century this act was an unmistakable statement of allegiance to Christ.

THE LORD'S SUPPER

Baptism is a one-time symbol signifying Christian conversion. God's people repeat the Lord's Supper as a symbol of ongoing allegiance to Christ. Our Lord gave his disciples this meal on the eve of his crucifixion, which was also the occasion of the Passover—the Jewish celebration remembering God's deliverance of Israel from Egypt by a "Passover" sacrifice. Jesus gives us a *new* meal to remember a new and greater deliverance: from sin, death, and hell.

> When the hour came, Jesus and his apostles reclined at the table. And he said to them, "I have eagerly desired to eat this Passover with you before I suffer. For I tell you, I will not eat it again until it finds fulfillment in the kingdom of God." After taking the cup, he gave thanks and said, "Take this and divide it among you. For I tell you I will not drink again from the fruit of the vine until the kingdom of God comes." And he took bread, gave thanks and broke it, and gave it to them, saying, "This is my body given for you; do this in remembrance of me." In the same way, after the supper he took the cup, saying, "This cup is the new covenant in my blood, which is poured out for you."
>
> —LUKE 22:14–21

By speaking of a *new covenant* in his blood, Jesus explicitly interpreted the meaning of his life and death as fulfilling everything that God had promised in the Prophets. Jesus is our Passover Lamb who dies in our place.

What is the meaning of the Lord's Supper? Like baptism, the Lord's Supper points us in four directions. First, the Lord's Supper reminds us to look *backward* in remembrance of Jesus' death, his body broken and his blood shed for us. We are a forgetful people! Yet in God's kindness, this symbol fixes our hearts and minds on the object of our faith, Jesus. Second, the Lord's Supper reminds us to look *forward*. As Jesus instituted the Supper, he said that he would not eat it again "until the kingdom of God comes" and he returns in glory. Third, in instructing the early church in the proper use of the Lord's Supper, Paul spoke to the *inward* aspect of the sign: "So then, whoever eats the bread or drinks the cup of the Lord in an unworthy manner will be guilty of sinning against the body and blood of the Lord. Everyone ought to examine themselves before they eat of the bread and drink from the cup" (1 Cor. 11:27–28). Fourth, the Lord's Supper reminds us to look *outward*. As we partake, we bear witness to the gospel. Paul states it this way: "Whenever you eat this bread and drink this cup, you proclaim the Lord's death until he comes" (11:26).

We must mention one more direction that applies to both signs. Baptism and the Lord's Supper, as received by Christians, also have an *upward* look. They are acts of worship that please the Lord and are a means of grace to help us grow in Christ.

THE CHURCH IN CAPTIVATING BEAUTY

The church is what she is because Jesus is who he is. Just as Jesus is a savior with unsearchable riches, so the church is a people of unsearchable beauty. Describing her is like describing a brilliant wedding dress—its patterns, textures, shape. All of these facets combine to make a captivating presentation. In this section, we will pull on eight threads from the Bible's story to describe the church.

The Bible's thematic strands—types and patterns—unfold through the covenants. But when these themes are viewed through the prism of the gospel, a rainbow of color is visible, giving us a picture of the church in its full, God-ordained beauty. Just as each Christian receives his or her identity from Christ, the church is the corporate expression of that identity. May her beauty captivate us as we make these connections, from the identity of Jesus, to the Christian, and then to the church.

We Are Christ's Radiant Bride

Here's how much joy the Lord has over his church: "As a young man marries a young woman, so will your Builder marry you; as a bridegroom rejoices over his bride, so will your God rejoice over you" (Isa. 62:5). The Lord said that through the prophet Isaiah. How much does our bridegroom love his people? We need only to look at the cross. For it was on the cross that "Christ loved the church and gave himself up for her to make her holy, cleansing her by the washing with water through the word, and to present her to himself as a radiant church, without stain or wrinkle or any other blemish, but holy and blameless" (Eph. 5:25–27).

The cross was horrific, but it revealed the depth and strength of Jesus' love for his bride. He was the bridegroom come for his bride, and he would take her away to be with him at any cost (Matt. 9:15; Rev. 19:7; 21:2).

As his bride, we look forward to the day when all of heaven will say, "Let us rejoice and be glad and give him glory! For the wedding of the Lamb has come, and his bride has made herself ready. Fine linen, bright and clean, was given her to wear" (Rev. 19:7–8). These fine linens are the righteous deeds of the church that we perform in this age as we ready ourselves to meet our groom face to face.

Jesus is the bridegroom, *every Christian* his treasured possession, and *the church* is his people pursued, purified, and presented to him in splendor.

We Are Family in Christ

In a healthy family, children feel safe with Mom and Dad. It doesn't matter where they are—a place familiar or unfamiliar, a deep forest or a busy street corner. Children trust that things will be okay if their parents are with them. To comfort suffering Christians, Paul tells us that we are part of the family. Writing of our adoption, he says, "The Spirit you received brought about your adoption to sonship. And by him we cry,

'Abba, Father.' The Spirit himself testifies with our spirit that we are God's children. Now if we are children, then we are heirs—heirs of God and co-heirs with Christ" (Rom. 8:15–17).

In the gospel, Jesus calls us brothers and sisters. This isn't an informal gesture or something nice to encourage us. It's an actual relational commitment, a matter of our eternal identification and comfort (Heb. 2:10–11). By adoption, every Christian inherits every blessing that is in Christ.

This love shapes our relationships with one another as brothers and sisters in his family. Consider the simplicity and depth of these words: "Follow God's example . . . as dearly loved children and walk in the way of love, just as Christ loved us and gave himself up for us as a fragrant offering and sacrifice to God" (Eph. 5:1–2). Together, we are joint heirs with Christ, our elder brother, and we are objects of the Father's eternal protection, his perfect discipline, and his tender love (Heb. 12:4–13).

Jesus is the Son of God, *every Christian* is an adoptive son or daughter, and *the church* is the family of God, a people adopted as sons and daughters through union with Jesus Christ.

We Are a Living Temple

Made with real stones, the temple was a concrete experience—God's people could see it and touch it. Layers of access, systems of sacrifice, elaborate furniture, and the detailed clothing for the priests all signaled that this was a special place. The temple's imagery was reminiscent of Eden, but the temple with its structure and systems could not return us to Eden. As glorious as the temple was, it also had limited access to God's covenantal presence, and it served as a daily reminder that access into the Most Holy Place was not yet a reality (Heb. 9:1–10). As it reminded the people of Eden, it also reminded them of the problem of sin that ever stands between God and us.

Consider these words from the apostle Peter to first-century Christians: "As you come to him, the living Stone—rejected by humans but chosen by God and precious to him—you also, like living stones, are being built into a spiritual house to be a holy priesthood, offering spiritual sacrifices acceptable to God through Jesus Christ" (1 Peter 2:4–5; cf. 1 Cor. 6:19–20; Eph. 2:19–22). Jesus' death tore the temple curtain in two, signifying that the way to God's presence was now open (Matt. 27:51).

Jesus is the cornerstone, *every Christian* is a stone for his temple, and *the church* is the temple, stones joined together for the place of God's presence.

We Are Members of Christ's Body

We all have a body. If the temple feels like an ancient image, something that few of us can relate to today, the imagery of a body is always relevant. The New Testament authors often pull in the image of a body to describe the church. By nature, a body represents unity in diversity because many different parts work together to form a coherent organism. Each part of the body, however big or small, serves and depends on the rest of the body. This image reminds us that each of us is needed. It also puts us in our place, since we are also needy and dependent on others (Rom. 12:3).

Just as a body is an organism ordered and led by its head, so the church is a covenant people ordered and led by its head, Christ. He is its source and its goal! As we "[speak] the truth in love, we will grow to become in every respect the mature body of him who is the head, that is, Christ. From him the whole body, joined and held together by every supporting ligament, grows and builds itself up in love, as each part does its work" (Eph. 4:15–16).

Jesus is our head and Lord, *every Christian* is a uniquely functioning body part, and *the church* is Christ's body, a people united to him by faith and joined together, growing into maturity in him.

We Are Christ's Flock

Unless you live on a farm or were born into a family of shepherds, you've probably had little to no contact with sheep. Each animal has its distinct qualities, but the Lord has identified his people as *sheep*. Why sheep? For several reasons. Sheep are vulnerable, undiscerning, and easy prey. But the Lord, like a shepherd, is both tender and tough in his leadership. One of the Bible's most famous psalms begins this way: "The LORD is my shepherd, I lack nothing. He makes me lie down in green pastures, he leads me beside quiet waters, he refreshes my soul. He guides me along the right paths for his name's sake" (Ps. 23:1–3). Sheep don't lie down unless they are secure, untroubled, and fed. Such is the care our shepherd has for us. He knows us by name and leads us. These pastures are not pastures for the stomach but pastures for the soul, and so even though we walk "through the darkest valley," we have nothing to fear, for he is with us (23:4).

It's no surprise that in the Old Testament, Israel's false priests and kings were described as wicked shepherds who abandoned or even ate their sheep (Ezek. 34:1–10). The Lord would come for his sheep, they would hear his voice, and he would lead them (34:11–25). When Jesus said, "I am the good shepherd" (John 10:11), he was making a claim. He is the Lord come for his sheep, the Davidic king and shepherd (11–18). Today, Jesus' shepherding care for his flock is expressed through the appointment of undershepherds (1 Tim. 3:1–7). This is where we get the term *pastor* (1 Peter 5:1–4). Pastors "shepherd" their people, leading them according to Christ's Word, not under compulsion but willingly.

Jesus is the good shepherd, *every Christian* is his sheep, and *the church* is his flock, a people led by the Chief Shepherd and by undershepherds he appoints.

We Are Outposts of Christ's Kingdom

The word used for "church" in the New Testament is *ekklēsia*, a common word for a gathering or assembly. This term was applied to Israel under the old covenant and the church under the new, highlighting the continuity of the one people of God. But as it's applied to the church, it speaks not only of the one people of God through time and scattered across the earth but also of our participation in the heavenly Jerusalem now. Wherever God's people are on earth, they now gather as local outposts of the heavenly Jerusalem to which we belong (Heb. 12:22–24).

Christ is the King who has risen and taken his throne, and his people meet as an embassy of his kingdom on earth. After the church was born at Pentecost, they gave themselves to the teaching of the apostles, to sharing in the Lord's Supper, and to prayer (Acts 2:42–47). As the old covenant community set aside the last day of the week as a Sabbath, the new covenant community gathered on the first day of the week, the Lord's Day.

Jesus is the King, *every Christian* is his subject, and *the church* is his new assembly, a people gathered in his name, an outpost of the new creation living on earth and awaiting the consummation of the age.

We Are Christ's Ambassadors

After Jesus' burial, he rose from the grave, the victorious Savior and King over death. Furthermore, after Jesus rose, he ascended to heaven and was seated on his throne. As a result of his work, all authority in heaven and on earth was given to him as the Messiah. Yet before he ascended, he addressed his disciples with these words: "All authority in heaven and on earth has been given to me. Therefore go and make disciples of all nations, baptizing them in the name of the Father and of the Son and of the Holy Spirit, and teaching them to obey everything I have commanded you. And surely I am with you always, to the very end of the age" (Matt. 28:18–20).

In that moment, Jesus extended his royal authority to his disciples for a mission with a message to proclaim. While the church gathered is an embassy of Christ in this world, the church scattered is a team of ambassadors representing Christ wherever they go. More than representing Christ, they speak for him with his message of salvation. This is what Paul had in mind when he wrote that God "reconciled us to himself through Christ and gave us the ministry of reconciliation . . . We are therefore Christ's ambassadors, as though God were making his appeal through us" (2 Cor. 5:18–20). In fulfillment of Isaiah's promise, Jesus is the light of the world, and by extension, his church is the light of the world, a city on a hill for salvation to all who see and believe (Isa. 60:1–6; Matt. 5:14–16).

Jesus is the Savior and Victor, *every Christian* is his messenger, and *the church* is his team of ambassadors, a people sent with his message to the ends of the earth.

We Are Christ's Exiles

As God's new creation people, a new humanity, ambassadors of the King, and an outpost of heaven on earth, the church is never fully at home in this fallen world. The church exists as sojourners and strangers in a world that is passing away, awaiting the new creation yet to come. If you have ever traveled to a foreign country where the language and customs are unfamiliar, you may know something of what it's like to be a stranger in a foreign land.

That's what it's like to be a Christian as we await the coming of Christ. Although God's saving reign in Christ has arrived, until Jesus returns there is an overlap of the ages. The new age has dawned, but the old era of sin and death remains. Our identification is with Christ, and we are no longer in Adam. We have been transferred from the kingdom of this world to the kingdom of Christ, yet until Christ's kingdom comes in its fullness, we remain strangers in the world (John 17:15–19).

When Peter addressed his readers, he called them "foreigners and exiles" (1 Peter 2:11). As exiles, we take comfort as we remember those who were exiles before us. Many before us died in faith, but "they did not receive the things promised; they only saw them and welcomed them from a distance, admitting that they were foreigners and strangers on earth" (Heb. 11:13).

We, however, not only look back to those who were exiles before us and follow their example by trusting all of God's promises but also have greater confidence because Christ has come and will come again. Even now, as we await the consummation of the age, we begin to live as God's new creation, knowing that the finality of our inheritance is certain. As Paul wrote, "Our citizenship is in heaven. And we eagerly await a Savior from there, the Lord Jesus Christ" (Phil. 3:20). The more faithfully we wait together, the more ready we will be.

Jesus is reigning in heaven, *every Christian* is a stranger in this age, and *the church* is a community of Christ's exiles who now participate in Christ's reign.

Chapter 15

NEW CREATION

A World Full of God's Glory

REVELATION

At the end of your life, the things you do—those habits that rise to the surface when you are medicated and lying in a hospital—can reveal a great deal about who you are. Two things marked Dave Steele, a dear friend of Trent's. First, as he was lying in his hospital bed, Dave would fish. He would "cast" his sheets, tie jigs, and report on his fishing trips: "Wasn't that a great trip with the Lord!" Second, Dave would preach. He would quote verses from the book of Revelation, hold up his hands as if holding a Bible, and shout, "This is how it's going to be!" It's been said that "the best moment of a Christian's life is his last one, because it is the one that is nearest heaven."[6] That proved true for Dave.

As we have raised them, our children have often asked us what heaven is like. There are a few ways to answer that question based on what we learn in the Scriptures. We can answer by pointing out the centrality of God in heaven: "Well, how much of the sea is covered by water? That's how much the glory of God will cover the earth! 'For the earth will be filled with the knowledge of the glory of the LORD as the waters cover the sea'" (Hab. 2:14). While this is good news, it's not specific. What makes it difficult to answer when children ask is that where the Bible *does* get specific, it's usually cryptic, especially when we turn to the book of Revelation. Despite the cryptic nature of some of the descriptions we find here, though, Revelation offers us some of the best insights about heaven. We just need to read them and interpret them carefully. One helpful place to learn about heaven in Scripture is Revelation 21–22. John gives us a glorious vision of "a new heaven and a new earth," a vision that beautifully concludes the Bible's story (Rev. 21:1).

First, let's review some things we've already learned. We know that the Lord Jesus Christ is the first man of the new creation and that he has inaugurated the new creation by his redemptive work. By Christ's life, death, resurrection, and the pouring out of the Spirit, the new creation is here in us as individuals and in the church as his corporate people. But we still await something more.

The new creation has come *in a person* in Jesus. In the church it has come *in a people*. Now we await its consummation *in a place*.

When Christ returns, what he inaugurated he will complete, and the whole earth will be filled with the glory of the triune God. When Christ returns in majestic power, he will completely transform and renew this world and create a new creation (Matt. 24:29–31; 2 Peter 3:10–13). Words cannot fully exhaust the beauty and glory of that final age, but God has given us words that faithfully capture something of it.

It should not surprise us to find that, in describing something of the reality of the new creation, God has chosen to employ a unique genre of writing suited for such otherworldly descriptions. We'll get to the vision of the new creation and what it means before this chapter is over. But before we jump into that and experience the sights, sounds, and tastes of heaven, we need to talk about the book of Revelation and how to read it properly.

PERFECT WORDS FOR A PERFECT WORLD

Most readers are confident that they will never fully understand the book of Revelation. Admittedly, Revelation is one of the more difficult books to understand. There is nothing quite like it in current literature. It contains dragons, angels, beasts, and locusts with human faces. While all of this sounds strange to our ears, this kind of literature was common for its original readers. And in keeping with his wise purposes, God chose to use *this* literary form to unveil Christ's glory and the glory that awaits us.

The Book of Revelation Is for You

Much of Revelation is difficult to understand, but the apostle John gives us an important clue to understanding the book when he opens with these clear words: "The revelation from Jesus Christ, which God gave him to show his servants what must soon take place. He made it known by sending his angel to his servant John, who testifies to everything he saw—that is, the word of God and the testimony of Jesus Christ. Blessed is the one who reads aloud the words of this prophecy, and blessed are those who hear it and take to heart what is written in it, because the time is near" (Rev. 1:1–3).

Notice a few things in what John writes. He says that this book is "the *revelation* from Jesus Christ." As a "revelation," or "unveiling," it's intended to be understood. This means that we must not approach the book as if God is hiding things from us. God gave us the book of Revelation to reveal truth and to encourage the church to remain faithful as we live between Christ's two advents.

The risen and exalted Christ says that he gave this revelation for "*his servants.*" The first servants who received this book were the "seven churches" that John mentions in the following verse (1:4) and that we read about in chapters 2–3. Look at how Jesus ends each letter to these first-century churches: "Whoever has ears, let them hear what the Spirit says to the churches" (2:7, etc.). Not only is this "revelation" given to encourage and warn these churches, but by extension it is also given to us. The threat of death from Rome was real for the early church, but the beast who stood behind Rome, Satan himself, is at work in our day just as well. Revelation is for *all* of God's people, in every era, as we await Christ's return.

John also tells us *why* this revelation was given: "to show his servants what must soon take place" (1:1). Our Lord doesn't want us stumbling around in the dark. He says that he's going to show us "the things" (1:1 ESV) that must take place to remind us that our triune God is on his throne and working out his sovereign purposes in every event of history.

John also tells us the book's kind of literature or literary form (genre). He says that Jesus "*made it known* by sending his angel to his servant John."

"Made it known" can also be translated as "signified." This is a book of *symbols*. John received a vision from Christ, mediated by angels, and this vision is written in a literary form that the original readers were familiar with, called apocalyptic literature. The last thing we learn from these initial verses is that Revelation is *to bless* those who *hear it* and *keep it*, believe it and obey it. Ultimately, this is what God wants from us as we study this book: to hear it, to obey it, and to have greater confidence in our sovereign God, who is working out all his good and glorious purposes in Christ.

Symbolic, Beautiful, and True

Apocalyptic literature is also found in the Old Testament. The book of Daniel is another example of this literary form, one that was popular in the time immediately preceding and following the time of Christ. The original readers would have understood its symbolism and message.

For us today the experience of reading apocalyptic literature is most similar to reading science fiction. The key difference is that apocalyptic literature gives us a symbolic universe that *points to and interprets reality as it is*. Science fiction is fiction; apocalyptic writings found in the Bible convey truth about reality and God. We must read Revelation with the background of the first-century world in view, yet as we read, we discover that it is God's truth for the church in every age. Revelation pulls back the veil of this world to show us God on his throne and the spiritual battle that is at work in the world. It does so with symbolism that is beautiful, awesome, and true.

Revelation, in its own unique way, gives us a glorious vision of the new creation to come. This vision is rooted in Old Testament imagery, and it leads us to imagine a world beyond our greatest imagination. We must exercise caution *not* to read Revelation like a historical narrative, such as we might find in the history books or the Gospels. At the same time, Revelation is a book written for the church in *every* age. It is prophetic, narrative in form, and full of symbols.

This literary form has six unique features. Since apocalyptic literature is unfamiliar, we'll compare it to six things that *are* familiar. Our goal is to learn how to "correctly handl[e] the word of truth" (2 Tim. 2:15).

1. *Apocalyptic literature is like an onion.* Books written in this genre have many layers.[7] In the textual layer we have the inspired and God-given text Jesus ensured John would write. We read about a slain lamb on the throne, for example. The visionary layer is what John actually saw: a slain lamb on a throne. The referent layer is the reality represented in what John saw. John may see a lamb in his vision, and that lamb is Christ. Yet Christ isn't a physical lamb. Finally, there's the significance layer. That Christ is pictured as a lamb on the throne means that his victory and rule were established through his substitutionary death.

2. *Apocalyptic literature is like a comic book.* When I [Trent] was a kid, my dad would say, "I swear someone from my office writes *Dilbert*." What did he mean? Was there a talking dog in his office? No. Good comics interpret the world. The reason we "get" them is that they "get" us. Comics are unreal, yet profoundly true. In a comic book, we find extravagant pictures, characters, and stories with development. Consider now how John describes Jesus: "The hair on his head was white like wool, as white as snow, and his eyes were like blazing fire. His feet were like bronze glowing in a furnace, and his voice was like the sound of rushing waters. In his right hand he held seven stars, and coming out of his mouth was a sharp, double-edged sword. His face was like the sun shining in all its brilliance" (1:14–16). Christ sees everything perfectly. He's majestic. He speaks a sure word. He is the radiant image and glory of God. In an allegory, there is no textually derived relation between the symbol and the thing symbolized. But in apocalyptic writings there are real historical and contextual clues for interpreting its symbolic imagery. For example, John writes, "Grace and peace to you from him who is, and who was, and who is to come, and from the seven spirits before his throne, and from Jesus Christ, who is the faithful witness, the firstborn from the dead, and the ruler of the kings of the earth" (1:4–5). Seven is a number of completion. In creation, there were seven days. It's like our number ten. Ten fingers. Ten toes. Seven spirits means the one and only Spirit of God.

3. *Apocalyptic literature is like surround sound.* The subwoofer emits a different sound from the right, left, or back speakers. Each speaker highlights a different frequency or a different instrument. Yet it's the same song. In parts of Revelation, it's like a song is on repeat and the fade dial keeps moving to a different speaker with each play. In apocalyptic literature, you often have "story circles." The author tells a story, and then starts right back at the beginning and retells the story from a different angle or focus. Yet if you read straight through, you get an overwhelming sense of the whole. Apocalyptic literature is like that. As we read it, we can't always assume a strict chronological telling of events; often the author cycles back and tells the events from another, complementary focus.

4. *Apocalyptic literature is like a satellite.* Revelation gives us the cosmic perspective on things, what we often call a "God's-eye view." Revelation describes things truly, but from the perspective of the eternal One who plans, knows, and sees all things. In visionary form, John enters heaven and sees things from the perspective of God's throne. Behind the curtain of the world, John shows us history from the perspective of eternity. We learn who is behind the suffering of Christians. We see the battle happening behind the battles and the characters behind the characters. We learn to look at life from God's perspective and begin to see how everything fits into its proper place, despite not knowing all that is occurring in the outworking of God's sovereign purposes.

5. *Apocalyptic literature is like a war speech.* It comes at a time of crisis. It's not surprising that Revelation is most popular among persecuted Christians. We can't imagine a battle scene in a film without a war speech to the troops before the rush. Apparently, we take it for granted that when we face a seemingly impossible task, we need someone to tell us how it really is, what's truly important, and how things could be. Then people do extraordinary things. Scriptwriters understand this about us, and so does God! In

times of crisis, we need encouragement about how to live, how to face suffering, and how to do so by viewing our lives from God's perspective. As we grow more confident in God and his promises, we live according to the truth that God is working all things according to "the purpose of his will" (Eph. 1:11).

6. *Apocalyptic literature is like a blender.* That's what this genre does with its content. It takes a whole bunch of ideas and shuffles them together to make something that is simultaneously chaotic and perfectly smooth. Throughout Revelation, we might find as many as four Old Testament images converging in a single verse. So if you read this book and think, *I'm confused*, your next thought should not be, *This is an impossible book*, but instead, *God wrote a complex masterpiece, so I need to keep reading it.*

Sometimes people puzzle over whether to interpret Revelation literally or symbolically, but that's not a proper distinction. To read Scripture literally means we interpret Revelation according to the author's intent, which takes into account the kind of literature he chose to write. If the author writes poetry, to read it literally is to read it *as poetry*. And if a speaker or author says he "gave an arm and a leg," he doesn't likely intend to say that he sacrificed his limbs. Rather, he speaks metaphorically to measure cost. That's what he literally intended to communicate by his use of a metaphor. Our responsibility as interpreters is to discern intent in a writer's words. In Revelation, John chose a literary form that must be interpreted apocalyptically.

The visions in Revelation are unique, but the significance is plain: The bad guy loses badly, along with all those who are with him. Conversely, the good guy wins big, and so do all those who are with him.

But there is a reason God didn't just give us one page with the words "Jesus wins!" He wants to encourage us with the truth of Jesus' victory through the means of apocalyptic literature to enflame our hearts, fire our imaginations, and create in us a longing for Christ's return. This literary form is perfectly suited to achieve that end, and it will bless us if we read it and take it to heart.

With all of this in mind, Revelation may be easier to grasp than we originally thought. Yet there are still difficulties. We encourage you to dig into Revelation to understand what it has to say, but for the purposes of this book, we're going to limit our focus on two big, future realities that all Christians eagerly anticipate: *full and final judgment* and *full and final salvation*.

THE LAKE OF FIRE

The Bible's vision of the future is terrible before it's beautiful. History is moving toward a moment of judgment, something we've known since the days of Genesis. If the world is to be remade like Eden, then sin, death, and Satan must be destroyed and finally defeated. Although the thought of divine judgment is terrifying, it is also good, right, and glorious. It's good that our triune God will not let sin and evil have the final word. It is good that God will be true to his character, and that he will balance the books to usher in an age of glory.

The prophets spoke of the "Day of the LORD," when the Lord would tread the winepress of his wrath and his fury would rage so that the moon and the stars of heaven would go black (Joel 3:13–15). They spoke of such a day in positive terms because only in such a day can all that opposes God be finally defeated. Our Lord Jesus also spoke of the same day when he "comes in his glory" to separate sheep from goats, and to send the goats "into the eternal fire prepared for the devil and his angels" (Matt. 25:31, 41). Paul also wrote of "the end," when Christ "hands over the kingdom to God the Father after he has destroyed all dominion, authority and power. For he must reign until he has put all his enemies under his feet. The last enemy to be destroyed is death" (1 Cor. 15:24–26).

Decisive judgment happened on Christ's cross, a foretaste of what will occur in the final judgment. Just when Satan thought he killed God's Messiah, the Father took death out of his hands and threw it back at him. Satan has been judged. He lives still, and yet his time is short. A final judgment is coming, and that is a good thing. Here's the apocalyptic vision John saw: "I saw an angel coming down out of heaven, having the key to the Abyss and holding in his hand a great chain. He seized the dragon, that ancient serpent, who is the devil, or Satan . . . And the devil, who deceived them, was thrown into the lake of burning sulfur, where the beast and the false prophet had been thrown. They will be tormented day and night for ever and ever" (Rev. 20:1–2, 10).

Satan, that ancient serpent, the deceiver of the world, will deceive no more! God's judgment is just, good, eternal, and terrible. It's for the devil and those who follow him. Here's what John saw next:

> Then I saw a great white throne and him who was seated on it. The earth and the heavens fled from his presence, and there was no place for them. And I saw the dead, great and small, standing before the throne, and books were opened. Another book was opened, which is the book of life. The dead were judged according to what they had done as recorded in the books. The sea gave up the dead that were in it, and death and Hades gave up the dead that were in them, and each person was judged according to what they had done. Then death and Hades were thrown into the lake of fire. The lake of fire is the second death. Anyone whose name was not found written in the book of life was thrown into the lake of fire.
>
> —REVELATION 20:11–15

There is some debate over how all of this unfolds, but for our purposes, one thing is clear: the glorious triune God will make all things right. He brings final justice to the source of everything bad and cruel—rape, murder, hate, deceit, adultery, and pride. He deals final justice to all those who, with the breath God has given them, have chosen to believe Satan's lies and joined him in his rage. God restores the universe to its proper order with all glory resounding to his holy name! This is a God-centered universe where God is loved, adored, and obeyed for who he truly is, and his covenant people are at rest in perfect relationship with him.

SALVATION WITH ALL OUR SENSES

Peter says we have new birth "into a living hope through the resurrection of Jesus Christ from the dead, and into an inheritance that can never perish, spoil or fade." This inheritance, he says, "is kept in heaven for you" (1 Peter 1:3–4). It will last forever, it will keep its shine, and it will never get old. This is profoundly encouraging to know, but in Revelation we get to see a picture of it. We have seen a vision of full and final judgment. Now we see a vision of full and final salvation.

Don't forget that these visions are sensory experiences for John. The final vision of the new creation comes to us from Revelation 21:1–22:5, and we'll briefly explore it with 21:1–6 as our primary focus.

> Then I saw "a new heaven and a new earth," for the first heaven and the first earth had passed away, and there was no longer any sea. I saw the Holy City, the new Jerusalem, coming down out of heaven from God, prepared as a bride beautifully dressed for her husband. And I heard a loud voice from the throne saying, "Look! God's dwelling place is now among the people, and he will dwell with them. They will be his people, and God himself will be with them and be their God. He will wipe every tear from their eyes. There will be no more death or mourning or crying or pain, for the old order of things has passed away." He who was seated on the throne said, "I am making everything new!" Then he said, "Write this down, for these words are trustworthy and true." He said to me, "It is done. I am the Alpha and the Omega, the Beginning and the End. To the thirsty I will give water without cost from the spring of the water of life."
>
> —REVELATION 21:1–6

Here's how all of this is going to *look*, *sound*, *feel*, and *taste*.

How It's Going to Look

What will we see? God's world, remade and stunning. John sees a new heaven and a new earth, and interestingly, it doesn't have a sea. In the ancient world, the sea symbolized chaos and trouble. To say that the new creation does not have a sea is not to say there is no water there, but it is to say that all disorder, chaos, and trouble are gone!

John mixes images as he speaks of the new creation in a variety of complementary ways. He sees "the Holy City, the new Jerusalem" coming down from heaven, but then immediately describes a city "prepared as a bride beautifully dressed for her husband" (Rev. 21:2). What is the point of this mixture of imagery? In the Old Testament, the city of Jerusalem stood for the historic city, plus it became symbolic of God's people. The heavenly Jerusalem is the people of God, who from another perspective is a bride beautifully dressed for her husband. If ever there was a sight of beauty, this is it. This is Christ's bride—beautiful, perfect, and ready—the people of the new creation.

Parts of John's new creation vision come into vivid focus from the background we've established in Ezekiel's prophecy. Although Revelation never directly quotes the Old Testament, the visions of Ezekiel, Isaiah, and Daniel inform its entire presentation.

In Revelation 21:10, John writes, "He carried me away in the Spirit to a mountain great and high, and showed me the Holy City, Jerusalem, coming down out of heaven from God." You'll remember that Ezekiel was taken to a high mountain overlooking Jerusalem. John describes what he saw in his vision: "It had a great, high wall with twelve gates, and with twelve angels at the gates. On the gates were written the names of the twelve tribes of Israel. There were three gates on the east, three on the north, three on the south and three on the west. The wall of the city had twelve foundations, and on them were the names of the twelve apostles of the Lamb" (Rev. 21:12–14).

Sound familiar? This is very similar to what Ezekiel saw, yet there's an important addition: the names of the apostles. This represents the perfection and completeness of God's people. Remember the measuring man? He's in John's vision too: "The angel who talked with me had a measuring rod of gold to measure the city, its gates and its walls. The city was laid out like a square, as long as it was wide. He measured the city with the rod and found it to be 12,000 stadia in length, and as wide and high as it is long" (21:15–16).

At first, we might think that its many measurements are uninspiring. Who needs to look at the blueprints when you can look at the finished product? But in apocalyptic literature, numbers are deeply symbolic, and that is certainly the case here. First, it is important to recognize the significance of the number twelve and multiples of twelve, symbolizing the completion of God's people, the twelve tribes of Israel from the Old Testament alongside the twelve apostles of the church. This is a reminder that throughout the ages, there has always been only one people of God.

Not only are God's people perfected and beautiful, but they are complete. They're all there. None is lost! Everyone whose name is in the book is in the city. Perfect, beautiful, and complete—that's the people of God in the new creation.

But a second point must not be forgotten in the description of the new Jerusalem. Did you notice that the city is laid out like a square and that its length, width, and height are equal? It's a perfect cube. What does this picture? The entire city is pictured as a perfect cube that is also co-extensive with the entire new creation. The only place we find a perfect cube in Scripture is the holy of holies in the temple, the place where God uniquely manifested his covenantal presence. It was a microcosm of Eden, but under the old covenant, full access to God's presence was not possible. Only the high priest, once a year on the Day of Atonement, could enter this place, signifying that full access to God's presence was not yet ours.

In Christ, this has all changed. As we have discovered in previous chapters, in Jesus and his work, the old covenant and its priesthood are fulfilled. By Christ's cross, he has fulfilled the purpose of the temple and torn down the curtain. Through him and by the Spirit, we—as new-covenant believers united to Christ, our head—have full access to God's presence and the throne room of grace. Yet there is more! In the creation of a final *place*, the entire new creation *is* the holy of holies, where the triune God in all his glory manifests his unique covenantal presence with us. No longer is God uniquely present merely in Eden, or in a tabernacle-temple structure after the fall. The significance of the new creation is that Eden and the holy of holies are now extended to the *entire* universe. What God created us for in the first place, namely, to dwell in his presence as his people, is now fully and finally realized. Heaven is not a far-off place with clouds and floating and harps. Heaven is the new creation where God's people, the bride, have full access to their bridegroom, Christ, and experience forever the presence and fellowship of the triune God! This is how it's going to look.

How It's Going to Sound

What will we hear? A loud voice with good news: "Look! God's dwelling place is now among the people, and he will dwell with them. They will be his people, and God himself will be with them and be their God" (Rev. 21:3). In the course of our lives, we may hear all kinds of good news. We may get the news that we've been accepted into a certain school, or that we've landed a certain job, or that the romantic interest we've been pursuing said, "Yes!" But this announcement tops them all! Sin is undone. God and his people are one. The impossible is made true.

In John's visionary experience, he sees a future world, but something central is missing: "I did not see a temple in the city, because the Lord God Almighty and the Lamb are its temple. The city does not need the sun or the moon to shine on it, for the glory of God gives it light, and the Lamb is its lamp" (Rev. 21:22–23). This description makes sense in light of what we have already seen. The new Jerusalem is a perfect cube, but it has now been extended to the entire new creation. In the new creation, God's covenantal presence is fully experienced, so there is no longer a need for a temple. The temple was the place where God met with his people, but now in Christ all those shadows and types have been fulfilled. God has created a place for us to dwell where we will experience the immediate presence of the glory of God. John now sees what the Old Testament looked forward to—the glory of God filling all the earth and God's people at rest with him.

Jonathan Edwards famously described heaven this way: "The enjoyment of God is the only happiness with which our souls can be satisfied. To go to heaven, fully to enjoy God, is infinitely better than the most pleasant accommodations here. Fathers and mothers, husbands, wives, or children, or the company of earthly friends, are but shadows, but God is the substance. These are but scattered beams, but God is the sun. These are but streams. But God is the ocean."[8]

In this fallen world, we lose loved ones, and if they died in Christ, we look forward to seeing them again. Yet our reunion, as joyful as it may be, is not the greatest reason for rejoicing. Those we love here are important, but they do not compare to knowing and experiencing the undiluted presence of the triune God. If the God of the Bible were not there, the new creation would *not* be heaven, because he is what makes heaven good. He is what makes heaven wonderful. As the psalmist writes, "Better is one day in your courts than a thousand elsewhere" (Ps. 84:10). A test of Christian growth is the measure of our anticipation of Christ, even over the other joys we'll know in the new creation.

What is central to the new creation, then, *is the triune God himself.* It is only in our experience of dwelling in his glorious presence forever that the very purpose of our creation and redemption is fully realized. In the new creation we will know God in perfect love, peace, and joy, and experience perfect truth, justice, holiness, wisdom, goodness, glory, and beauty.

Our songs about heaven often miss the most important thing about heaven. Too often they are human-centered rather than God-centered, missing what is central to heaven. A hymn by Anne Cousin (1824–1906), "The Sands of Time Are Sinking," beautifully captures what the new creation is all about—living in the presence of our great and glorious God.

> The sands of time are sinking, the dawn of heaven breaks,
> the summer morn I've sighed for, the fair sweet morn awakes.
> Dark, dark has been the midnight, but dayspring is at hand,
> and glory, glory dwelleth in Emmanuel's land.
>
> The King there in his beauty without a veil is seen,
> it were a well spent journey though seven deaths lay between.

The Lamb with his fair army doth on Mt. Zion stand,
and glory, glory dwelleth in Emmanuel's land.

O Christ, he is the fountain, the deep sweet well of love.
The streams of earth I've tasted more deep I'll drink above.
There to an ocean fullness, his mercy doth expand,
and glory, glory dwelleth in Emmanuel's land.

The bride eyes not her garment, but her dear bridegroom's face.
I will not gaze at glory, but on my King of grace.
Not at the crown he gifteth, but on his pierced hand:
the Lamb is all the glory of Emmanuel's land.[9]

What this hymn communicates beautifully in song, we also hear in the
book of Revelation. In that place we hear the sound of the saints praising
the Lord and the Lamb. In Revelation we have the lyric sheet for the songs
we'll sing along with untold thousands of others rejoicing in the Lord:

> You are worthy to take the scroll
>   and to open its seals,
> because you were slain,
>   and with your blood you purchased for God
>   persons from every tribe and language and people and
>   nation.
> You have made them to be a kingdom and priests to serve
> our God,
>   and they will reign on the earth . . .
>   Worthy is the Lamb, who was slain,
>   to receive power and wealth and wisdom and strength
>   and honor and glory and praise! . . .
>   To him who sits on the throne and to the Lamb
>   be praise and honor and glory and power,
> for ever and ever!
>
> —REVELATION 5:9–13

Christ, the Lamb of God, will be worshiped forever, along with the Father and the Spirit. The glory of heaven is God himself, and we will forever sing the triune God's praises as we live for his glory and fulfill the purpose of our creation as image-bearers and adopted sons and daughters.

Why do we experience all of this? Not because of anything we have done, but solely because of God's sovereign grace. *He* is the one who has chosen us, redeemed us in Christ, and made us alive by the Spirit. The song of heaven will be of our grateful praise to the Lord and the Lamb. This is how it's going to sound.

How It's Going to Feel

What will we feel? We will feel the strong and gentle touch of God on our cheeks as he wipes away "every tear" from our eyes (Rev. 21:4). This represents the very removal of every bad and sad thing that we know in this world: "There will be no more death or mourning or crying or pain, for the old order of things has passed away" (21:4). Whatever is sad in this life is gone. Whatever is difficult, painful, tragic, and devastating is no more. Your tears? They're wiped away. Death? It's no more, because it has been defeated and destroyed. Mourning, crying, or pain? They have all passed away. This is a place filled with joy, and it's a place emptied of sorrow.

In John's final vision of the new creation is a familiar symbol that we can't miss: the tree of life. "The angel showed me the river of the water of life, as clear as crystal, flowing from the throne of God and of the Lamb down the middle of the great street of the city. On each side of the river stood the tree of life, bearing twelve crops of fruit, yielding its fruit every month. And the leaves of the tree are for the healing of the nations" (Rev. 22:1–2).

That river reminds us of the river in Eden and the river in the temple vision given to Ezekiel. By this river is a tree whose leaves heal the nations, a beautiful picture of what the Lord does for his people.

This future should capture our imaginations and enflame our love, trust, and confidence in God. Saints before us have meditated deeply on heaven, and there is much to learn from them. Here is another example from Jonathan Edwards: "The blessedness of Heaven is so glorious that when the saints arrive there they will look back upon their earthly pilgrimage, however wonderful their life in Christ was then, as a veritable Hell. Just as truly, on the other hand, will those who perish in Hell look back on the life in this world, however miserable it may have been, as veritable Heaven."[10] This is how it's going to feel.

How It's Going to Taste

How will it taste? We are born with stomachs, and we eat and drink every day to stay alive and healthy. In this life, we are preoccupied with finding good food to taste, new flavors to try. Interestingly, eating and drinking is one way the Bible teaches us about the world to come. We are born as people to be satisfied. So when John hears Jesus say, "To the thirsty I will give water without cost from the spring of the water of life" (21:6), this is an exciting promise. The Lord fed his people in the wilderness so they would know that they live on his Word. Jesus lived on "every word that comes from the mouth of God" (Matt. 4:4) and offered himself as the very "bread of life" (John 6:35). And to the Samaritan woman he offered the water that wells up to eternal life (4:13–14).

In this fallen world, we may not always feel that Jesus is enough. In this age, we are often parched and tired, physically and spiritually. Yet Jesus tells us he will satisfy our thirst in the age to come. Physically, we will have no needs, but more important, spiritually, he will satisfy us in every way. God's salvation rest is ours fully in Christ. J. I. Packer writes, "Hearts on earth say in the course of a joyful experience, 'I don't want this ever to end.' But invariably it does. The hearts of those in heaven say, 'I want this to go on forever.' And it will. There can be no better news than this."[11]

We do not deserve such wonder, nor could we ever earn it! This is why the gift of eternal life in God's presence is available to us "without payment." How can this be? The answer to that question must be fixed firmly in our minds. The cost of salvation is clear in the Bible's story, and that cost is ever before us, even to the Bible's last page.

How is there a future for sinners, given our sin before God? If receiving the new creation and our reconciliation to God is without payment, then is God really just, righteous, and good? We should not fool ourselves: there will be no sin in the new creation. Jesus' words should cause us to shudder for those who will not be in the new creation: "Those who are victorious will inherit all this, and I will be their God and they will be my children. But the cowardly, the unbelieving, the vile, the murderers, the sexually immoral, those who practice magic arts, the idolaters and all liars—they will be consigned to the fiery lack of burning sulfur. This is the second death" (Rev. 21:7–8).

This is what sinners deserve; this is what we deserve. Yet this is not what all sinners get. Why? Because of God's amazing grace centered in Christ, the Lamb.

- "Then the angel said to me, 'Write this: Blessed are those who are invited to the wedding supper of the Lamb!'" (Rev. 19:9).
- "I did not see a temple in the city, because the Lord God Almighty and the Lamb are its temple. The city does not need the sun or the moon to shine on it, for the glory of God gives it light, and the Lamb is its lamp" (Rev. 21:22–23).
- "Nothing impure will ever enter it, nor will anyone who does what is shameful or deceitful, but only those whose names are written in the Lamb's book of life" (Rev. 21:27).

A marriage supper. A city without a sun. A book of life. The one thing each of these has in common is this Lamb. Eternity goes in one of two directions, depending on our relationship to the Lamb. What is a lamb doing in this vision of John's? We know the answer. A lamb—the Lamb—is the answer to Scripture's great question: How can sinners be made right with a holy God? This Lamb is our salvation, and forever he will be our song.

In this new creation we will be happy in Christ, and he will forever be happy in us. As a bride is happy in her groom, so we will be happy in him. And as a groom rejoices over his bride, so our triune Lord will rejoice forever over us. There has never been any competition in his heart for us, and in this consummated age, there won't be any competition in ours. Finally, our joy in him will be a truly *pure* joy and satisfaction because of the glorious work of the Lamb.

How we long for that day! As a bride waits for her groom, so we wait for Christ's return. And as we do, we cling to his parting words with great hope: "Look, I am coming soon! . . . I am the Alpha and the Omega, the First and the Last, the Beginning and the End" (Rev. 22:12–13).

CONCLUSION

Finding Our Story in His

What did Jesus pray for on the eve of his arrest? *Who* was he praying for? What incredible petitions did he bring to his Father as he faced down his impending death? Just as our own prayers reveal our deepest desires, the prayers of Jesus reveal the very heart and mind of Christ.

We have learned much about Jesus—*who* he is, *what* he said, and *what* he did for us in his entire work. But one chapter in Scripture, John 17, reveals Jesus in a unique and special way. John 17 records one of the prayers of Jesus on the night of his arrest. As Jesus celebrated the Passover and prepared for his death, he taught his disciples one last time in the Upper Room by praying aloud—for *them*. In truth, the rest of the New Testament and our very lives today are an answer to this prayer. This prayer reveals more than Jesus' inner thoughts; it unveils God's plans for his people.

As we close this book, we want to offer you a meditation on what Jesus said to his Father that night. Looking at the prayer of Jesus helps us understand what it means to be a Christian and what it means to be the church.

God, through his Word, never lets us read the Bible and walk away unchanged. Jesus did not come so that we could merely know about God and about his promises. God the Son, our Lord Jesus Christ, came so we could know *him* and *become* a new creation. Jesus came so that we, as the church, would be an outpost of that future age, living now in the world as we await his return. The Bible is more than a story about Christ; it's God's love letter to you!

You've read the story of Scripture. It's now time to settle the question of Jesus Christ for yourself.

DO YOU KNOW JESUS CHRIST?

Here's how Jesus begins his prayer:

> Father, the hour has come. Glorify your Son, that your Son may glorify you. For you granted him authority over all people that he might give eternal life to all those you have given him. Now this is eternal life: that they know you, the only true God, and Jesus Christ, whom you have sent. I have brought you glory on earth by finishing the work you gave me to do. And now, Father, glorify me in your presence with the glory I had with you before the world began.
>
> —JOHN 17:1–5

Jesus is fixated on his own glory, but not just for himself! He will later say, toward the end of his prayer, "I desire that *they also*, whom you have given me, may be with me where I am, *to see* my glory" (17:24 ESV, emphases added). He sees the finish line of his own work on earth, and with it the culmination of the Father's eternal plan, or what he calls "the hour." Bound up with that plan and "hour" are the people Jesus came to save. He prays that those whom the Father has given him would know the Father and know him. *To know* the triune God is the very reason for our creation and redemption in Christ.

Here's the question each one of us must answer: Do *I* know Jesus Christ? That may not be the question you asked when you opened this book. You certainly had questions about the Bible, and perhaps some questions for God. Yet as we read the Bible, we discover that it asks questions of us as well. Jesus himself asks questions of us, and the most important question in all of life is about our relationship to the most important person in the Bible and in all of history, Jesus Christ the Lord.

Jesus is the Bible's answer to the problem of our sin and God's holiness. He is the one to whom the entire story of the Bible leads. He is the

one we were made to know. The work Jesus came to do was not impersonal but deeply personal. The divine Son didn't become incarnate, live,
die, and rise from the dead as a mere assignment. From eternity past,
and in his entire life on earth, he had on his mind his Father's glory and
a relationship with those he came to save.

This covenant relationship is the very definition of "eternal life."
When we think of eternal life, we tend to put the emphasis on "eternal,"
and while eternal life refers to a quantity of life, it especially refers to its
quality—life to the full. This is life that the prophets announced, tied
to God's promise to save, restore, and remake us after the image of the
Son. As he prays, Jesus shares his desire to join his Father, but not alone.
He wants us with him. The Bible presents us with more than a story;
it introduces us to a person.

Do you know Jesus? Are you one of those the Father has given to the
Son? There's an easy way to know! Keep listening to Jesus' prayer:

> I have revealed you to those whom you gave me out of the world.
> They were yours; you gave them to me and they have obeyed your
> word. Now they know that everything you have given me comes
> from you. For I gave them the words you gave me and they accepted
> them. They knew with certainty that I came from you, and they
> believed that you sent me.
>
> —JOHN 17:6–8

Do you accept the words that Christ spoke about himself? Do you
believe that Jesus came from the Father?

This kind of believing means believing certain things *about* Jesus—
that he is who he said he is, the divine Son of God, that he is the Messiah
long promised (John 20:30–31). Do you believe that Jesus lived and
died for your sin? Do you believe that his death and resurrection are the
only means of salvation? When you look at the cross, do you see there a
picture of where your sin leads and what your sin deserves? When you
look to the cross, do you also see the sheer grace and mercy of God for
sinners? Do you agree that "salvation is found in no one else, for there

is no other name under heaven given to mankind by which we must be saved" (Acts 4:12)?

Knowing Christ means believing things about him. It also means that we trust in him. It's personal. It means renouncing our own glory for his. It means valuing him above all else. It means trusting in his righteousness above our works. Here's how Paul put it: "Whatever were gains to me I now consider loss for the sake of Christ. What is more, I consider everything a loss because of the surpassing worth of knowing Christ Jesus my Lord, for whose sake I have lost all things. I consider them garbage, that I may gain Christ and be found in him, not having a righteousness of my own that comes from the law, but that which is through faith in Christ—the righteousness that comes from God on the basis of faith. I want to know Christ" (Phil. 3:7–10). Believing in Christ means repenting of your self-righteousness and trusting in Christ's righteousness alone.

You may feel that it is too late to believe, or perhaps you believe your sins are too great for Christ to forgive. But neither is true! Jesus said to the thief who hung next to him on the cross, "Today you will be with me in paradise" (Luke 23:43). It wasn't too late for him. Peter preached to those who killed Jesus: "You killed the author of life, but God raised him from the dead . . . Repent, then, and turn to God, so that your sins may be wiped out" (Acts 3:15, 19). God's grace is greater than all our sin. The offer was open to them, and the offer is open to you. It's never too late, and your sin is never too great. To you, Jesus says, "Come to me, all you who are weary and burdened, and I will give you rest" (Matt. 11:28).

We are wired as humans to fix problems. But your sin is not a problem you can fix. You must be saved from it. You need a rescue! That's why Scripture says, "Everyone who calls on the name of the Lord will be saved" (Rom. 10:13). So call on him today and believe. "To those who believed in his name, he gave the right to become children of God—children born not of natural descent, nor of human decision or a husband's will, but born of God" (John 1:12–13).

GROWING TOGETHER IN HIS JOY

Jesus continues his prayer, and we learn that the eternal life he gives to us changes us. Jesus doesn't leave us as we were. We belong to him now, and as those who belong to him, we belong to another age—to the new creation. As those who belong to the new creation, we are being renewed into a new humanity, conformed into his image, and transformed into his likeness. We remain in the world, but we don't remain the same. Here's how Jesus prays:

> I will remain in the world no longer, but they are still in the world, and I am coming to you. Holy Father, protect them by the power of your name, the name you gave me, so that they may be one as we are one. While I was with them, I protected them and kept them safe by that name you gave me. None has been lost except the one doomed to destruction so that Scripture would be fulfilled. I am coming to you now, but I say these things while I am still in the world, so that they may have the full measure of my joy within them. I have given them your word and the world has hated them, for they are not of the world any more than I am of the world. My prayer is not that you take them out of the world but that you protect them from the evil one. They are not of the world, even as I am not of it. Sanctify them by the truth; your word is truth.
>
> —JOHN 17:11–17

This prayer is encouraging because it shows us that Jesus wants many things for us: his joy, our unity, the Father's protection, our sanctification—that we would be *made holy* by the word of God. But this prayer is also sobering, because Christ knows better than we do the dangers that lurk in this world and the forces set against us. Remember what Peter called us: "foreigners and exiles" (1 Peter 2:11). "Your enemy the devil prowls around like a roaring lion," he wrote, "looking for someone to devour" (5:8).

Jesus' work secures two things that are the object of Satan's destructive lust: our unity and joy together in him (John 17:11, 13). Not surprisingly, Jesus preoccupied himself with these themes earlier that evening, as he taught the disciples:

> As the Father has loved me, so have I loved you. Now remain in my love. If you keep my commands, you will remain in my love, just as I have kept my Father's commands and remain in his love. I have told you this so that my joy may be in you and that your joy may be complete. My command is this: Love each other as I have loved you. Greater love has no one than this: to lay down one's life for one's friends ... This is my command: Love each other.
>
> —JOHN 15:9–17

Our joy in Christ and our unity with one another are likely far more important than we typically realize. Jesus wants his full measure of joy to be known in us. What incredible joy that must be! And this joy is intimately connected to our unity with one another in the love of Christ. The new covenant community, the church, is more than a helpful resource for Christian growth; it's the only context for all true and lasting transformation. Christianity cannot be conceived apart from the church any more than the Father and the Son can be separated in the life of the Trinity (John 17:11). No doubt, this is what Paul had in mind when he wrote to the church at Ephesus to "be completely humble and gentle; be patient, bearing with one another in love" (Eph. 4:2). This doesn't mean that we pursue unity at the expense of truth as revealed in God's Word. Paul roots Christian unity in the triune relations in the Godhead and the certainty of the salvation God grants. Notice what Paul writes: "There is one body and one Spirit, just as you were called to one hope when you were called; one Lord, one faith, one baptism; one God and Father of all, who is over all and through all and in all" (4:4–6).

Our joy and our unity are beautifully mingled, and they will only increase throughout eternity. Satan hates them both. Yet with the sobering reality of Satan's purpose against us comes a comforting assurance that the glorious God of the Bible is *for* us. As Jesus kept his own disciples by his name, so the Father will keep his people by the power of his name (John 17:11–12). Our joy and our unity are under threat, but they are ultimately secure.

In his prayer, Jesus also asks for the Father to sanctify us in truth. This is a prayer that we would be made into a truly mature humanity. The New Testament describes Christian maturity in a variety of ways. Paul writes about presenting his readers "fully mature in Christ" (Col. 1:28), and elsewhere as being "conformed to the image of [the] Son" (Rom. 8:29). Peter encouraged Christian growth in the church with these words: "Grow in the grace and knowledge of our Lord and Savior Jesus Christ" (2 Peter 3:18). We come to know Christ, and we never stop growing in that knowledge.

How does God mature, grow, sanctify, transform, and confirm us into Christ's image? Jesus told us, "Sanctify them by the truth; your word is truth" (John 17:17). What God first used to bring order out of chaos at creation, he now uses to bring beauty out of the brokenness of our sin-torn lives. The serpent used a lie to deceive the first human couple, but salvation brings a return to Truth, a return to the trustworthy and true Word of God as the source and satisfaction for all of life.

In the book of Romans, Paul spent eleven chapters explaining God's grace to sinners in the gospel, and then he made this urgent plea: "Therefore, I urge you, brothers and sisters, in view of God's mercy, to offer your bodies as a living sacrifice, holy and pleasing to God—this is your true and proper worship. Do not conform to the pattern of this world, but be transformed by the renewing of your mind. Then you will be able to test and approve what God's will is—his good, pleasing and perfect will" (Rom. 12:1–2).

The gospel that saves results in our transformation in Christ and by the Spirit. It makes us worshipers of the living God. By the renewing of our minds, which happens by reading and obeying Scripture, we are transformed so that our lives reflect that which is good, pleasing, and perfect. All of this pleases the Lord.

If you have been saved by God's amazing grace, are you also being changed by that same grace? Are you seeking to be transformed by the

Spirit by giving yourself to the means of change ordained by the Spirit, God's Word? Are you bearing the fruit of the Spirit and so showing yourself to belong to Jesus who sent him? Are you putting off the old ways that belong to Adam and this fallen and fading age, and are you putting on the new ways that belong to Christ and the new age he brings (Eph. 4:22–28)? Are you following Christ? We pray the answer is yes! And remember, "He who began a good work in you will carry it on to completion until the day of Christ Jesus" (Phil. 1:6).

SPREADING CHRIST EVERYWHERE

Jesus called his first disciples by calling out to them with his own voice. How does he call his disciples *after* his resurrection and ascension? He calls out to them with his own voice *through the voices* of his people. When he called out to two fishermen, "Follow me," he continued, "and I will send you out to fish for people" (Matt. 4:19). Men who worked nets would become networkers for the gospel, and today you and I are messengers for Jesus just the same.

As Jesus prayed for his disciples that evening, he prayed also for those who would become disciples *through their word*.

As you sent me into the world, so I have sent them into the world. And for their sake I consecrate myself, that they also may be sanctified in truth. I do not ask for these only, but also for those who will believe in me through their word, that they may all be one, just as you, Father, are in me, and I in you, that they also may be in us, so that the world may believe that you have sent me. The glory that you have given me I have given to them, that they may be one even as we are one, I in them and you in me, that they may become perfectly one, so that the world may know that you sent me and loved them even as you loved me. Father, I desire that they also, whom you have given me, may be with me where I am, to see my glory that you have given me because you loved me before the foundation of the world. O righteous Father, even though the world does not know you,

I know you, and these know that you have sent me. I made known
to them your name, and I will continue to make it known, that the
love with which you have loved me may be in them, and I in them.

—JOHN 17:18–26 ESV

What begins with a small band of disciples around the table with
Jesus eventually spreads throughout the world and across centuries to
create one perfectly happy and beautifully unified people: the church.
Through their words, these people communicate his gospel. Through
their lives, and more specifically their life together, they commend the
goodness of that gospel. They share it with words, and they show it off
with their lives.

Jesus prayed for this mission on the eve of his arrest, but he gave it
in explicit terms days later on the cusp of his resurrection. Matthew's
Gospel ends with what is rightly called "the Great Commission": "All
authority in heaven and on earth has been given to me. Therefore go
and make disciples of all nations, baptizing them in the name of the
Father and of the Son and of the Holy Spirit, and teaching them to obey
everything I have commanded you. And surely I am with you always, to
the very end of the age" (Matt. 28:18–20).

The call to discipleship was and still is a call to disciple making, a call to
spreading the glory of Jesus Christ everywhere. Jesus' Great Commission
represented a climactic moment for the disciples in what was a several-
year training program. How did Jesus make these followers into fishers of
people? How did he prepare lowly fishermen for so great a calling?

In between Jesus' call to discipleship and this Great Commission
is a story of preparation for that mission. The disciples began by drop-
ping their nets and following Jesus as he taught and performed works
throughout all Galilee (Matt. 4:23; 9:35). But after some time, Jesus sent
his disciples out to do the same work he had done (Matt. 10:5). In doing
this, he extended his words and his works into the world. The initial
mission was like a training program, a boot camp for what was to come.
It was a shotgun start for the race that would take Jesus' disciples to the
very ends of the earth.

Just as Jesus commissioned his disciples in the first century and provided them with what they needed for the task, today he continues that work by commissioning you and me and giving us all we need to do his work. Jesus gives us more than a charge to "go." He gives us his authority and his presence by his Spirit, who came upon those first disciples with "power" so they would be witnesses to Christ "in Jerusalem, and in all Judea and Samaria, and to the ends of the earth" (Acts 1:8). This witness is a witness of words, for the good news of Jesus' life, death, and resurrection is indeed *news*. But the gospel is also to be lived as God's people before the watching world. As our Lord reminds us, "A new command I give you: Love one another. As I have loved you, so you must love one another. By this everyone will know that you are my disciples, if you love one another" (John 13:34–35). Our life as the church commends the gospel and compels the world to believe.

Jesus, the light of the world, shines his light into the world by lighting us up like little torches of his glory. Now, in everything we do and everywhere we're found, we radiate his beauty, and his truth, and his goodness. We see Jesus' glory, we are transformed by that glory, and we emanate that glory into every dark corner of the earth. We, his people, are a foretaste of the joy and peace and unity that Christ will bring when he returns.

Until that day when we see Christ in all his glory, we imitate Jesus by praying earnestly to the Father. For our neighbors and for the nations, we pray as Paul did, "that God may open to us a door for the word, to declare the mystery of Christ" (Col. 4:3 ESV). We pray that we may declare that gospel "boldly, as [we] ought to speak" (Eph. 6:20 ESV). And in all things we pray as Jesus taught us:

> Our Father in heaven,
> hallowed be your name.
> Your kingdom come,
> your will be done,
> on earth as it is in heaven.
> Give us this day our daily bread,

> and forgive us our debts,
> as we also have forgiven our debtors.
> And lead us not into temptation,
> but deliver us from evil.

—MATTHEW 6:9–13 ESV

May he grant it all. Amen.

NOTES

1. These contexts are adapted from Richard Lints, *The Fabric of Theology: A Prolegomenon to Evangelical Theology* (Grand Rapids, Mich.: Eerdmans, 1993).
2. Mortimer J. Adler and Charles Van Doren, *How to Read a Book: The Classic Guide to Intelligent Reading*, rev. ed. (New York: Simon and Schuster, 2014), 75.
3. These metaphors are taken from John R. W. Stott, *The Cross of Christ*, twentieth anniversary edition (Downers Grove, Ill.: InterVarsity, 2006), 107–11.
4. This paragraph is indebted to John R. W. Stott, *The Message of Ephesians* (Downers Grove, Ill.: InterVarsity , 1979), 91.
5. This section is taken from Stott, *Message of Ephesians*, 91–92.
6. C. H. Spurgeon. "The Dumb Become Singers," a sermon delivered at the Metropolitan Tabernacle, published December 12, 1912. Metropolitan Tabernacle Pulpit, Sermon #3332, www.spurgeongems.org/vols58–60/chs3332.pdf.
7. This way of describing visionary layers in apocalyptic literature is taken from Vern S. Poythress, "Genre and Hermeneutics in Rev 20.1–6," *JETS* 36 (1993): 41–42.
8. Jonathan Edwards, "The Christian Pilgrim, Or, The True Christian's Life a Journey toward Heaven" (September 1733), available at www.sermonindex.net/modules/articles/index.php?view=article&aid=3416.
9. Anne R. Cousin, "The Sands of Time Are Sinking," *Hymns for the Living Church* (Carol Stream, Ill.: Hope Publishing, 1974), 535.
10. Jonathan Edwards, from an unpublished manuscript available at www.the-highway.com/theology8_Gerstner.html.
11. J. I. Packer, *Concise Theology: A Guide to Historic Christian Beliefs* (Wheaton, Ill.: Tyndale, 1993), 267.

SCRIPTURE INDEX